ADR AND COMMERCIAL DISPUTES

Edited by RUSSELL CALLER
Senior Partner, Gillhams Solicitors
Managing Director, Dispute Mediation Limited

LONDON
SWEET & MAXWELL
2002

Published in 2002 by Sweet & Maxwell Ltd of
100 Avenue Road
London NW3 3PF
Typeset by Servis Filmsetting Ltd, Manchester, U.K.
Printed in England by Athenaeum Press Ltd, Gateshead, U.K.

No natural forests were destroyed to make this product; only farmed timber was used and replanted.

A CIP catalogue record for this book is available from the British Library

ISBN 0 421 76300 0

ISBN 0-421-76300-0

9 780421 763005

FOREWORD

SIR GAVIN LIGHTMAN

Mediation (a term which for this purpose includes other forms of alternative dispute resolution) only a few years ago was a theoretical option for the parties to a dispute, but an option rarely invoked, of limited (if any) interest to the court or the legal profession and of minimal practical significance. The traditional forms of litigation were the norm. The spiralling costs of contentious litigation, and the delays, uncertainties and lasting acrimony which such litigation occasions, have however over the past 20 years led to the increasing recognition by the judiciary, legal advisers and the disputants themselves that contentious litigation itself should be recognised as the option of last resort, and every facility should be afforded by the legal system, and every effort should be made by legal advisers, to achieve by alternative means a resolution of disputes which both parties can accept. This new approach was decisively endorsed by the Woolf Reforms, which came into effect in April 1999 and gave mediation a central role. There is no going back. Neither the public nor the private purse can afford the financial costs nor can society afford the social costs of the traditional forms of contentious litigation where an alternative method of dispute resolution is available. There can be no doubt that mediation, of all recent developments in English law and procedure, affords the greatest potential benefit and saving for disputants and the public generally.

The central role of mediation in today's legal system calls for attention to the possibilities for the use of mediation in the many and different areas of law where disputes arise. This work is written by experienced and well respected specialists in fields where there is scope for mediation as the favoured approach for resolving disputes. Their insight provides valuable guidance for practitioners as to the means of achieving for their clients when parties to a dispute the benefits which mediation affords—benefits in terms of saving time and money and safeguarding business relationships. I recommend this work as a "first port of call" for those considering the use of mediation in the wide range of situations covered by it.

Sir Gavin Lightman
Royal Courts of Justice
Strand
London
October 2001

INTRODUCTION

RUSSELL CALLER

"All government, indeed every human benefit and enjoyment, every virtue and every prudent act, is founded on compromise and barter."

This could be a soundbite from a recent speech by the United States administration in respect of its continuing diplomatic efforts to resolve the conflicts in any world flash point. In fact, these words were spoken by Edmund Burke in a speech in the House of Commons, on conciliation with the American Colonies as far back as March 22, 1775.

Mediation is not new. The resolving of disputes by shuttle diplomacy, compromise and conciliation and just plain talking has been around for generations, but perhaps it is only now at the very outset of the twenty-first century that the commercial world is just waking up to see the real value of resolving commercial disputes in this way as opposed to taking an adversarial approach through the court system.

As with all social change, many different factors have to be in place before true revolution occurs and it would be folly to say that all those factors are yet in place, but the change is certainly coming.

It might be helpful to stop a minute and consider what changes have occurred and indeed what changes have yet to occur in order for commercial mediation to prosper.

Lord Woolf has created the backdrop for the resolution of disputes by mediation. With the introduction of his reforms in April 1999, a clear signal has been given to litigants and their advisers that the settling of disputes in court should be a last resort and that mediation should be used at the earliest opportunity. However, the introduction of legislation on its own does not have sufficient impact without other factors also being in place.

Professional advisers, and in particular lawyers, are notoriously slow in encompassing change. Sadly, this is reflected to some degree, throughout the U.K., at the present time.

I have been in mediations where lawyers have become almost deliberately destructive in assisting in the resolution of a dispute because either the lawyer in question has been brought up on the principle that the rule of law is the only safe way to resolve a dispute and any other course of action in his or her opinion simply does not provide the correct result, or more cynically he or she can see many hundreds of thousands of pounds worth of fees slipping away if a dispute is resolved at the mediation.

There is a real fear that if mediation takes off the result will be an enormous reduction in the amount of litigation being conducted and this will have a direct impact on the lawyer's fee income. The reality is that if the individual lawyer spent more time harnessing new alternative approaches to dispute resolution then the loss in litigation fee income might be replaced by offering new varied professional services that encourage ADR. One thing is for sure, the Luddites did not prevent industrial revolution occurring in the early nineteenth century and it is unlikely that lawyers who adopt an obstructive approach to alternative forms of dispute resolution will prevent a fundamental change in approach to the settling of commercial disputes in the twenty-first century.

The driving force that is already in place to encourage alternative forms of resolving disputes is the general concern of businesses and the public at large at the enormous cost of litigation. By this I mean not only the vast professional fees that are charged during the conduct of litigation but equally (if not more so) the enormous cost in management time by businesses in spending three or four years in receiving and considering professional advice and providing instructions to its professional advisers. Perhaps this loss of management time would be acceptable if more often than not the result of the litigation is beneficial to the business, but experience says otherwise.

However, at the time of writing, the managing directors, the financial directors, the human resource directors and the general managers of business have yet to fully take on board the benefits of the resolution of disputes by means other than the courts or tribunals. The key to the dispute resolution revolution is that the end users are properly educated in the real value of ADR. I strongly believe that once these end users understand the time and money savings that can be achieved, they will jettison the old adversarial court approach and value the new change.

What this book seeks to achieve is to continue the education process of the professional adviser and the end user in the value of ADR and in particular mediation in the resolution of commercial disputes. Whether you are a sole practitioner, partner in a small firm, in-house counsel or partner in a large city professional practice, this book can be of significant practical use to you.

It should be emphasised that this book is not a "novel" to be read from cover to cover because each chapter is self-contained. As a result there may be some repetition. The idea has been to choose a number of areas that commonly create commercial disputes and to examine the nature of those commercial disputes and how they inter-relate to resolution of those disputes by the courts and tribunals and also how those disputes can be resolved by ADR.

The busy practitioner needs a book which can be picked up at ease and can be "dipped into" quickly and easily to provide the reader with the practical information necessary to advise clients which form of ADR should be used to assist in the resolution of the particular dispute.

It is a commonly held belief that in order to mediate a dispute, it is not necessary to have a detailed knowledge of the subject matter. I do not subscribe to that view.

I believe the greater the knowledge and experience there is in relation to the subject matter of the dispute, the greater the understanding of the dispute and thus the greater the chance of the matter being resolved. Accordingly, each of the chapters have been written by people who are well respected within their profession and have a detailed knowledge and understanding of their subject and simultaneously have been accredited as a mediator by one of the leading mediation training organisations in the U.K.

Each chapter loosely follows the same structure so that if the reader wishes to compare and contrast different approaches that are taken in respect of different types of commercial disputes, then he or she can easily do so. However, the final chapter is quite different in that it is a case study of a particular Wills and Probate dispute which shows how mediation actually works in practice.

In addition, there is one separate chapter which is devoted entirely to looking at alternative dispute resolutions generally and in isolation to any particular commercial dispute. It is hoped that this chapter will provide the reader with a general overview of ADR.

It is appreciated that the reader may be sceptical about the true value of resolving commercial disputes by means other than the courts or tribunals. Let me leave you with the following thought.

In 1990 hardly anyone had ever heard of, let alone used, the internet; as we embark upon the twenty-first century the use of the internet has become part of our daily routine. It is impossible to know where ADR and in particular mediation is on the time line of this analogy but there is little doubt in my mind that resolution of commercial disputes by ADR has arrived and sooner rather than later will be embraced by businesses as their main approach to resolving commercial disputes.

PROFILES OF GENERAL EDITOR AND CHAPTER AUTHORS

General Editor

Russell Caller

Russell Caller is a Solicitor and Senior Partner of Gillhams Solicitors, a niche commercial practice based on the Park Royal Business Park in West London. Russell is a CEDR accredited mediator and a founder member and Managing Director of Dispute Mediation Limited, being a recently formed mediation service company involved in organising and advising on commercial mediations. Russell is also Vice Chairman of the Association of Mediation Solicitors.

Chapter Authors

Jonathan Arkush

Jonathan Arkush has more than 20 years' experience as a barrister specialising in commercial and chancery litigation. His main areas of work are disputes involving property, contracts, wills and trusts. He became an accredited Mediator in 2000. He practises from 11 Stone Buildings, Lincoln's Inn, from where he has both advised parties to mediations and acted as Mediator in cases involving companies, individuals and families. Jonathan is a panel mediator of Dispute Mediation Limited.

Philip Bartle

Philip Bartle has been a barrister for 25 years. He is a member of Littleton Chambers and specialises in professional negligence litigation. He lectures on professional negligence and civil procedure and contributes case reports to Lloyds' Professional Negligence Law Reports. He is an accredited mediator with ADR Chambers, has taken part in several mediations and is a member of the Bar Council's ADR Ethical Guidance Working Group.

Catherine Bloomfield

Catherine Bloomfield joined Ince & Co in 1996 upon qualification as a solicitor. She is a senior assistant who advises on a wide range of contentious matters and specialises in the areas of shipping, insurance and international trade.

John Bowers

John Bowers Q.C. practises primarily in employment law from Littleton Chambers. He is co-ordinator of the Workplace Mediation Project and a CEDR accredited mediator. He is Chairman of the Employment Law Bar Association and Legal Advisor for Public Concern at Work, the whistleblowers' charity. He is a part-time employment tribunal Chairman and the author of several books including *Bowers on Employment Law* and *Human Rights and Employment Law*. He is a member of the Standards Board for England, the Government body overseeing ethical standards in local government. John is also a panel mediator of Dispute Mediation Limited.

Simon Davis

Simon Davis is a commercial litigation partner at Clifford Chance. He specialises in the resolution of commercial disputes, regularly with an international element. Simon is an accredited CEDR mediator and has participated in the Central London County Court and Court of Appeal Mediation Schemes. He is treasurer of the London Solicitors Litigation Association Committee. Simon is also a panel mediator of Dispute Mediation Limited.

Christine Derrett

Christine Derrett is a Solicitor and Partner in the Commercial Litigation Department of DJ Freeman. She has specialised in insolvency litigation over the last 12 years and is very experienced in dealing with complex multi-jurisdictional, multi-party insolvency disputes. She has recently been appointed a Deputy Bankruptcy Registrar and will be sitting in the High Court dealing with bankruptcy matters. Christine is a CEDR accredited mediator.

Clive Freedman

Clive Freedman was called to the Bar in 1978 and took silk in 1997. He is also a Recorder. He is a member of Littleton Chambers, and an associate member of chambers in Manchester. He is a commercial litigator covering a wide variety of business disputes including disputes relating to franchising. He is a CEDR accredited mediator, and a panel member of Dispute Mediation Limited. He has conducted a number of mediations as a mediator as well as appearing in mediations as a barrister.

Peter Garry

Peter Garry is a partner in the Commercial Dispute Resolution Department of Cripps Harries Hall, one of the leading firms in the South East region, where he is one of several partners dealing with partnership, shareholder and boardroom disputes, arising throughout the South East and also in London. He is a CEDR accredited mediator and is also on the mediation panels of Dispute Mediation Limited and The City Disputes Panel.

Michèle Gill

Michèle Gill is a mediator specialising in workplace and employment disputes. She has worked with a number of public and private sector organisations conducting mediations as well as facilitating the resolution of conflict within teams and large groups. Michèle is a CEDR accredited mediator. She is a panel member of the Workplace Mediation Project, co-ordinated by John Bowers Q.C. and offering mediation for the resolution of harassment and discrimination cases in the workplace. Michèle is also a panel mediator for Dispute Mediation Limited.

Geoffrey Greenhouse

Geoffrey Greenhouse is a solicitor in private practice specialising in trust probate and charity law. He trained as a mediator at Harvard Law School (advanced mediation certificate) and is a CEDR accredited and registered mediator. He is chairman of the Association of Mediation Solicitors and a member of the Law Society's working party on ADR. Geoffrey is also a panel mediator for Dispute Mediation Limited.

Tim Hardy

Tim Hardy heads up the Litigation and Dispute Resolution Department of CMS Cameron McKenna and has more than 20 years' experience advising corporations on contractual and commercial disputes. He has been practising as a mediator since July 1998 in the field of commercial disputes. He has particular experience of representing clients in mediations relating to the failure of major infrastructure IT systems. Tim is an accredited mediator for both ADR Group and CEDR. He is also a panel mediator for Dispute Mediation Limited, Intermediation and ADR Chambers.

David Leibowitz

David Leibowitz is a solicitor and a CEDR accredited mediator. He is a partner in the Corporate Recovery department at Berwin Leighton Paisner and specialises in banking and insolvency dispute resolution. He has experience both as a mediator and as a lawyer representing clients at mediations. He is a committee member of the London Solicitors Litigation Association, the co-author of a recent book entitled *Getting out of a Contract* and writes regularly on insolvency and mediation issues. David is also a panel mediator of Dispute Mediation Limited

Claire Lester

Claire Lester is a senior assistant solicitor in the Litigation and Dispute Resolution Department of Berwin Leighton Paisner. She obtained a Master's degree in law from London University in 1999 specialising in ADR and international commercial arbitration in which she was awarded a merit. She has wide experience in general commercial litigation, with a particular interest in international arbitration and mediation.

Jonathan Lux

Jonathan Lux qualified as a Solicitor in England in 1977 and Hong Kong in 1986. He joined Ince & Co in 1975 and became a Partner in 1983. Jonathan has been involved in a number of the landmark cases, acting for the major P&I Clubs, their shipowner or Charterer members, cargo interests and cargo sellers and buyers. Jonathan is an accredited mediator and heads Ince & Co's ADR Group. Jonathan is also a panel mediator of Dispute Mediation Limited.

Jeremy Manuel

Jeremy Manuel OBE co-founded Manuel Swaden Solicitors in 1989. He specialises in property law, particularly as it relates to property investment, development and trading. He serves a wide range of clients including major PLCs, property investment and development companies and individuals. Jeremy is committed to the idea of effective dispute resolution and is a CEDR accredited mediator. Jeremy is also a panel mediator of Dispute Mediation Limited.

William Marsh

William Marsh is a senior assistant solicitor at Ince & Co. where he has worked since 1990. He specialises in commercial litigation and arbitration, concentrating on shipping and marine insurance. He regularly handles all aspects of dry shipping, with particular emphasis on carriage of goods by sea, charterparty, shipbuilding and ship sale and purchase disputes.

Michael Wood

Michael Wood has over 20 years' experience of litigation, arbitration and mediation. He is a Fellow of the Chartered Institute of Arbitrators and an ADR Group accredited mediator. He is Head of Dispute Resolution at Gardner Weller, Solicitors, and has wide experience of the resolution of international and domestic insurance disputes. Michael is also a panel mediator of Dispute Mediation Limited.

CONTENTS

TABLE OF CASES

Bandar Property Holdings Ltd v. J.S. Darwen (Successors) Ltd [1968] 2 All E.R. 305; 19 P. & C.R. 785, QBD 9.2.9
Batchelor (T.B.& S.) & Co. Ltd v. Owners of the SS Merak (The Merak) [1965] P. 223; [1965] 2 W.L.R. 250; [1965] 1 All E.R. 230; [1964] 2 Lloyd's Rep. 527; 108 S.J. 1012, CA 11.2.1
Blythe v. Sams [1999] C.L.Y. 322 .... 2.8.3
Charman v. Guardian Royal Exchange Assurance [1992] 2 Lloyd's Rep. 607 .... 7.3.1
Commercial Union Assurance Co. Plc v. NRG Victory Reinsurance Ltd (Joined Cases: Skandia International Insurance Corp v. NRG Victory Reinsurance Ltd) [1998] 2 All E.R. 434; [1998] 2 Lloyd's Rep. 600; [1998] C.L.C. 920; [1998] Lloyd's Rep. I.R. 439; *The Times*, March 19, 1998, CA 7.3.1
Dyson and Field v. Leeds City Council [2000] C.P. Rep. 42, CA 2.8.2, 8.3.3
Finchbourne Ltd v. Rodrigues [1976] 3 All E.R. 581, CA 9.2.9
Havenridge Ltd v. Boston Dyers Ltd [1994] 49 E.G. 111; [1994] E.G.C.S. 53; [1994] N.P.C. 39; *The Times*, April 1, 1994 .... 9.2.9
Insurance Co. of Africa v. SCOR (U.K.) Reinsurance Co. Ltd [1985] 1 Lloyd's Rep. 312, CA 7.3.1
Kinstreet Ltd v. Balmargo Corp. Ltd Transcript:95 K 4271; [1999] C.L.Y. 322, Ch D 2.8.3,7, 7.2.4
Kwik Fit Insurance Services Ltd v. Bull Information Systems Ltd Transcript: HT 99-178, QBD (T&CC) 8.1
Mather v. Barclays Bank Plc [1987] 2 E.G.L.R. 254, DC 9.2.13
Mirror Group Newspapers v. Kevin and Ian Maxwell and the Personal Representatives of Robert Maxwell (Deceased) [1998] 1 B.C.L.C. 638; [1998] B.C.C. 324; *The Times*, July 15, 1997 .... 6.3
Morgan v. Stainer [1993] 33 E.G. 87; [1992] E.G.C.S. 162 .... 9.2.9
Muman v. Nagasena [2000] 1 W.L.R. 299; [1999] 4 All E.R. 178, CA 2.8.3
Pegler Ltd v. Wang (U.K.) Ltd (No.1) [2000] B.L.R. 218; 70 Con. L.R. 68; [2000] I.T.C.L.R. 617; [2000] Masons C.L.R. 19, QBD (T&CC) 8.1
Rotadata Ltd, Re [2000] 1 B.C.L.C. 122; [2000] B.C.C. 686, Ch D (Companies Ct) 2.8.3
Thomas (T.W.) & Co Ltd v. Portsea Steamship Co. Ltd (The Portsmouth) [1912] A.C. 1, HL 11.2.1
Walford v. Miles [1992] 2 A.C. 128; [1992] 2 W.L.R. 174; [1992] 1 All E.R. 453; (1992) 64 P. & C.R. 166; [1992] 1 E.G.L.R. 207; [1992] 11 E.G. 115; [1992] N.P.C. 4; *The Times*, January 27, 1992; *The Independent*, January 29, 1992, HL 8.3.3

TABLE OF CASES

TABLE OF STATUTES

1890 Partnership Act 1890 (53 & 54 Vict., c.39) 10.3.1
1927 Landlord and Tenant Act 1927 (17 & 18 Geo.5, c.36)
s.18(1) 9.2.13
s.19(1) 9.2.6
1954 Landlord and Tenant Act 1954 (2 & 3 Eliz.2, c.56) 7.2.6, 9.2.11, 9.6.9
s.30(1)(a) 9.2.11
(b) 9.2.11
(f) 9.2.11
(g) 9.2.11
1971 Carriage of Goods by Sea Act 1971 (c.19) 11.1.1
1975 Inheritance (Provision for Family and Dependants) Act 1975 (c.63) 12.4
Employment Protection Act 1975 (c.71) 4.2.1
1977 Unfair Contract Terms Act 1977 (c.50) 5.7.2
1979 Merchant Shipping Act 1979 (c.39)
s.17 .... 11.1
Sched.4 .... 11.1
1981 Supreme Court Act 1981 (c.54)
s.20 .... 11.1
s.21 .... 11.1
s.38 .... 9.2.7
1984 County Courts Act 1984 (c.28)
s.138 .... 9.2.7
s.139 .... 9.2.7
1985 Companies Act 1985 (c.6)
ss.459-461 .... 10.3.3
Landlord and Tenant Act 1985 (c.70)
ss.18-20 .... 9.2.9
1986 Insolvency Act 1986 (c.45) 6.1, 6.1.2, 6.1.3, 6.1.13, 6.2
s.167 .... 6.1.5
s.168 .... 6.1.5
s.238 .... 6.2
s.239 .... 6.2
s.314 .... 6.1.14
Sched.1 .... 6.1.2
para.14 .... 6.1.1, 6.1.2
para.18 .... 6.1.1, 6.1.2
para.23 .... 6.1.1, 6.1.2

1986 Insolvency Act 1986 (c.45)—*cont.*
Sched.4 .... 6.1.3
Pt.I 6.1.3
para.2 .... 6.1.4
para.3 .... 6.1.5
Pt.II 6.1.3
Pt.III 6.1.3
para.13 .... 6.1.6
Sched.5 .... 6.1.8, 6.1.14
Pt.I 6.1.8
para.6 .... 6.1.9
para.7 .... 6.1.10
para.8 .... 6.1.11
Pt.II 6.1.8
Pt.III 6.1.8
1988 Landlord and Tenant Act 1988 (c.26) 9.2.6
1995 Merchant Shipping Act 1995 (c.21)
s.185 .... 11.1
Sched.7 .... 11.1
Landlord and Tenant (Covenants) Act 1995 (c.30)
s.19(1A) 9.2.6
1996 Employment Rights Act 1996 (c.18) 4.6.11
Arbitration Act 1996 (c.23) 11.2.1, 11.3.2
s.1 .... 11.2.3, **11.3.1**
s.33 .... 11.3.2
(1) 11.2.3
(b) 11.3.2
(2) 11.3.2
Housing Act 1996 (c.52) 3.9.2
Housing Grants, Construction and Regeneration Act 1996 (c. 53) 8.2.7
1998 Employment Rights (Dispute Resolution) Act 1998 (c.8) 4.2.2
Human Rights Act 1998 (c.42) 7.5.6
2000 Financial Services and Markets Act 2000 (c.8) 2.13.1
Limited Liability Partnerships Act 2000 (c.12) 10.1.1

TABLE OF STATUTORY INSTRUMENTS

TABLE OF INTERNATIONAL TREATIES AND CONVENTIONS

1924 Hague Rules (the Brussels Convention 1924) 11.1, 11.1.1

1950 Convention for the Protection of Human Rights and Fundamental Freedoms 7.5.6
- Art.6 ....2.8.2

1952 International Convention for the Unification of Certain Rules Relating to the Arrest of Sea-going Ships (the Arrest Convention) 11.1

International Convention on Certain Rules Concerning Civil Jurisdiction in Matters of Collision (the Collision Convention) 11.1

1957 International Convention Relating to the Limitation of Liability of Owners of Sea-going Ships 11.1

1958 Convention on the Recognition and Enforcement of Foreign Arbitral Awards (New York Convention) 2.5.3

1965 Washington Convention 2.5.4

1968 Hague-Visby Rules (the Hague Rules as amended by the Brussels Protocol (1968)) 11.1, 11.1.1

1974 York-Antwerp Rules 11.1.1

1976 Convention on Limitation of Liability for Maritime Claims 11.1, 11.2.7

1978 UN Convention on the Carriage of Goods by Sea (the Hamburg Rules)..11.1.1

CHAPTER 1

ADR: WHAT IS IT AND WHAT ARE THE PROS AND CONS?[1]

SIMON DAVIS

INTRODUCTION 1.1

All practitioners should have a working knowledge of what is meant by Alternative Dispute Resolution ("ADR"). They should also know what the advantages and disadvantages of the process are. Otherwise a transaction lawyer will not be able to advise a client whether to seek to include an ADR clause in a contract or to object to its inclusion. Similarly a litigator will not be in a position to advise a client whether to suggest ADR to the other side or how best to respond to a request from the other side or a direction from the court that ADR take place.

WHAT IS ADR? 1.2

In order for this book to be useful to a range of practitioners the acronym ADR is defined as including arbitration, which in truth is an alternative to county or High Court litigation.

When advising a client, however, many practitioners might find it easier to explain that ADR is a method of assisting the parties to settle their differences with the involvement of a third party mediator, but without any binding determination taking place. This would exclude arbitration from the definition.

ADR is a form of facilitated settlement, which is confidential and without prejudice. Consequently the contents of the process need not usually be disclosed to a court. Because it is a form of settlement process the client is not at risk of being bound to an unfavourable outcome by a third party's decision.

If agreement is reached, a binding settlement agreement can be entered into. If it is not, the fact that ADR has taken place but

[1] Simon Davis is the Treasurer of the London Solicitors Litigation Association. This Chapter is an updated version of the submission he prepared in March 2000 for the LSLA to the Lord Chancellors department concerning ADR.

failed can be disclosed to the court, but usually not the reasons why.

Because the process is without prejudice and non-binding, the client does not lose control of the process, as contrasted with what happens when court proceedings are commenced and proceed to judgment at trial.

1.3 How does it work?

There are three principal kinds of ADR: mediation, neutral evaluation and executive mini-trial.

Mediation is the most common. Once the parties have agreed that a mediation should take place, the first step is to appoint a mediator. There are a number of mediation bodies and an even larger number of individual mediators, most of which can be instructed without the need to involve one of the mediation bodies.

The chosen mediator will usually have a meeting in person or on the telephone with the lawyers for both sides, with a view to agreeing the mediation procedure. The procedure can be agreed by exchanges of correspondence between the parties, but that is sometimes time consuming and inefficient. Oral communication between the parties and the mediator tends in any case to facilitate a successful mediation. The parties will sign a mediation agreement.

1.3.1 The mediator will normally be provided with a core bundle of documents agreed between the parties. This might include the pleadings, if a case is already commenced. Almost more important are the key documents in the case. In addition, the parties will often exchange a written statement of their views on the merits.

A mediation is intended to be short: usually one day. It is attended by both parties and their legal representatives. Taking into account that the purpose of the ADR is to achieve a binding settlement, the presence of the lawyers will normally be essential.

The representative(s) from the client should be a decision-maker, able to negotiate and then bind the client. Otherwise momentum will be lost if the client representative has to take instructions at the conclusion of the ADR process. The presence of a decision-maker is also important for further reasons explored later in this chapter.

At the mediation, the mediator will usually invite a short opening statement from each of the parties. There is no set form for this. It might consist of a short resumé of the merits, a statement as to why a party considers it is morally in the right and a statement of commitment to achieving settlement if possible now, given the cost and uncertainty of litigation.

1.3.2 The opening statements should be made without interruption from the other side. The mediator may then ask clarification questions and sometimes even seek a short response from the other party. The most important work, however, is then done in "caucus".

This means that the mediator spends time with each side separately. These separate sessions are confidential. The mediator will test informally the merits of the case and seek potential areas of common ground. The mediator will also try to find creative solutions based on the mediator's own experience, including for example, stage payments, discounts on future business, apologies and revised business terms.

The mediator will then obtain authority from each side to disclose each side's thinking to the other. During the course of the day(s), the mediator will often reconvene the parties together with a view to summarising progress and increasing common ground. If the mediation is successful, the parties will seek to agree and to sign a settlement agreement immediately.

Neutral evaluation is a variation of the mediation process, where the parties invite the mediator to give a view, orally or in writing, on the outcome of the case were it to go to trial. The parties could agree to this at the beginning of the process or during the course of the mediation could reach an agreement that it would be appropriate for the mediator to give this view. This might happen, for instance, if little progress has been made but the parties wished to continue with the mediation. A non-binding evaluation or prediction from the mediator is likely to assist in resolving an impasse.

A further variation is an executive mini-trial. The parties agree to form a panel, which consists of the mediator and a decision-maker from each side. It is that panel which considers written and oral submissions from the parties and their legal representatives and then seeks to assist in bringing about a settlement. It can be particularly helpful in assisting each side to understand better the other side's position.

The advantages of ADR 1.4

Some advantages of ADR over the court process are immediately obvious. If successful an acceptable outcome would have been achieved that is more straightforward, less stressful, less public and far cheaper than proceedings culminating in a trial with an uncertain and unacceptable outcome. Taking into account, however, that almost all cases settle anyway, comparing ADR with the court process is only the beginning of the comparison. The comparison will only be complete if it includes an analysis of the benefits of ADR over the orthodox approach: where settlement is achieved, unassisted by third parties, but often at an advanced stage of a litigation—all too often at the door of the court or even after the trial has commenced, but prior to judgment.

Timing

1.4.1 One of the reasons why cases often settle at a late stage is because neither party has wanted to make the first move—fearing that it might be perceived as a sign of weakness. Taking into account that parties are expected by the Civil Procedure Rules ("CPR") and by the courts to have considered ADR, a suggestion of mediation has less chance of being construed as a sign of weakness in the same way. This risk can be avoided altogether where the mediation suggestion comes from the court.

Understanding the other side's position

1.4.2 The ADR process brings the parties and their lawyers together, in one room or a series of rooms, for a sustained period of time. This process, particularly if the mediator is skilled, enables a party to understand the strength of feeling (and sometimes of case) on the other side better than is usually the position perceived from their respective lawyers' offices.

Focus

1.4.3 An ADR lasting even only a day will require both parties to prepare with great care in advance. Knowing that this day is likely to result in the end of the dispute (approximately 85 per cent of mediations are successful) both parties must focus carefully in advance on the factual and legal issues involved, what commercial principles are at stake and what the parties are prepared to accept as an alternative to an uncertain and expensive determination process.

The preparation involved prior to the sending of a settlement letter or a holding of a settlement conversation may not be as dedicated. The parties may often take the view that settlement negotiations initially are mere skirmishes and that the bottom line of the parties will not really emerge until after their commitment to the litigation process has been thoroughly tested.

The intensity of the effort and focus required for a one-off alternative dispute resolution process increases significantly the chances that a settlement will be achieved during the course of that process.

Commitment

1.4.4 Orthodox settlement discussions conducted on the telephone and by correspondence, often by lawyers, require little in the form of commitment to the process by either the clients or their lawyers. They will typically be conducted while the client and the lawyer are dealing with a series of other matters, sometimes unconnected with the case. Their attention might not be exclusively on those settlement discussions.

In the case of the client in particular, the person having the day-to-day conduct of the action may not be the person or persons who will decide whether a case should be settled.

An in-house lawyer, for example, devoting even 100 per cent of his time to a litigation, may be enthusiastic about achieving a settlement. It will enable that person to become free to carry out work which may be of far more benefit to the client than the ongoing litigation.

The position may be quite different for those who are to make the financial decision. Those individuals, possibly at board level, may have a preconceived idea as to the merits of the case. The issue of settlement of the case may be only one of many items on a busy agenda. They might devote one hour of their time to discussing it or even less. Little commitment in terms of time or energy is therefore required of the decision-makers. They will be making a decision second hand, based only on reports as to what the other side's case and attitude might be. **1.4.5**

Contrast this with the ADR process: as indicated, the person attending from the clients must usually have authority to settle. This may mean that the in-house lawyer brings a senior executive to a mediation. This will require the executive to spend a great deal of time understanding thoroughly the issues in the case, reviewing the facts and merits, and deciding what would be acceptable.

The executive in question then devotes at least an entire day to the ADR process, possibly 12 hours or more, with the parties and the lawyers for both sides. This commitment in terms of time and energy will inevitably increase the chances that the decision-maker will resolve the dispute during the ADR process, possibly on terms which might otherwise have been regarded as unacceptable based on substantially less commitment of time and energy.

The decision-maker may form a different, possibly more realistic, view of the merits of the case in light of the representations made by the other side during the mediation or by having the case "tested" by the mediator. Previously entrenched positions may shift.

The role of the mediator

The importance of having a thoroughly trained, experienced mediator is hard to exaggerate. If, in the early stages of the mediation, the mediator is able to obtain the respect of the parties, there can be an immediate change in the attitude of those parties to that which is present in a settlement negotiation. **1.4.6**

In a settlement negotiation, even where both parties and their legal representatives are present, feelings may run high. Parties may threaten to storm out, extreme positions may be adopted, posturing may take place. As indicated, there will usually be no commitment to seeking to achieve a resolution at that meeting—it will only be part of settlement "talks"—and an acrimonious breakdown may delay settlement talks for a lengthy period.

If the mediator is credible the parties might often in an ADR process seek to impress the mediator with their decency and reasonableness. Threats to storm out may be bitten back. Strong words might be avoided. At the very least the letting off of steam (which may itself be a good thing—see below) will be in a managed environment. The mediator can suggest "time out". He will spend time with each party separately and act as a buffer between them.

The geography of the day

1.4.7 An ADR process will typically involve there being three rooms: one for plenary sessions and the other two for caucuses. This has the advantage of giving the parties thinking time and keeping them separate from the other side. It also enables the mediator to control the process, raising and lowering the temperature as he considers best with a view to achieving a settlement. The presence of separate rooms is sometimes a feature of unassisted settlement negotiations but this kind of structured face-to-face negotiation is not the norm.

Letting off steam

1.4.8 As meetings between both parties may have been relatively rare, particularly meetings between decision-makers occupied by their lawyers, the ADR process gives the parties an opportunity to let off steam. They can complain about the conduct of the other parties and receive at least a sympathetic hearing from the mediator. Neither party expects any sympathy from the other side's lawyers and their own lawyers have natural loyalties. It may well assist a client to be able to say to a third party why it considers that the other side has behaved badly and to obtain some cathartic benefit from receiving an independent hearing.

Testing the merits

1.4.9 During the course of a determination process, the way in which the merits are tested ultimately is at the determination hearing. Along the way the parties might seek to test objectively the merits of their case by internal meetings and perhaps by the involvement of Counsel.

An experienced mediator need not, and probably should not without the consent of the parties, seek to pass any informal judgment on the merits during the course of the ADR process. On the other hand, he can quite reasonably ask the lawyers in the caucus sessions to explain how confident they are of success, why they feel confident of success (if they do), what "guarantees" or percentages of success they are giving their clients and then to ask the clients to compare that confidence with what could happen if the case were to be lost. An experienced mediator can take the parties and the lawyers through best and worst case scenarios (even the "best" case is likely to involve a loss in the form of irrecoverable costs).

This does not mean necessarily that either party considers after a discussion with the mediator that the case is stronger or weaker than they imagined. This may be unrealistic if the mediator has no legal background and in any event it is unnecessary. The point is more for the parties to appreciate the risks of failing to settle on the day.

This kind of worst/best case scenario exercise regularly goes on between lawyers and their clients in any event. The chances of it assisting in reaching a settlement can often be increased when conducted in the presence of or by an experienced mediator during the course of a day expressly intended to bring about a settlement that very day.

Mutual goal

ADR processes tend sometimes to be successful because both parties at the beginning of the day state that their combined goal is to achieve a settlement. The mediator can justifiably remind them of this during the course of the day. It is rare that two parties in an orthodox settlement meeting announce that their goal is to achieve a settlement that very day without proceeding any further. 1.4.10

Flexibility of outcome

A court determination is generally black or white. It will decide on the law and the facts, not impose an equitable solution. The obvious advantage of a settlement is that a solution can be achieved which is tailored to the needs of the parties. This is particularly appropriate where the two parties have an ongoing business relationship and all kinds of creative solutions can be devised. A mediator's experience in assisting in many complex settlements will be well placed to assist in devising such solutions. 1.4.11

THE DISADVANTAGES OF ADR 1.5

The take-up of ADR is increasing, but is still relatively low compared with the number of disputes which become the subject of proceedings. It follows that the process is perceived by many practitioners and clients as having potential draw-backs when compared first with the court/determination process and then with an unassisted settlement.

The determination process

Urgent Court Order required

A party to a dispute may urgently require an Order compelling another party to do or desist from doing some kind of act. Whereas it is of course possible for the parties to a settlement, and therefore 1.5.1

ADR, to agree to do or desist from doing something, this may be too slow. In those circumstances it may be inappropriate to expect the parties first to take part in some kind of ADR process.

No pleadings

1.5.2 A party might often wish to test the other side's resolve or at least to understand the nature of their case, by waiting until proceedings have been served or a Defence has been served before even considering an ADR process.

No disclosure

1.5.3 One party might often prefer to delay settlement or ADR process until after disclosure has been given. Even with the more limited forms of disclosure now available, a party might wish to see whether the other side's documents support the case which is being advanced.

No expert evidence

1.5.4 The case may be very heavily dependent on the evidence of experts. Many accounting disputes, for example, may turn on the professionalism, experience and expertise of particular experts. A party may not want to take part in an ADR process before it has been able to consider the view of the other side's expert or even a court appointed expert if that is appropriate.

No witness statements

1.5.5 A party may wish to see whether the other side's witnesses support a case which is being advanced. Again, consideration of ADR may be perceived as premature.

No cross-examination of witnesses

1.5.6 One party may be convinced that another party's witness will not appear or will not support that side's case when cross-examined under oath. This may be a reason why a party does not wish to take part in an ADR process at all, preferring to take his chances at the determination process.

No precedent

1.5.7 Similarly, a party may wish to obtain a judgment which establishes a matter of principle and precedent for use in his future dealings with the other side or generally. A binding judgment may also be required by a party for use or export overseas. This may not be available through the ADR process.

Size of award

A party who has persisted through to a final determination may have done so because he has a strong sense of grievance or a strong sense that the merits are on his side. This may turn out to be justified as the amount or the result if successful will generally (but not always, *i.e.* where the loser is legally aided or insolvent) be better than would have been achieved through ADR. **1.5.8**

Cost

It is too simplistic to say that ADR is cheaper than a determination process. As already indicated, if properly conducted an ADR is very time consuming for parties and their respective lawyers. The amount of cost can be quite substantial, certainly far exceed the cost of unassisted settlement and will only add to the cost of the determination process if unsuccessful. **1.5.9**

All the above factors may be perceived by parties as a drawback to an ADR process. There will be many (but not all) occasions where that perception is not justified. In many cases the parties or their lawyers may be missing the point. Focusing exclusively on the merits for example assumes that the case will go to trial. Since it is overwhelmingly likely that the case will in fact settle, a party's efforts may better be focused on considering what it would be prepared to pay or accept now as compared with the costs and uncertainties of proceeding further.

Unassisted settlement

Lack of familiarity

An experienced lawyer who has achieved settlements in a cost-effective manner for his clients over many years may see little point in recommending that his client take part in a process with which the lawyer is unfamiliar. **1.5.10**

By way of example, a lawyer of 20 years' experience, but who has never taken part in a mediation, may be reluctant to do so where the other party's lawyer is not so experienced in the world of litigation or unassisted settlement but has a substantial body of mediation experience. The experienced lawyer may consider, not unreasonably, that he will achieve a more satisfactory outcome for his client outside the ADR process.

Commitment

The commitment in time and energy in an ADR process is often intensive. If the parties can achieve an unassisted settlement without this kind of commitment it is not surprising that they choose to do so. **1.5.11**

The commitment required may be what the clients have sought to avoid. The role of the lawyer may be to conduct the brunt of the work without requiring substantial commitment from the clients, whose efforts are being devoted to the running of a business. An experienced lawyer may be able to achieve a cost-effective, satisfactory resolution for the clients without unnecessary demands being placed upon them. If a lawyer can achieve such a settlement for his client without going through the ADR process, it is understandable that he does so.

Abuse of the process

1.5.12 It is sometimes said that ADR cannot be abused, since it is only a settlement process and the parties are free to leave at any time or decline to reach a settlement with both parties being represented by lawyers.

This is too simplistic. The parties will have devoted substantial energies in preparing for the day; their avowed aim is to reach a settlement; the mediator is often seeking quite forcibly to persuade the parties to settle. The client, during the course of the day would have had explained to him the alternative, in terms of costs, expense, and management time of "failing" to reach a settlement. The pressure on the client will be substantial.

In those circumstances there is a possibility that a client may enter into a settlement which is less favourable, perhaps significantly so, than might have been achieved through an unassisted settlement. Apart from the pressures, the decision-maker may not have a thorough grasp of the facts or merits of the case and may reach a decision which undersells the merits of the case.

Abuse of the principle

1.5.13 A party with a weak case or who has no intention of proceeding with it (whether by way of claim or Defence) may seek to use ADR to his advantage. Cloaking the weakness with an expressed desire to participate in an ADR process in accordance with Woolf principles, the weak party may strive for the opportunity in an ADR process to obtain a settlement which may not reflect the merits.

Inadequate mediator

1.5.14 A mediator knows that his role is to seek to achieve a settlement. A mediator may be proud of a successful track record and be keen to maintain it. This may lead, inadvertently, to the mediator overly pressurising the parties into reaching a settlement. The mediator may be more experienced and articulate than the parties before him. His persuasiveness may lead to one or other party entering into a settlement which could have been bettered for him in an unpressurised situation. The mediator is of course in a difficult position. He is there to use his skills to achieve a settlement, and must not hold back from being forceful when necessary. On the other hand, he must be careful not to overstep the mark by pressurising the parties unduly.

WHY IS ADR SELDOM USED? 1.6

The use of ADR is steadily increasing. At an early stage in the proceedings the parties must confirm to the court that ADR has been considered. It is likely that any General Pre-Action Protocol introduced will contain a similar requirement. This will increase further the use of ADR processes and techniques. So far, however, the overall take-up compared with the number of disputes is relatively low.

Earlier in the chapter perceived drawbacks are summarised. Added to this can be: conservatism, inertia, too busy or too reluctant to learn new methods and a lack of familiarity.

Overriding all of this, ADR is rightly regarded by the parties and their lawyers as a settlement process. As such, when a party or parties have no current wish to settle they will not wish to pursue ADR for the time being. On the other hand, if both parties wish to settle, they and their lawyers may feel able to achieve that settlement without the need of the intervention of a third party or any formal process which may add unnecessary expense.

This chapter is intended to enable practitioners to feel more comfortable and familiar with what is involved in ADR and to be able to advise their clients accordingly. It is also hoped that it is shown that in many cases those parties rejecting ADR as not acceptable or necessary as no more than a settlement process are overlooking its benefits. 1.6.1

First, parties who initially have no wish to settle, and therefore reject ADR, all too often change their minds as the determination date fast approaches, only after significant expense has been incurred. Second, those parties who seek to settle without the intervention of a third party, ignore the possibility of using ADR once orthodox settlement talks have failed or even using it as a substitute, taking into account the advantages outlined of assisted over unassisted settlement.

Elsewhere in this book practitioners will find guidance on the use of ADR to govern specific situations. It is hoped that this chapter will provide practitioners and their clients with sufficient knowledge concerning ADR and its advantages and disadvantages to enable an informed choice to be made. While ADR should not be regarded as the panacea for all the problems associated with litigation, properly used it can provide many clients with a controlled, cost-effective and far less painful outcome.

Chapter 2

BANKING AND FINANCE DISPUTES

DAVID LEIBOWITZ AND CLAIRE LESTER

2.1 Introduction

The primary objective of this chapter is to introduce the reader to the concept of using ADR mechanisms and, in particular, mediation in banking disputes. We will briefly examine different types of ADR processes, and look at the advantages and disadvantages of ADR as a mechanism to resolving banking disputes. We will also consider the effect of the CPR on ADR processes and look at the procedural process of mediation in practice.

The principles that we will address in this chapter broadly apply equally to banks and financial institutions (*i.e.* building societies, investment management companies, securities and futures companies, deposit taking institutions, etc). To avoid the repeated use of the phrase "banks and financial institutions", for the most part, we shall simply refer to these types of businesses collectively as "banks".

2.2 Banks and dispute resolution

Banks are regular users of the court system. Take a typical High Court or county court civil daily listing anywhere in the U.K. and you can be sure that the banks will feature. Hundreds of thousands of banking transactions are conducted on a daily basis. Whether the transactions be business to business or consumer to business, it is no surprise that large numbers of disputes arise. Financial disputes are an inevitable consequence of the nature of their business.

2.3 Types of disputes involving banks and financial institutions

More often than not, the banks will be claimants (for example looking to recover an unpaid loan or mortgage arrears). However, banks have deep pockets. This makes them an attractive target for an unsatisfied party looking for a large corporation upon whom to pin the blame when a transaction goes wrong.

We have listed below some of the types of legal actions and complaints that banks experience on a regular basis:

(a) recovery of loans;

(b) enforcement of security;

(c) disputes relating to personal guarantees;

(d) disputes relating to letters of credit;

(e) claims against banks for negligent advice;

(f) claims against banks in relation to pension and mortgage mis-selling;

(g) disputes between banks resulting from bank to bank transactions;

(h) customer complaints on overcharging;

(i) customer complaints concerning calling in a loan and/or appointing a receiver too early.

The range is large. Some of these disputes are business to business. Others are business to consumer. Some are modest in terms of quantum. Others can be multi-million pound actions. It simply depends upon the facts. This chapter is about whether mediation is suitable for these types of disputes. The writers take the view that the value of mediation as an ADR option is not limited to a particular type of case. In general terms, if the parties are willing to try mediation then the prospects of success should be fairly favourable irrespective of the size and nature of the dispute.

TRENDS 2.4

Litigation against banks rose dramatically in the 1980s in both the U.S. and the U.K. and continues to do so in terms of both the number of actions and the size of the banks' potential financial exposure. Litigation involving banks used to be relatively straightforward. Typically the case involved the lending process and the borrower's default. However, the variety and complexity of disputes has grown as the banks and financial institutions have provided an increasingly wide variety of products and services to customers.

This trend has coincided with developments by the courts of new theories of "lender liability" often based upon the concept that financial institutions owe fiduciary duties to customers. At the same time, customers have become increasingly sophisticated and are increasingly prepared to exercise their rights against nationals or multinationals.

Whilst banks must be resigned to the fact that they will inevitably always be heavy users of the dispute resolution procedures, evidence suggests that the banks are exploring methods beyond conventional litigation and are increasingly looking to alternative forms of dispute resolution.

2.5 What is ADR?

ADR is a generic term and covers a large number of different processes, ranging from unstructured purely voluntary processes, such as negotiation and mediation, to more structured forms which result in binding decisions, such as arbitration and expert evaluation.

ADR processes have enjoyed increasing popularity in Great Britain over the last 20 years. Long before the implementation of the Civil Procedure Rules 1999 ("CPR"), many family disputes have been resolved through mediation and employment disputes through the conciliation methods adopted by ACAS. The late 1980s saw the introduction of dispute resolution groups such as CEDR, IDR Europe Limited, the ADR Group and Dispute Mediation. In England and Wales alone there are now approximately 20 such groups and the number continues to rise.

In terms of non binding processes, mediation is the most widely used method of ADR and in our view has considerable advantages over other forms of ADR. In order to understand why this is so it is necessary to briefly consider the way in which different ADR processes work.

Negotiation

2.5.1 Negotiation is the most obvious way of resolving disputes without the need for court intervention. Negotiation is effective if the parties are prepared to co-operate with each other and can agree the issues in dispute. It is most successful where there are external constraints placed on the parties, such as costs, lack of time and resources to resolve the dispute. However, negotiation alone as a means of resolving disputes may not work if the parties have poor negotiating skills, unrealistic expectations of the outcome or where there is a power imbalance betweeen the parties as is often the case between a bank and a debtor.

Mediation

2.5.2 The definition of mediation is not without difficulties, because of the blurring of its boundaries. In its purest form it can be described as the facilitation of negotiations by a neutral third party who has no decision-making power and therefore does not adjudicate on disputed issues. He informally assists the parties to voluntarily reach a mutually acceptable settlement by structuring the mediation and identifying issues. It is a voluntary, confidential process. Usually the mediator will be trained and ideally will have a background knowledge of the particular industry with which the dispute is concerned.

As a non partisan facilitator of negotiations the mediator is better placed to help the parties achieve a settlement than through negotiations alone. Specifically he may be able to focus the parties' attentions on the particular issues, identify and evaluate the options open to each party by probing each party's case for strengths and weaknesses, assist the parties in the bargaining process by exploring various proposals for settlement including those not previously considered and finally to help the parties formulate an agreement.

Arbitration

Arbitration is the process by which parties by agreement refer their dispute to an impartial third person, or panel, selected by the parties to give a decision on their dispute. The decision or award, although the result of a private agreement, may be recognised and enforced by legal proceedings in the national courts where enforcement is sought.[1] 2.5.3

Whilst arbitration and mediation have a number of features in common such as relative informality when compared to litigation, privacy and the ability to chose the mediator or arbitrator, the main feature distinguishing arbitration from mediation is the adjudicatory nature of arbitration. However, some matters are non arbitrable or difficult to arbitrate and certain matters may be subject to restrictions or a complete ban. Depending on the circumstances arbitration can be expensive, particularly institutional arbitration and the procedure agreed upon by the parties may be just as lengthy as litigation.[2]

International Centre for Settlement of Investment Disputes ("ICSID")

ICSID was created by the World Bank and formally established by the Washington Convention of 1965 in order to foster international co-operation for economic development. The Convention 2.5.4

[1] The provisions of the New York Convention 1958 which deals with the recognition and enforcement of foreign arbitral awards are effective in many countries of the world.

[2] There may also be domestic laws which are disadvantageous to arbitration such as the " single action" rule adopted in many U.S. states. For further discussion see "ADR for Financial Institutions"—R. M. Smith (West Group 1998), Part 5:11.

addresses the role of private investment in respect of disputes which may arise in connection with such investment between contracting states and nationals of other contracting states. In order to provide a uniform forum for settling such disputes, ICSID was established.

ICSID promotes settlement of disputes through two different procedures—conciliation and arbitration. However, the procedures are only available if:

(a) the parties agree to submit their dispute to ICSID;

(b) the dispute is between a contracting state (or one of its sub divisions or agencies) and a national of another contracting state;

(c) it is a legal dispute arising out of an investment.[3]

An ICSID arbitration is governed by international law rather than any national systems and the Convention provides that each contracting state shall recognise an award as binding and enforceable as if it were a final national court judgment. Although over 80 states have ratified the ICSID Convention, there have been very few arbitrations since its inception.

Early neutral evaluation

2.5.5 This procedure is intended to encourage each party to better understand its own legal position by providing a forum in which the parties present their respective cases to an independent third party (often a retired judge) and receive an independent neutral assessment of the likely outcome. It is a confidential non binding process, the goal of which is to assess the relative strengths and weaknesses and encourage a settlement. However, unlike a successful mediation it will not necessarily result in settlement between the parties.

How does mediation compare with other forms of ADR?

2.5.6 Of all of the above, negotiation is the most satisfactory form of dispute resolution. However, in the heat of a dispute, parties may not be able to settle without third party help. Of the various forms of ADR identified above, mediation and the flexibility that the procedure offers, has proved to be particularly attractive to those parties that have tried it. A successful mediation can help to focus the parties towards the future and away from the events of the past.

[3] "Investment" is not defined but is taken to cover investment of services and technology as well as capital investment.

WHY HAVE BANKS TRADITIONALLY FAVOURED LITIGATION OVER ADR? 2.6

The traditional stance taken by banks, particularly those involved in international banking transactions, has been to avoid any dispute resolution procedure other than litigation.

As frequently there is a significant imbalance of power between the parties in favour of the bank, the bank's choice of dispute forum will prevail. There are various reasons why banks have traditionally favoured litigation over ADR (and mediation in particular).

In relation to commercial banking disputes regarding loan markets, the position adopted by the Loan Market Association ("LMA") may help to shed light on this. The LMA was set up in 1996 with the objective of " fostering an environment in the Euro markets that would facilitate the constructive development of a secondary market for loans". Amongst its initial aims was the standardisation and simplification of the sale of loan assets and to this end a documentation committee was set up, the object being "to achieve and maintain effective standard forms of documentation for the Primary and Secondary loan markets, responsive to changes in the legislative, regulatory, taxation and market environments".[4]

The members of the LMA are wide-ranging, from City law firms, to central banks, to industry organisations, such as the British Chamber of Commerce and Chartered Institute of Bankers, and various European and world-wide stock exchanges. It is therefore interesting to note that the LMA's standard facility agreement, developed by a working party consisting of members of the LMA, the British Bankers' Association, the Association of Corporate Treasurers and several City law firms, provides for the settlement of disputes through litigation[5] in English courts with no reference whatsoever to any form of ADR.

It is not known why the LMA have adopted this stance, nor indeed whether any review of its standard form documentation is intended in the near future. However, its stance may be due to various perceived disadvantages of ADR, some of which are discussed below.

Perceived disadvantages of ADR

Default by the debtor and/or inability to pay

The traditional bank view has been "If we are owed the money we sue. Why bother with ADR?" Default by the debtor often results from an inability to pay rather than any complex dispute in relation to contractual terms. There is a perceived risk that ADR may put the 2.6.1

[4] Information taken from the LMA website.

[5] Clause 38 of the LMA's standard Multicurrency Term and Revolving Facilities Agreement.

bank under pressure to take a "split the difference" approach which the bank may feel does not reflect the strong legal merits of the bank's case.

Summary procedures/injunction

2.6.2 Litigation provides the ability to use summary procedures to obtain a quick judgment against a debtor where there is no defence to a claim or for the enforcement of promissory notes, letters of credit or to freeze assets by way of injunction.

Publicity/precedent

2.6.3 Litigation proceedings are heard in public. The bank may consider that the publicity is welcome because it may put additional pressure on the debtor to settle. Publicity may also be welcome if the bank is looking to set a precedent.

Jurisdiction

2.6.4 Litigation provides the opportunity to commence court action in the jurisdiction where the debtor's assets are located. This will almost certainly be an option if security has been given by the debtor over the asset in question. This jurisdictional benefit can avoid later problems on enforcement.

Conservatism

2.6.5 The reluctance to try any "new" method of resolving disputes. If litigation has by and large served the purpose in the past, why change tactics?

Cost of ADR

2.6.6 On very low value cases, it may not necessarily be cost-effective to proceed by way of ADR. Use of the county court small track or fast track procedures may prove to be more cost-effective.

Abuse of the ADR process

2.6.7 The ADR process may be abused by one of the parties who has no intention of settling but is looking to find out all he can as to the other party's case and to ascertain their "bottom line".

No court order

2.6.8 A successful mediation will result in a contractual settlement agreement between the parties. However, the settlement agreement does not have the force of a court order. Mediation may be inappropriate if one of the parties cannot be trusted to honour a voluntary settlement.

Whilst it must be recognised that ADR will not be appropriate in every case, the writers of this chapter believe that many of the disadvantages cited above are misconceived and must be balanced against the considerable advantages ADR and, in particular, mediation can offer.

ADVANTAGES OF ADR AND IN PARTICULAR, MEDIATION, IN BANKING DISPUTES 2.7

Flexibility

As with all ADR processes, there is a degree of flexibility in media- 2.7.1
tion which is not available in litigation. Creative settlement terms can be agreed in mediation which may be outside the ambit of that available to a court. For example, agreeing business deals for the future, profit sharing solutions or tying in a third party in order to achieve objectives.

Maintaining relationships with clients

Litigation typically destroys relationships. If it is important to the 2.7.2
bank to maintain a relationship with a commercial borrower, the ADR techniques may offer the best option.

Alternatively, if the bank no longer wishes to maintain its relationship with a borrower, ADR can provide a fast, efficient cost-effective way for the bank to extract itself from the relationship.

Parties retain control

Mediation is a consensual process which is essentially driven by 2.7.3
the parties themselves, rather than their lawyers.

Banks are typically organisations with significant financial and political power. On one level they are well able to cope with the high stakes "winner takes all" environment of the courtroom. However, clients are becoming more educated and knowledgeable about legal matters. Clients in this sector will want, where possible, to retain control over the dispute resolution process. Litigation is typically run by the lawyers. Banks can experience a loss of control over the dispute resolution procedure. Client control over the outcome is one of the key features that distinguishes ADR from litigation.

Mediation can save banks money

The use of mediation can save banks money. Speedy and cost- 2.7.4
effective mediation allows banks get on with their business.

Speed

The slow pace at which civil courts operate can cause problems for 2.7.5
banks. Typically, funds are limited when a borrower is in default.

Delay may result in a decrease in value of both the bank's security and the borrower's business.

A successful mediation can save months or years of trial preparation. This saves both management time and legal costs. Because it is a consensual process, the parties can dispense with the time and expense of preparing and exchanging witness statements and disclosure if they so choose and can set a deadline for the length of the mediation.

Disputes *between* banks often need to be resolved particularly speedily. For example, there may be some uncertainty as to the accounting position between two banks. For the parties, it may be the uncertainty itself that is the most pressing problem. They have to close the position. A speedy resolution is the paramount concern.

Publicity and confidentiality

2.7.6 Particularly in cases where a sustainable claim has been made against a bank, it may be particularly important to the bank not to have the evidence aired in open court. ADR provides the benefits of confidentiality.

2.8 THE COURT'S POWERS IN RELATION TO ADR

> "Litigation is a socially inefficient method of resolving disputes . . . It must surely be regarded as the remedy of last resort, and to save the social cost every endeavour must be made to encourage the parties to take advantage of alternate dispute resolution and most particularly mediation."[6]

This powerful passage delivered by Mr Justice Lightman in 1998, highlights the central role that ADR now plays in the new post-Woolf landscape.

The overriding objective set out in the CPR is to enable the courts to deal with cases justly.[7] This includes, *inter alia*, saving expense,[8] dealing with the case in ways which are proportionate to the amount of money involved, the importance of the case, the complexity of the issues and the financial position of the parties.[9] In managing cases that are to come before the court, the court must be alert to the possibility of directing the parties to attempt to resolve their dispute by ADR or any other means at their disposal so that the court can manage its resources. Accordingly, the more

[6] Mr Justice Lightman, Chancery Bar Association Spring Lecture—"Civil Litigation in the 21st Century" (1998) 17 C.J.Q. 391.

[7] CPR 1.1.(1).

[8] CPR 1.1(2)(b).

[9] CPR 1.1(2)(c).

cases that can be dealt with by ADR, the less strain will be placed on the court's other resources.

To further the overriding objective, the court now has a duty to actively manage cases and should encourage parties to use an alternative dispute resolution procedure if the court considers that appropriate and to facilitate the use of such procedure.[10] The following are particularly relevant in this regard: **2.8.1**

(a) Reference to ADR is incorporated into the allocation questionnnaire. The parties are invited to agree a stay to try to settle the case by ADR. The court has power to order a stay for that purpose.[11]

(b) Matters the judge may take into account in deciding whether to grant a stay may include such things as the value of the claim, how the claim is being funded, time the case will take at trial, possible outcome at trial and the financial ability of the parties to satisfy a judgment entered against them.[12]

(c) The court has a discretion as to the type of ADR process to be followed. If one party wants a stay to try party and party negotiations as a means of settlement, but the other wishes to use mediation, the judge will have discretion to follow a particular settlement route.

(d) In assessing costs the court is to have regard to a number of factors including the conduct of the parties before as well as during proceedings and the efforts made, if any, before and during the proceedings in order to try to resolve the dispute.[13]

Encouragement or coercion?

The conventional view is that ADR is a consensual process and that it is fundamental to that process that ADR should not be mandatory. If a party agrees to mediate and then fails to turn up or uses the mediation for an ulterior motive, that party has contravened the CPR and should rightly be penalised. However, that scenario has to be distinguished from the right of a party to decide whether his case is suitable for ADR. This decision is probably best left to the parties. Threats by the courts to impose substantial penalties on parties who elect litigation over ADR almost amounts to compulsory ADR. It is our belief that if the courts confuse encouragement with coercion, it will not be long before a dissatisfied party alleges **2.8.2**

10 CPR 1.4 (2)(e).

11 CPR 26.4.

12 "Alternative Dispute Resolution Under the New Civil Rules—Some Guidelines for Lawyers and Judges" by D. I. Shapiro (1999) 18(7) *Litigation—the Journal of Contentious Business*.

13 CPR 44.5(3).

a breach of Article 6 of the Convention on Human Rights (*i.e.* the right to a fair trial).

It is interesting to consider the court's attitude to the use of ADR since the introduction of the CPR. Several judgments in the course of the last year have been of particular note.

In one Court of Appeal judgment[14] where a retrial was ordered due to the trial judge's failure to explain his reasons for preferring one party's expert evidence over another, Ward L.J. stated:

> "this is pre-eminently the category of case in which consistent with the overriding objective of the CPR and the court's duty to manage cases . . . we should encourage the parties to use an ADR procedure to bring this unhappy matter to a conclusion . . . the court has powers to take a strong view about the rejection of the encouraging noises we are making, if necessary by imposing eventual orders for indemnity costs or indeed ordering that a higher rate of interest be paid on any damages which might at the end of the day be recoverable".

Both Lord Woolf and Laws L.J. were eager to associate themselves with Ward L.J.'s "warning of dire consequences" if such encouragement was not heeded.

2.8.3 In another case,[15] the Court of Appeal made an order that charity proceedings brought by trustees pending authorisation of the proceedings be stayed. The court then went on to provide that during the course of the stay, the parties must attempt to resolve the dispute by mediation. In some instances the courts have been prepared to do more than simply encourage ADR and have gone as far as ordering ADR on a reluctant party.[16]

In a share valuation case[17] where the costs of the action were likely to exceed the value of the shares in question, Neuberger J. reminded the parties that a refusal to use ADR could be taken into account by the court in considering costs.[18]

2.9 ADR CLAUSES

Why draft an ADR clause?

2.9.1 Agreement to any form of alternative dispute mechanism is very difficult once a dispute has arisen as the parties are likely to be so entrenched in their respective positions that any attempt at agreeing a mechanism other than litigation for settling a dispute is likely to prove fruitless. Accordingly, it makes sense to negotiate precise details of the way in which the dispute resolution procedure is to

14 *Dyson and Field v. Leeds City Council* [2000] C.P.Rep. 42.
15 *Muman v. Nagasena* [2000] 1 W.L.R. 299, CA.
16 *Kinstreet Ltd. v. Balmargo Corporation Ltd.* [1999] C.L.Y. 322.
17 *Re Rotadata* [2000] 1 B.C.L.C. 122.
18 See also *Blythe v. Sams* [1999] C.L.Y. 322.

operate before any dispute has arisen. This will often involve an ADR clause being inserted in the contract governing the parties' relationship.

There are a wide variety of clauses, some simple and some complex. A clause that provides for a non-binding ADR procedure such as mediation can only require the parties to attempt to resolve disputes through ADR. A clause containing a binding ADR procedure such as adjudication, can oblige the parties to comply with the outcome of an award.

The growth of ADR will depend largely upon the willingness of lawyers and their clients to draft these types of clauses into their contracts. Studies have shown that a litigant's lawyer is the most significant determinant of the parties attitude to ADR and therefore, their perspective on ADR is of vital importance.

The writers' experience is that when parties are negotiating contracts sometimes late into the night, the dispute resolution clause is often the very last issue to be addressed. At this stage it will probably be simpler for the parties to insert a simple and familiar jurisdiction and governing law clause than a less familiar and possibly lengthier ADR clause.

Some commentators suggest that an ADR clause is in a sense 2.9.2
contrary to the philosophy of ADR. Successful mediation requires the parties to be willing to mediate. The prospects of a successful mediation are low if one party is only attending the mediation because he is contractually obliged to do so.

However, the benefit of the ADR clause is that it puts ADR "on the agenda". The parties clearly thought that ADR was a sensible option when they negotiated the contract. The fact that a clause is in place overcomes the reluctance to suggest ADR when a dispute arises. In such a circumstance, a party need not be concerned that proposing ADR is a "sign of weakness"—it is a contractual obligation.

There is some evidence from the U.S. that including an ADR clause in loan documents may have a deterrent effect upon lender liability actions. The Bank of America has reported a decline in lender liability law suits since its inclusion of arbitration clauses in its loan documentation.

Banks will want to ensure that whatever their approach to dispute resolution, they preserve rights to repossess secured assets, exercise set-off, freeze accounts, etc. A sensibly drafted ADR clause will not prohibit a bank from exercising their rights.

What points should the ADR clause cover?

A well drafted ADR clause should cover the following: 2.9.3

(a) a clear description of the issues/disputes to be decided by ADR;

(b) the type of ADR process to be adopted;

(c) the procedure under which the ADR process will operate, (*e.g.* whether a particular ADR provider is to designate the procedural rules; if mediation is the chosen process, how to chose a mediator; length of mediation; scope of intervention of the mediator; costs position; will lawyers be involved; forum of mediation, etc).

2.10 THE MEDIATION PROCESS

Having examined the advantages and disadvantages of ADR and in particular mediation, we now turn to the mediation process itself. Mediation practices encompass diverse styles and methods largely due to the informal nature of mediation. For parties contemplating mediation, the following points should be borne in mind:

Facilitative or evaluative mediation

2.10.1 There are two main forms of mediation:

(1) facilitative;

(2) evaluative.

At one end of the spectrum the mediator will maintain a low profile with only minimal interruption when the parties are communicating. His role is to help the parties to reach a settlement by oiling the wheels of communication but to hold back from expressing his own views or opinions. This is facilitative mediation in its purest form.

At the other end of the spectrum is evaluative mediation. A mediator's role becomes evaluative if he is asked by the parties to express an opinion on the relative strengths of some or all of the issues between the parties.

When setting up a mediation, it is important to agree a framework for the mediation with both the other party and the mediator. A key issue that needs to be addressed pre-mediation, is the role that the parties wish the mediator to take. Where on the spectrum between facilitative and evaluative mediation does the mediator's role lie?

There are no fixed rules as to when to select evaluative over facilitative mediation. However, in general terms, the writers favour mediation towards the facilitative end of the spectrum. The essence of mediation is that the mediator controls the process and the parties control the outcome. The primary advantage of mediation and negotiation over other forms of ADR is that the parties take responsibility for the solution. It is not imposed upon them.

A mediator who expresses a view favouring one party's arguments over the other risks being perceived as favouring one party over the other. The mediator runs the risk of no longer being of a neutral party.

If a deadlock position is reached during the course of a facilitative mediation, it may be appropriate for the mediator to discuss with the parties whether to switch towards a somewhat more evaluative approach. Flexibility of approach is one of the primary attractions of mediation.

Selecting a mediator

Once the parties have agreed to mediate they need to select a **2.10.2** mediator. Mediation organisations such as Dispute Mediation and CEDR have panels of accredited mediators. These organisations will help the parties, if help is required, to select a suitable mediator for the dispute in question.

For banking and finance disputes, a suitable mediator is likely to be a lawyer and/or a practitioner within the industry. However, the most important single qualification required is that the proposed candidate is a skilled mediator. Unless the dispute is highly technical and/or the parties are looking for an evaluative mediation, the mediator need not have an in depth knowledge of the industry.

Preliminary contact between the parties and the mediator

Once a suitable mediator has been selected, there are certain pre- **2.10.3** liminary matters that need to be discussed between the parties and the mediator. On a small scale mediation, this contact may be by telephone and/or by correspondence. However, a preliminary meeting is preferable on larger matters. Issues to be addressed at this preliminary stage include:

(a) level of mediator's fees (usually split equally between the parties);

(b) mediation agreement to be signed;

(c) venue to be agreed;

(d) length of mediation to be agreed (usually no more than a day);

(e) role of mediator to be agreed (*i.e.* where on the spectrum between facilitative and evaluative?);

(f) documentation available at the mediation to be agreed (*e.g.* are the parties going to provide case summaries and/or bundles and if so by when?);

(g) ensuring that those present at the mediation will have authority to settle.

The mediation

2.10.4 Most mediations begin with an initial joint meeting between the parties and the mediator. The mediator opens by explaining the process and answering any questions that the parties may have. Even at this stage, it is not uncommon for the parties to be expecting that towards the end of the day the mediator will be making a "ruling". It is essential that the mediator explains the fundamentals of a mediation to the parties at the beginning of the day.

The parties need to know that:

(a) all discussions are on a strictly without prejudice basis;

(b) the parties are free to walk away from the mediation at any point in time;

(c) all conversations in private session between the mediator and any one of the parties are strictly confidential;

(d) the mediator will be helping the parties to find their own solution to the dispute, he will not be adjudicating on the merits of the case;

(e) if terms are agreed, they will be recorded in a written settlement agreement which will be binding on the parties.

After this introduction by the mediator, each party will then have an opportunity to make an uninterrupted opening statement setting out how they see the position. Each party will be given an equal period of time, typically say 15 minutes or so.

In most mediations, the mediator will then ask the parties to retire to separate rooms so that the mediator can have private and confidential meetings with each of the parties in turn. The essential feature of these meetings (often referred to as "caucuses") is that all matters discussed in caucus are entirely confidential. Each party can speak frankly with the mediator with the confidence that nothing said will be related to the opposing party without his express consent. This confidentiality and trust is at the heart of the mediation process.

2.10.5 If and when the mediator considers it appropriate to do so, he may decide to bring the parties together again for a joint session. The pace of the mediation is a factor that falls under the control of the mediator and can make the difference between settlement and a missed opportunity. The parties must have sufficient time to put their case to the opposition and to cover the ground that they consider necessary with the mediator. The mediator needs to be a good listener.

Clearly at some point (and not too late during the day), the bargaining has to begin. An inexperienced mediator may be tempted to do too little listening and try to push the parties towards exchanging offers and counter offers before they are psychologically ready to do so.

Mediation has shown itself to be a successful form of dispute resolution. Most mediations result in settlements on the day of the mediation. Some result in settlement in the days and weeks following the mediation. As and when terms are agreed, the mediator will help the parties draw up a settlement agreement. If the parties are legally represented, the drafting of the agreement is usually left to the lawyers. The settlement constitutes a binding contract between the parties. If confidentiality is an issue (and it frequently is) a settlement agreement will typically provide that all matters discussed at the mediation remain confidential and that the terms of the settlement remain confidential.

If no settlement is achieved, time and money may have been lost but little more. Most importantly, all discussions that took place during the course of the mediation were on a without prejudice basis and cannot be relied upon by either party in subsequent court proceedings without the consent of the other. Even a mediation that does not result in settlement, may help to identify the issues between the parties (*i.e.* both the issues that are common ground and those that are in dispute).

THE RIGHT TIME TO MEDIATE 2.11

Care needs to be taken in selecting the right time to mediate. Views vary on this issue. The obvious advantage of mediating early is that if the mediation is successful and the dispute settles, time and costs have been saved. However, earlier mediation carries certain risks. In some disputes, it may be important for one or both parties to have "fought" for a period of time before they are psychologically ready to settle. In some cases, an early mediation may come at a time when the parties simply have insufficient information about their opponent's case to make a realistic assessment of the merits. For this reason it may on occasions be wise not to mediate until disclosure and/or exchange of witness statements (whether fact or expert) have been completed.

CHANGE OF ATTITUDE BY THE BANKS AND CURRENT PRACTICE OF U.K. CLEARING BANKS 2.12

Evidence of change

Notwithstanding the LMA's standard documentation and the traditional views expressed by banks in the past, banks and financial institutions have been significant users of mediation over the last 2.12.1

couple of years. The Woolf reforms and the increasingly important role played by ADR generally coincide with cultural changes within the banks in relation to their approach to dispute resolution.

CEDR 2000 statistics show that six per cent of all disputes referred to CEDR in the financial year 1999/2000 were banking and finance disputes.

We spoke to a number of U.K. clearing banks about their experience and use of mediation. The approach and experience of these banks was for the most part fairly consistent. Some of the more important observations are summarised below.

Barclays Bank Plc is one of the banks that has been particularly proactive in the ADR field. Barclays is a founder member of CEDR and in 1996 Barclays won the Industry ADR Excellence Award. The Barclays legal risk management guidelines state:

> "... disputes should be resolved as cost effectively and quickly as possible ... negotiation, whether informed or in the context of ADR is normally the preferred way of resolving a dispute".[19]

Early settlement before involvement of external lawyers

2.12.2 From our discussions, it is clear that where possible the banks are looking for quick and cost-effective resolutions. There are significant benefits in terms of cost saving, time saving and public relations in achieving a satisfactory early settlement.

Claims made by or against the banks are typically never handled at branch level. They are handled by case managers who have been trained in the art of negotiation. The aim is to try to get the disputes settled in-house at this stage without having to use external lawyers.

Panel solicitors and ADR

2.12.3 Inevitably however, all of the banks that we spoke to rely heavily on the use of external solicitors to pursue or defend claims on behalf of the banks. Banks put their work out to tender and appoint a small panel of solicitors. All of the banks that we spoke to required their panel solicitors to demonstrate a willingness and capacity to resolve disputes by way of mediation in appropriate cases. One bank reported that no firm gets on the panel without having an accredited mediator on the team. LloydsTSB reported that panel solicitors instructed by the recoveries team out of Bristol are required to receive regular six-monthly training by one of the ADR organisations.

Although external lawyers are required by the banks to be recep-

[19] "The Woolf inside the Barclays Group" by Miryana Nesic in *Resolutions* issue no. 24.

tive to the ADR options that are now available, it is rare for a bank to dictate to an external solicitor that he should take the ADR route. The decision as to whether to offer ADR is usually left to the discretion of the external solicitor.

All those we spoke to accepted that flexibility of approach was important and that the merits of using ADR had to be assessed on a case by case basis.

Economic factors

We are presently experiencing a benign economic environment. 2.12.4
One case manager we spoke to on the debt recovery side explained that where possible it was important for the bank to "give the debtor a chance". If the debtor runs into financial difficulty it is almost always preferable for the bank to try to reschedule the debt and reach a satisfactory accommodation with the debtor rather than to litigate.

Where possible the bank is looking to retain an ongoing relationship with its clients and to preserve and promote the public image of the bank in the wider community.

However, the case manager in question commented that the approach may alter if the economy slows down or indeed if the U.K. experiences a recession. In that event, the banks may elect to be less concerned about their public image and focus more tightly on maximising their short-term recovery.

Maintaining the relationship

All of the banks that we spoke to recognised the importance, where 2.12.5
possible, of maintaining a relationship with the client. In simple financial terms, an ongoing relationship gives the bank an opportunity to continue to benefit from a client's business. The client remains a potential buyer of the range of products that the bank has to offer. Banks no longer simply take deposits and grant loans. Most of the clearing banks now have a large portfolio of financial products available to clients.

Perceived image of the bank

Banking is a competitive market. The clearing banks in particular 2.12.6
are very aware of the importance of projecting an efficient but caring image in the market place. This is particularly important in relation to consumer and small business clients. By way of illustration, one of the banks we spoke to wanted us to understand just how exceptional it is for his bank to seek an eviction order after possession proceedings. An application for such an order has to be sanctioned at the very highest level.

Similarly, banks in the current climate are sensitive about the adverse publicity that they may attract on the appointment of receiver over a company or by petitioning for the bankruptcy of a judgment debtor.

Where possible more creative positive solutions are being sought. The banks are doing more talking and are less trigger happy.

Case management

2.12.7 All those we spoke to observed that when the CPR came into force in April 1999, the expectation was that judges would be referring disputes to mediation on a regular basis. However, this has not proved to be the case. Both District Judges and High Court Judges have left it to the parties to take a view as to whether they wish to try mediating the dispute.

As mentioned above, there is a good deal of judicial attention at present regarding the degree of encouragement/coercion to be imposed by the courts on the parties. Whilst the experience of those banks that we spoke to suggests that judges are currently proceeding cautiously, the writers suspect that the more senior members of the judiciary will lead the way towards a more robust approach in the near future.

All of the banks that we spoke to had considerable mediation experience. Whilst the number of mediations was lower than had been anticipated when the Woof Reforms came in, mediation nevertheless continues to provide an important method of dispute resolution for the banks.

Selection of mediators

2.12.8 We discussed with the banks how mediators were selected and who attended at the mediation. In almost all cases, the bank leaves the selection of the mediator to their external solicitor. Mediators selected have tended to be lawyers. Bank practice is that case handlers (and/or line managers) attend at the mediation with the external solicitor but branch managers and branch staff do not attend.

Costs

Typically, there is a significant imbalance of power between the parties in favour of the bank. This is one of the reasons why the banks frequently offer to meet the costs of the mediation rather than the typical 50/50 split between mediating parties.

One banker commented that because of this imbalance of power, his experience was that mediators frequently put pressure on banks during the course of the mediation to be financially generous when it came down to concluding terms of settlement.

BANKING MEDIATION IN ACTION 2.13

The changing attitudes to the use of mediation in banking disputes has resulted in various initiatives to attract more users to mediation. Some of these are set out below.

The Financial Services Authority

The activities of banks, building societies and insurance companies 2.13.1
are regulated by the Financial Services Authority (the "FSA"). All businesses that fall under the FSA umbrella must satisfy the FSA that their rules and arrangements provide adequate investor protection. The FSA must ensure that firms meet the minimum requirements of all relevant legislation and codes of practice.

Financial institutions cannot trade without FSA authorisation. To do so is a criminal offence. The system is policed by the FSA through their enforcement procedures.

The Financial Services and Markets Act 2000 ("FSMA") gives the FSA a range of disciplinary powers.[20] These include:

(a) withdrawal of authorisation;

(b) a public statement of censure;

(c) imposition of a financial penalty.

Before imposing such a penalty, the firm in question is served with an FSA "Warning Notice". The notice sets out the proposed action to be taken by the FSA and the reason why. The addressee then has a limited amount of time in which to make representations to the FSA. The notice provides that a person who is or may be subject to enforcement action may discuss the proposed penalty with the FSA staff, on an informal basis.

If it is not possible to reach an agreed settlement of the case by informal discussions, the FSA staff and the person concerned may agree that it is appropriate to submit the case to mediation.[21] The FSA has developed a special mediation procedure for disciplinary cases, involving a panel of independent mediators. The party to be disciplined is not obliged to go to mediation but the scheme is available if the party wishes to use it. The mediator's costs are split equally between the FSA and the firm or individual.

Mediation will not be available in cases involving allegations of a criminal offence, impropriety or dishonesty.

Under the mediation scheme, confidentiality is limited in that if any information indicating potentially criminal conduct is disclosed to the mediator, the mediator will not be required to keep that matter confidential (and may choose to terminate the mediation).

[20] *FSA Enforcement Manual*—August 2000.

[21] *FSA Enforcement Manual*, Annex 6G—August 2000.

Terms of any settlement will only be binding if ratified by the Regulatory Decisions Committee ("RDC") of the FSA.

The use of mediation in the disciplinary context is a novel approach in the area of financial regulation, but reflects current trends in civil litigation. The FSA is currently operating the mediation scheme on a pilot basis. The success of the scheme will be assessed by the FSA within the next 12 months.

The City Disputes Panel ("CDP")

2.13.2 In 1994, a solicitor and former merchant banker, Richard Freeman conceived the idea of an organisation specialising in the resolution of City disputes. It was set up for the banking and financial institutions. At that time few banks or financial institutions were aware of the growing importance of ADR. However, there was a recognition that for London to retain its position as a premier world-wide financial centre, the City institutions had to explore ways of resolving disputes in a cost-effective and speedy manner. Lengthy and expensive litigation damages the reputation of the City.

CDP has a panel of lawyers, retired judges and City experts available for all forms of ADR.[22] One of CPD's major successes was in managing to broker a deal following on from the collapse of Barings Bank. More recently, in the run up to the millennium, CDP set up a panel of lawyers and IT consultants to help resolve disputes involving financial institutions resulting from Y2K problems.

The CDP has an impressive list of members including all the U.K. clearing banks, the leading financial institutions and firms of lawyers and accountants. The CDP is a non-profit making organisation. Members pay an annual charge to cover administrative costs.

2.14 OTHER METHODS OF RESOLVING BANKING DISPUTES

Banking Ombudsman Scheme ("the Scheme")

Who can use the Scheme?

2.14.1 The Scheme is available to help resolve complaints against banks in the U.K. The service is free to complainants. The Ombudsman has authority to award compensation up to £100,000 to the complainant. The banks are obliged to accept the decision of the Ombudsman. However, the complainants do not have to; they retain the right to go to court.[23]

The Ombudsman will deal with the complaints from individuals, sole traders, partnerships and clubs. It can also deal with com-

[22] CDP website at *www.disputespanel.com*.
[23] Office of Banking Ombudsman website at *www.obo.org.uk*.

plaints from companies if their annual turnover is less than £1 million.

The Scheme has a staff of 50. Whilst the management and operation of the Scheme is independent of the banks, it is funded by a levy on the banks.

The purpose of the Scheme is to deal with complaints. It does not have the power to make rules or recommendations in general terms for the banking industry.

All the major banks are covered by the Scheme, including those which were previously building societies. Ordinarily the complaint must be about something the bank did (or failed to do). The Scheme will consider complaints of maladministration or unfair treatment. However, there are some matters that fall outside of the remit of the Scheme (*e.g.* a complaint about a bank's commercial judgment as to whether or not to provide a loan).

The procedure

The complainant's first step is to complain to the bank. If the complainant gets to the end of the bank's complaints procedure without the complaint having been resolved, the bank will declare in a letter that the complaint has reached *deadlock*. The complainant then has six months within which to take up the complaint through the Scheme. **2.14.2**

The Ombudsman explores whether there is scope to resolve the complaint quickly by conciliation. If the complaint cannot be resolved by conciliation, it will be passed to the Scheme's investigation department. The Ombudsman may decline to conduct an investigation if satisfied that the bank has already offered the complainant adequate compensation.

When a complaint is passed to the investigation department, it is allocated to one of the Ombudsman's Adjudicators, who investigates the case fully. He then delivers his decision. In the majority of cases, once the adjudication has been made, both parties usually accept the verdict. Subject to any grounds for judicial review (which is very rare) the bank is bound by the verdict. However, the complainant is free to accept or reject the decision.

Does it work?

We spoke to The Royal Bank of Scotland ("RBS") about the Scheme. They explained to us that the Scheme plays a central role in their dispute resolution programme. Customer complaints usually start at the branch level. The complaints are channelled by managers through from branch level to a specialist customer relations department. Specially trained staff look to settle complaints internally from this centre. However, if terms cannot be agreed then a reference to the Banking Ombudsman typically follows. **2.14.3**

RBS commented that they thought that the Scheme worked well. One criticism is that some complainants are concerned at the perceived lack of independence of the Scheme. After all, essentially, the Scheme is funded by the banks. A second cause for complaint is that it can take several months for the Banking Ombudsman to reach a decision.

Nevertheless, large numbers of complaints at the lower end of the scale are conciliated or adjudicated by the Banking Ombudsman each year.

Under the FSMA, the Financial Ombudsman will replace the five existing Ombudsman schemes (*i.e.* banking, building societies, personal investment, pensions and insurance). Notwithstanding the name change, the Scheme will continue in its present form.

2.15 CASE STUDIES

Because of confidentiality issues it can be difficult to gather together information concerning mediations (whether successful or unsuccessful) that have taken place. However, within the banking field here are just a few examples of disputes that have been successfully mediated in the recent past.

A loan was taken for an office block which was syndicated to four banks. The borrower was in liquidation and the banks repossessed the building. The syndicate documentation failed to address procedures post repossession. For example, one bank was looking to suffer the loss quickly and organise a sale. Another wanted to take a long-term view, manage the property and only market it when the time was right.[24]

The banks were based in different jurisdictions and there was some doubt as to how long some or all of the banks could hold the property. A solution had to be found. The property could not simply be left in limbo. A cost-effective and speedy workable solution to the impasse was found through mediation which would simply not have been available in the litigation context.

As mentioned above, in 1997 the CPD was involved in facilitating a settlement between bondholders of Barings and the administrators of Barings. The dispute was one of many that followed the collapse of Barings in 1995 resulting from unauthorised trading by Nick Leeson in the bank's Singapore office. The issues between the bondholders, administrators, directors and advisers, were complex. On this occasion, with the help of the CDP the parties within the market were able to achieve a settlement.[25]

Both the Channel Tunnel Rail Link and the Docklands Light Railway involved large-scale financing projects. Disputes relating to

[24] Robert M. Smith *ADR for Financial Institutions* (West Group, 1998).

[25] *Daily Telegraph*, May 19, 1999.

these projects were settled partly by the use of mediation techniques.

British and Commonwealth Holdings Plc ("B&C") went into insolvent administration following the disastrous acquisition of Atlantic Computers ("AC"). The acquisition resulted in a number of large and very expensive disputes. One of the central disputes concerned B&C's bankers, (BZW), AC's bankers (Rothschild) and a number of magic circle auditors. The sum in dispute was £850 million. A trial would have lasted months. The dispute was successfully mediated in four days.[26]

One of the many complex cases concerning interest rate swaps (in this case between Bankers Trust and Proctor and Gamble) was successfully settled by mediation.

CONCLUSION 2.16

We hope that this chapter has demonstrated how ADR processes can resolve banking disputes and achieve results which would not be possible through litigation. However, whilst the use of ADR in banking disputes is on the increase in the U.K., it is still not widespread. The reason for this lies largely with lawyers responsible for drafting standard form documentation and a lack of awareness on the part of the institutions as to the value of ADR.

To embrace ADR may involve a complete change in the mindset of the lawyer who is used to the battle of litigation rather than trying to resolve the parties' problems. However, the growth of the ADR industry and the introduction of ADR into the CPR has served to increase awareness to the existence of alternatives to litigation.

In light of the trend towards firmer encouragement from the courts to try ADR and escalating costs of litigation, mediation will play an increasingly important role in dispute resolution for banks and financial institutions.

[26] "Atlantic Dispute sets ADR Record", *Legal Week* January 21, 1999.

CHAPTER 3

COMMERCIAL PROPERTY DISPUTES

JEREMY MANUEL

3.1 INTRODUCTION

From a mediation perspective property disputes are like any other commercial dispute. There are disappointed parties, unfulfilled expectations, loss (which may be financial or, for example, may be the loss of the benefit of use or a right of enjoyment or right of way) and the desire of one party to seek redress from another.

Litigation, arbitration or other third party determination would resolve the problem. However, the familiar encouragements for the parties to choose mediation to resolve their differences remain persuasive from a commercial point of view. Mediation can bring the problem to an end sooner than litigation, be far less costly than lengthy drawn out legal proceedings (even if the dispute is resolved by arbitration) and often as important to the commercial litigant as any other consideration, if successful, will allow the parties to get back to their business swiftly, thus avoiding having to spend huge amounts of management time preparing for the fight.

In this chapter I do not propose to define the mediation process and the roles of the mediator and the parties. I assume that the reader is familiar with mediation and how it works. Rather, I propose to illustrate by way of example and case study various techniques to assist the mediator and present ideas that are pertinent to commercial property disputes.

3.2 "TRANSACTION" OR "RELATIONSHIP" DISPUTE

Property disputes will fall into two categories. The first I will call "Transaction" disputes. This is where the circumstances are likely to have arisen from a transaction which has left one party unfulfilled (say in an agreement for sale and purchase) and that party seeks redress. In these cases a solution to the conflict is needed, a settlement (possibly involving the payment of money) would need to be reached and the parties can then move forward leaving the dispute behind them and effectively have nothing more to do with each other. There will be no need for the parties to have an ongoing relationship. If the mediator has been really successful he may even leave the parties with some positive perceptions of each other or even leave considering that they might do business together again or if that is too much to ask at least not bad mouthing each other. Such Transaction disputes often arise from the failure of the parties to manage and clearly understand each others expectations and later on in this chapter we will consider a situation which provides amongst other points a good example of how the failure of effective communication can lead to litigation.

In Transaction disputes the likely source of conflict is an alleged breach of agreement (the agreement being for a single purpose not envisaging any ongoing relationship); a transaction that has gone wrong leaving the parties at odds.

The second type of property dispute I term "Relationship" disputes and arise from what potentially would have been a long-term, perhaps even permanent, relationship. Such relationships will involve rights, obligations and duties on both sides. One party will contend that some or all of these have been broken. Relationships are susceptible to change; parties' needs change and their expectations alter. The parties to the legal relationship may themselves change; a tenant may assign the unexpired residue of his lease; a landlord could sell his interest subject to a tenancy; neighbours will move away from each other and new people will move in who may themselves have different needs, expectations and attitudes. Relationships between landlords and tenants, joint users of a shared right (perhaps an easement or right of way) do breakdown. Neighbour disputes may serve to feed the news media and represent captivating television viewing (*e.g.* "Neighbours from Hell") but they do not only arise in the residential settings and could arise between tenants of multi-let buildings or neighbours on an industrial estate and in any environment do pose real problems that interfere with the running of normal business and personal lives. **3.2.1**

Mediation provides the potential to find a way to address the differences whether arising from an agreement, a lease, a licence or a statute and to encourage the parties to accommodate a compromise really does add value to the resolution of the dispute.

The resolution of ongoing property relationships whereby foundations are rebuilt for a peaceful co-existence are the true challenge to those involved in mediation of property disputes. They provide the opportunity for successful structuring of a settlement which can result in the reality of preserved relationships and the establishment of a *modus vivendi* allowing parties to continue to "live" with each other in the future.

Thus, having identified that the types of potential property litigants can be divided into categories of "Transaction" disputes and "Relationship" disputes, before considering case studies for each of a Transaction and a Relationship dispute it is worth looking at some categories of the parties to disputes of a property nature (all of which may come under the general description of "Property Disputes"). It becomes apparent that the circumstances of the parties to a dispute do result in its being treated in a particular way and thus consideration must be given as to whether mediation is always the suitable method to employ in trying to resolve the particular question.

3.3 The parties and their perceptions

The historic nature of the legal process may compartmentalise the types of dispute into different areas of legal category. Clients will believe that they have a "property" dispute even if their legal advisers suggest that the law governing the transaction that has gone wrong or the relationship that has broken down will come under another legal category, *e.g.* "partnership" or "administrative law" (with the result it may be dealt with by a specialist in that field of law within the solicitors' practice). Interestingly the current trend of establishing multi-disciplinary departments within law firms reflects this client-focused perception rather than the rigidity of the structure of legal practice.

Property disputes between the buyers and sellers, landlords and tenants, and neighbours, are however just some of the categories of conflict that will fall under the heading "commercial property disputes" and there are a range of other types of dispute where the nature of the parties create a different balance of power and therefore different needs and expectations and thus different challenges in seeking to resolve the disputes.

First, there are disputes between property owners or occupiers and their advisers. This could for example be a negligence action against a solicitor, surveyor or architect or over fees that may be due to an estate agent or other intermediary.

It is worth noting that both the Royal Institute of Chartered Surveyors (RICS) and the National Association of Estate Agents (NAEA) have their own dispute resolution service although these do differ in the services provided.

3.3.1 Secondly, there are disputes with contractors. This could either come in connection with works being carried out by a developer or indeed between an individual or a company and their own builders. Everybody has their own builder story and it is never really clear whether people's reluctance to share details of their builders with colleagues and friends is because of fear of the blame that may follow if the contractor is inefficient or unreliable (or both) or whether once the details of a good builder arc passed on you can never get him back to work for you again as he is so busy elsewhere. However, a dispute with a contractor can be devastating to the commercial developer and the small business alike and result in significant loss. It is for that reason there are well-defined dispute resolution procedures with contractors with procedures laid down in most well drafted building contracts. In contracts for larger developments there are often sophisticated dispute (particularly mediation) schemes to resolve problems as they arise so that any delays are kept to the minimum and the Centre for Effective Dispute Resolution ("CEDR") has established a specialist service to the building industry. It has been suggested that the construction industry provides one of the largest sources of mediation referrals to CEDR.

Thirdly, there are disputes with "authorities". These can take the shape of disputes with the district surveyor over valuation or building regulation matters; with local authorities over planning, rating or the provision of accommodation and also with housing associations and other statutory providers of commercial or residential properties.

The method of dealing with a dispute with an authority will depend on the powers that particular authority have over the matter in question. If the authority is a decision-maker in this process (*e.g.* a planning authority) then there will be laid down statutory procedures to appeal against decisions that a party considers unfavourable. Historically there was no practical role for mediation in such situations once a decision had been given although the role of the mediator (and mediation skills) should not be underestimated in the negotiating with the relevant authorities prior to and at the time that the original application which is being decided is made. A skilled adviser will use mediation techniques in considering the needs and objectives of the relevant authority in preparing their application.

However, as the procedures now stand there may in future be a **3.3.2**
role for mediation once the potential for negotiation has passed. Previously, once a matter was determined by a tribunal the only next step if the decision was not accepted would be appeal. However the Lord Chancellor's Department has announced that government departments will promote mediation and other forms of non-litigious disputes resolution in place of litigation.

Another category of property matters involving "authorities" are housing matters. The Housing Ombudsman has operated a scheme for housing associations and other (non-private) owners of residential accommodation where disputes between tenants and their landlords are offered mediation prior to the Ombudsman's determination. Care should be taken in these matters to ensure the parties fully understand the mediator's role as circumstances have arisen where tenants in particular view the mediator as a "judge" and are disappointed by the process because they are not given a "judgment".

Thus having considered the two types of disputes (Transaction and Relationship) and differing types of parties to dispute a mediator needs to consider the stand point of each of the parties involved with the dispute concerning properties.

3.4 HISTORY MAKES US LITIGIOUS

The old adage "an Englishman's home is his castle" can equally be applied to business property. Humans are naturally territorial and as such can treat a property dispute as "personal" sometimes becoming irrational when dealing with their own property. It is necessary for the mediator to bear this in mind. Even the Law Society recognises the emotional nature of the buying and selling of property by laying down the strict guidelines on its members when dealing with contract races for the buying and selling of property which it does with no other contractual relationship.

A property will be either somebody's home or a place from which he does business. For a residential occupier (owner or tenant) a dispute will strike at the heart of the person's daily life. For the commercial owner or occupier a dispute will at best interfere with the running of his business, involve expenditure of time which the occupier should be spending on running the business and at worst threaten the very existence of that business.

For the developers or the landlords the same emotions may not apply. A landlord may feel proud of the building he owns and some sense of achievement in the portfolio of buildings that have been built up. He could genuinely believe that his actions are the appropriate commercial steps that should be taken to protect and maximise the value of his assets or of his investments. But ultimately his focus is likely to be different and in encouraging the parties to recognise the different objectives the mediator will enhance the likelihood of a successful mediation.

Landlords, developers, property investors and traders need to realise that the objectivity applied to decisions that they make over the commodity with which they deal commercially is received by their tenant or occupier subjectively. If a mediation in a property dispute is to succeed this difference in stand point must be understood by both parties. If it is not and the aim of one party is to give the other "a bloody nose" the mediation is doomed to failure.

3.4.1 Land owners have always had a privileged place in English society. Perceived as wealthy and influential, the land owner traditionally was master of his estate and historically also of the people who worked or lived on it.

Legislation was needed both in the commercial and the residential spheres to protect the tenant. In reality over 50 years of legislation has sought to balance the bargaining positions of the parties.

Some may argue that with residential property, the Rent Act 1967 and subsequent legislation which brought new protection for the tenant making his interest almost paramount, the balance was tipped in the tenant's favour and that the legislation ended up dissuading commercial landlords from the residential market resulting in further legislation in the form of the Housing Act 1988 attempting to encourage residential landlords back into the market.

But even at the end of the twentieth century whilst there may have been legislation in place to protect those in a weaker bargaining position, the legal process, because of its lack of speed and high cost, did not deliver what the social reformers set out to do.

The sophistication of twenty-first century life calls for different solutions. Just as developers and landlords are no longer feared and hated, buyers and tenants are now better advised and more focused on their objectives. **3.4.2**

Furthermore, clients are no longer afraid to challenge advice given by their lawyers and have identified that litigation should be avoided at all cost. This sentiment of course is echoed by the Lord Chancellor's Department in their assorted attempts to take pressure off the courts therefore the suggestion of mediation is now no longer perceived as a sign of weakness.

The RICS has championed the cause of alternative dispute resolutions and indeed have their own dispute resolution service offering arbitration, expert determination, adjudication, expert witness and their well known PACT (Professional Arbitration on Court Terms) for lease renewals as well as mediation. They publish a newsletter called "Dispute Resolution News" and it should be noted that the RICS services are designed for all property disputes not simply claims against surveyors. The National Association of Estate Agents mediation scheme is set up to deal with disputes over fees and does offer some form of evaluation of the dispute in addition to the mediation.

LITIGATE OR MEDIATE? **3.5**

To date mediation has been relatively slow to catch on with lawyers in resolving property disputes. However, in the same way that a land owner and his tenants are no longer viewed as a relic of feudal society, the "I'll show him" approach to property disputes leading to litigation will give way to the advantages of the more practical cost-effective and speedy resolution offered by mediation.

Consider the mediation of a dispute which arose between a landlord and tenant of a building where work was being carried out and the tenant claimed that noise and general disruption resulted in loss of profits. The same circumstances of course would apply to any neighbourly dispute be it commercial or residential.

Injunction proceedings were originally brought but went nowhere and the case drifted for nearly two years.

3.5.1 You can imagine the situation. A claim is made. "Your works are interfering with my business. My staff cannot work and I am losing profits. They must stop now and can only be carried out quietly and at times which do not disturb me". The landlord or neighbour's response would be something like "I'm entitled to carry out works in the building (the lease says so). If I limit the times the contractors can work or the noise that will be generated there will be significant impact on my business and costs will escalate. In any event the down turn in your business is nothing to do with us and is due to the market or is because of your sales force". The traditional litigation process causes each party to lose sight of the actual problem. The lawyers are now taking up their defensive and offensive positions. Half-hearted attempts to settle lead nowhere. The litigants themselves have stopped communicating; the tenant may even stop paying the rent. The parties are in a hole and instead of looking for a ladder to help them climb out, the traditional litigious approach keeps the parties digging and what's more throwing the contents of their shovels on each other.

So legal costs are mounting, relationships between the parties are at an all-time low and quite possibly the communication between the lawyers is now frosty. The parties however are probably beginning to think how they can get out of this. Time has passed, the works which were the cause of the dispute have long finished. The building is back to normal but the parties are left with litigation and the potential of huge costs. What's more their lawyers will not guarantee that they will win and have said that even if they do win they will still be left with a hefty legal bill. Management hours are being consumed in increasing amounts as the trial date gets nearer, forcing the litigants to place their business objectives secondary to preparing for such trial. Clearly the best advice to the parties would be to find a solution but traditionally the view was that the first side to propose settlement reveals their weakness (be it in their case, their stomach for the fight or depth of their pockets).

Once the parties have agreed to mediate and the day is set, case summaries are exchanged.

3.6 RULES OF PRESENTATION OF THE CASE—IMPRESS THE CLIENT, IMPRESS THE MEDIATOR

It is possible to set out in the case summary the goals of the mediation but more often the case summary tends to be a repeat of the claims and the counterclaims found in the proceedings (where proceedings have been issued) or of the early correspondence alleging breach or loss. The bundle, however, may include (because the mediation is "without prejudice" and is treated as confidential negotiations) any without prejudice offers that may have been made by either party.

Whilst the written case summaries (and the oral presentation made in the plenary session) can be a time when one party may express hopes and aspirations for the future, in reality an experienced advocate at a mediation is likely to save such proposals for the private caucus meeting with the mediator rather than reveal his hand at the first plenary session which from a negotiation position may be viewed as being too early.

On the day itself the parties themselves or more likely their advocate, will present each side's case at the plenary session. The dilemma is whether to be aggressive, conciliatory, neither or both. The advocate wants to impress the client and persuade the mediator.

Seeking to impress the client is an obvious objective. It is the **3.6.1** client who is paying the advocate's fees and clearly the advocate wants the client to feel he is getting his money's worth. Quite how he impresses the client will depend on the client's aims for the mediation which no doubt will have been discussed privately beforehand. Whilst the caucus is always perceived as the opportunity for the clients to have "their say" or "their day in court", the presentation must be sensitively phrased and be couched in more conciliatory tones if this plenary session is really to be the start of the settlement process.

The presentation of the opening statement may well give an early indication of the likely success (or otherwise) of the mediation. Where the parties' advocate aggressively restates their case position rejecting (or belittling) the other side's statement or presentation, the mediation is clearly not off to a good start and the mediator may well be advised in these circumstances to ask the client directly to contribute a few words to check whether the presentation is a true reflection of the client's own position or merely a negotiation stance on the part of their advocate.

On the other hand (and this is where the mediator is likely to be impressed) is when the case is put in conciliatory terms. For example, where the advocate in the presentation expresses a note of regret, not necessarily for the actions of the parties, but for the fact that the business relationship that was at one time viewed positively and with enthusiasm had reached the stage where an independent third party had to be brought in to resolve the parties' differences in the hope that court may be avoided.

The openings at the plenary sessions (and the earlier round of **3.6.2** telephone calls between the mediator and the parties) will not however always allow the mediator to predict the eventual outcome.

The statements of case by each side will have been sent to the mediator a few days before the mediation. These will have given the mediator an understanding of the facts of the case. The case study typically will contain a summary of each case, copies of any proceedings (with supporting documents). If the matter is nearing trial they may even take on the appearance of the first draft of the trial bundle. Copies of without prejudice correspondence will have been included by the parties probably to show how reasonable they are and how unreasonably the other side is behaving.

Neither the summary of case nor indeed the preliminary round of telephone conversations between the mediator and the parties' solicitors' advisers will tell the whole story. Just as an individual is often surprised when he meets for the first time somebody whom he has spoken to on the telephone, of whom a mental picture has been created but who turned out to be completely different in the flesh, so the first meeting and the opportunity to see the parties in private provides time for the mediator to establish an understanding of the background and allows him to probe and thus establish the real motivation behind the particular transaction or relationship that was proposed and what the parties expect or hope to achieve from the mediation.

Furthermore, whilst the mediator may carefully have considered the layout of the plenary room before the plenary session, deciding who will sit where, the reactions of the parties when they come together for the first time must be carefully observed by the mediator and if nothing else will give the lead as to the appropriate formality or informality to be employed.

3.7 What went wrong and why?—how did we end up here?

In many instances it is not difficult from the documentation to establish what was the parties' intention, for example the developer was to build the unit and put in the tenant (perhaps with a view to selling the building on to an institutional investor) and the tenant was seeking to relocate his business to these premises in order to achieve a business goal. But what needs to be understood by the mediator is the bigger picture. What the transaction/relationship meant to the parties, not just in the practical terms of a new office or factory and the potential to generate increased income, but in terms of the impact on the business or indeed way of life. Once this is understood and can be made known to the other side progress can be made. To give a party the tools to make them look at the situation from the other's point of view is valuable in understanding their actions.

Another useful key in unlocking the dispute is for the mediator to try and find out the point or points where things began to go wrong and thus explain the subsequent handling of events by each of the parties. The benefit of hindsight is a great thing and whilst it may be counterproductive to argue that if one party behaved in a different way at a certain point in time the dispute would never have reached the level it has reached, asking the other side (hypothetically) what they would have done in similar circumstances often results in some understanding of the other side.

The following scenario exemplifies a number of issues which are likely to rise in the negotiation of a Transaction dispute and offers some ideas to those trying to find a way to settle them.

Arising from what the parties no doubt described at the outset as a "simple" agreement by a developer to construct and let light industrial premises the parties found themselves locked in litigation each accusing the other of breach of agreement to lease. The events took place over a period of approximately two years.

A business was looking to relocate. It was expanding and needed **3.7.1**
more space. It was doing very well but in order to achieve the quantum leap set out in its business plan it needed a bigger facility with the ability to expand further.

The developers were experienced property professionals with a reputation of developing small to medium-sized light industrial units in out of town centre locations.

The tenant, a northern based supplier of equipment to the catering trade, had been searching for new premises for some time. Their accountants had advised them to buy a building but nothing suitable could be found. The worry of the potential loss of business because of inability to fulfil larger sized orders lead to an agreement to take space on a leasehold basis on the developer's newly built estate. The tenant was very clear as to his needs. He needed warehousing that had specific dimensions for layout to allow for the use of forklift trucks. He needed office space and the usual W.C.'s, rest rooms and kitchen facilities. One unit would not be big enough but two adjoining units would be suitable if they were reconfigured by moving the dividing wall between them thereby creating a warehousing space that was larger than one of the original planned units with a small space for the office and ancillary facilities. The negotiations between surveyors took some time. The specification of additional works were agreed and as is often the case by the time the solicitors were instructed, in the minds of the parties and their surveyors, the deal had been struck and all that was left was the sorting out of the paperwork and achieving exchange of contracts on what they saw as a "relatively straightforward" transaction. This had to be done swiftly.

Here of course lies the source of the first potential problem. The **3.7.2**
solicitors were provided with copies of the exchanges of the correspondence between the parties' surveyors which referred to the proposed specific requirements of the tenant. These letters were to be incorporated into the agreement and they were (by reference).

The developers' solicitors despatched the standard form agreement for lease which had been prepared for the development with the standard form lease annexed to the tenant's solicitors. The lease was negotiated relatively easily and non-contentiously although it was interesting to note that a tenant's solicitors not unusually proposed an amendment to the alienation provisions in the lease seeking to permit underletting of part of the premises which was later referred to in the pleadings as an indication of the tenant's intention to underlet part.

The tenant's solicitors raised enquiries, initiated searches and there was some negotiation over the terms of the agreement. When the dispute arose as is often the way both parties sort to rely on the specific terms of agreement and in purely the contractual terms on both sides there were legal arguments supporting parts of each sides position. There was no suggestion that the solicitors were negligent in the drafting or the negotiation of the agreement. The clients and their agents put a great deal of pressure on the solicitors to get the deal exchanged. The clients and their agents thought they had clearly understood the various requirements of the tenant but it did transpire that neither side had thoroughly analysed the impact of those requirements on the planning considerations and developers' ability to deliver the building for use as the tenant had in mind, indeed as the tenant required.

Both solicitors were given the same correspondence which amounted to the specification. Both solicitors assumed that the parties had fully considered what needed to be done and that the landlord would be able to comply with the specification and additional requirements. The solicitors amended the documentation and pushed ahead to exchange. In the mediation there was never any suggestion that the solicitors should have advised in different terms.

3.7.3 The agreement for lease was:

(a) conditional upon the landlord building the premises in accordance with the planning consent previously obtained and "such other consents as may be required and in accordance with the agreed specification";

(b) provided for additional works to be carried out (subject to obtaining consent for these additional works); and

(c) provided for completion to take place on 10 days' notice of practical completion (as determined by the landlord's surveyor).

Exchange of contracts took place at the beginning of January 1998 with a target completion date of the end of February. There was a "long stop" date of July 31, 1999 and if completion had not been effected by that time the tenant was entitled to service notice and withdraw.

The pre-existing planning consent authorising the construction of the industrial unit contained a number of planning conditions including the prohibition against the amalgamation of "two units" and specified the proportion of warehousing as a proportion of all ancillary uses of the units. The tenant's intention was that the two units together would operate as one business premises. The dividing wall between the two units had to be moved and although it was not the intention for the units to be "amalgamated" in the sense that the wall would be knocked down and they would become one unit, it was the intention that by connecting the two adjoining units they would be used for the purpose of one business.

Additionally, the landlords were aware that the tenant intended his part of their work to carry out alterations that would incorporate another floor into one unit. Although it was the tenant who was to carry out the works which were of a non-structural nature the landlord was to provide modifications to the structure to support the alterations. The tenant took the view that it was the landlord's responsibility to obtain any necessary consent required for the modifications even though they were not carrying out the alterations for which the modifications were being carried out.

The landlord's opinion was opposing. He took the view that as the reconfiguration of the premises as he was required to carry out did not require consent and it was not his obligation to obtain planning consent for the modifications which were required so that the tenant could complete his works. The target deadline came and went and eventually the landlord produced the required certificate of practical completion. This was, however, rejected by the tenant as being invalid as their own enquiries had established that extra consents may have been required for the building as it had now been built.

The tenant rejected the certificate of practical completion and 3.7.4
issued proceedings for breach of contract seeking specifically:

(a) damages for loss of profit that would have been achievable had the business been able to move into the larger premises;
(b) the wasted costs incurred in the purchase of materials for its own works which had been purchased, paid for and delivered to the site which could not then be used and which had indeed subsequently disappeared;
(c) general damages;
(d) costs.

The landlord counterclaimed that the tenant was in breach of contract (*i.e.* for not completing) and claimed payment for the rent that was lost from the date the completion should (in their view) have taken place until such time as the premises were re-let and in addition damages and costs.

There appeared to be no serious attempt to settle. The writ was issued in September 1999 and the time between the issue of the writ and the eventual mediation was spent in accumulating evidence to support the respective parties' claim and to diminish value in the strength of the other side's defence.

Thus just under two years after the initial projected completion date parties found themselves sitting around one of the conference rooms of a leading Central London firm of solicitors trying to mediate the dispute.

3.8 THE MEDIATION—PLENARY—CAUCUS—SETTLEMENT

On the claimant's side there was the claimant himself and with him came two solicitors, being the solicitor who originally handled the conveyancing and the solicitor who was in charge of the conduct of the litigation. Also available to him on the telephone was his financial controller who could substantiate the financial calculations which sought to approve the loss the business had sustained (which in part were profits that it could not make) due to the fact that the business could not move.

For the defendant landlord company the Company Chairman attended once again with the solicitor who acted in the conveyancing and the solicitor in charge of the conduct of the litigation.

The opening plenary session was civil and straightforward. To both sides the issues were clear. Both were alleging breach of contract, both were denying this. They each made clear that they performed their own side of the agreement, they themselves had done nothing wrong and briefly explained the losses they had sustained. Encouragingly, both stated at the end of their presentations that they hoped that mediation would be able to find a solution in order to put the dispute behind them.

3.8.1 The plenary session broke into individual caucus groups and the mediator visited each in turn.

After the preliminary discussions with each of the parties as to the history of the case some reality testing began. The claimant was challenged by the mediator to analyse his confidence in his own financial claim and whether this would be convincing in court. His lawyers were asked to express their level of confidence; and whether it was arguable that on simple construction of the wording of the contract he could be supremely confident on the merits of his case.

On the defendant/prospective landlord's side an admission that the counter-claim had only been made as a defensive position and would be dropped if the claimant would drop his claim came at their first caucus meeting with the mediator.

The conveyancing lawyers on both sides were most defensive of their position. They claimed that the contract they had prepared adequately protected their respective clients and dealt clearly with the issues that were at large. In each of the separate sessions where the strength of the individual cases was explored by the mediator with each party on both sides it was the litigation solicitor who was urging caution and recommending settlement.

Thus dynamics in both caucuses were similar. Each had a bullish **3.8.2**
conveyancer expressing confidence that "his" agreement would withstand the test of the court in his client's favour. Each had a litigator who knew that if this matter came to court he was charged with the responsibility of ensuring that the confidence of his professional partner was well placed and each had a client who at different times during the day had displayed irritation (and sometimes a little anger) and frustration at finding themselves caught in this situation and anxiety about the mounting costs. Both sets of clients expressed the need to move on and get on with their business.

Any settlement was likely to be a financial one. The premises in question had been re-let and there was no possibility of the landlord offering the tenant alternative premises and the tenant's attitude to letting premises had hardened and he now only wanted to buy business premises. The claim (and the counter-claim) were both for financial sums. The landlord, by conceding his counter-claim early on had made clear that he was not expecting to come away with any money. His proposal to drop this counter-claim when put to the claimant/tenant resulted in their reviewing again the amount they were claiming. Tasking the Financial Controller to break down in detail the claim and then asking the litigator to speculate as to how much of the sums would be accepted by the court brought a reduction in the amount required for settlement by the tenant. Things were beginning to move. The mediation had reached a point where it was down to finding a number which would be satisfactory to both sides. It was time for the mediator to ask both sides:

"How much will it cost you if you lose?"

SPECIFIC PROBLEMS—SPECIAL SKILLS—THE BENEFITS OF EXPERIENCE **3.9**

Although not apparent in this case as both sides were business professionals and had their own legal (and property) advisers, often the dilemma for the mediator is to determine which party is the most open to further negotiation once the horse trading starts. It is not appropriate simply for the mediator to put pressure on the weaker, more vulnerable or less articulate party in order to achieve a settlement. Where one party is not represented the mediator's problem is more acute. Often the unrepresented party asks for advice and the mediator must resist the temptation to offer this (however tempting it is if it will result in an increase in the number of his successes!). A useful technique is to "role play" with the party, asking for such advice, with the party playing the mediator and where the mediator plays the party. Once chairs have been swapped the mediator in the party's chair asks the party (now playing the mediator) "what do you think I should do?" A useful response may be elicited.

The perceived wisdom is that any skilled and experienced mediator is able to successfully mediate any type of dispute. It is the skill in the administration of the process, the mediator's approach and particular abilities that are the catalyst to settlement rather than his understanding of the technical nature of the dispute. In commercial property matters, however, an understanding of the way that the transactions operate, the jargon and the practice is a definite aid to the mediator in identifying areas where a party in caucus can be "reality tested". In the case in question an amendment was made to the lease where the tenant's solicitor sought and obtained an amendment which permitted underletting of part of the premises. The tenant's solicitor quite properly sought to obtain certain flexibility in the alienation provisions of the lease just in case there was excess space available to the tenant which he could usefully underlet achieving some rental income should the desire (or need) arise. In the litigation, reference was made to this lease amendment as evidence of the tenant's lack of commitment to the whole building and as an indication that the landlord was not fully aware of the tenant's real intention in respect of the whole building. An experienced commercial property lawyer would know that seeking such an amendment in leases where the size of the premises exceeds the immediate tenant's need (or even as a precautionary measure) is an act of commercial prudence rather than an expression of the tenant's intent. A mediator who is experienced in commercial property matters will have the experience to appreciate the significance of such proposed amendment and thus the advantage in challenging parties on the strength of the assertions that are being made.

3.9.1 In mediating "Relationship" disputes the result will not always lie with the "to-ing and fro-ing" of the financial settlement. In multi-let buildings or in cases where there are residential tenants a landlord is able (and indeed sometimes is obliged) to act in particular ways and this can cause conflict resulting in bad feeling from his tenant.

Commercial leases of multi-let buildings frequently provide that a dispute between tenants will be put before the landlord for determination and the result of such determination could well create hostility from the tenant whose behaviour has been objected to or criticised.

Thus landlords may well wish to consider abrogating the responsibility of determining inter-tenant disputes for fear of the damage that it may cause to his relationship with his tenant. Mediation could offer an avenue where there is at least a contractual obligation (embodied in the lease) to submit a difference to mediation before it is put to determination by a third party or to the landlord to determine.

Market conditions vary but commercial landlords in the future may not always wish to find themselves in a position where they can simply dictate terms to their tenant risking the result of damaged relationships.

The Housing Act 1996 established an approved Ombudsman Scheme which deals with disputes between landlords and tenants and under this scheme the Housing Ombudsman has jurisdiction over more than 2,000 landlords. 3.9.2

The Housing Ombudsman set up a pilot scheme whereby with the agreement of the parties matters that had been referred to the Ombudsman for adjudication would be sent for mediation in what appears to be an effort to achieve a more consensual resolution to a landlord and tenant dispute.

The mediation procedure under the Independent Housing Ombudsman Scheme procedurally adopts the usual characteristics of a commercial mediation save that the mediator's obligation of confidentiality to the parties was qualified by the Housing Ombudsman's right to request information about the content of the mediation.

Mediators of a commercial relationship dispute will have similar 3.9.3
characteristics of that in the residential schemes (although they will not have the additional responsibility to release information to the Ombudsman).

Previously discussed was the viewpoint of each of the parties but the significance of this in a "Relationship" dispute goes further.

Consideration will need to be given to the nature of the parties. On one side there will be a landlord who may be an individual institution or corporation. For the landlord the property in question is likely to be one of many for which he is (as actual owner or as employee of an institution or corporation) responsible. If the management of the property is delegated to a managing agent or member of staff of the corporate landlord they are likely to be under pressure to meet performance or other targets.

The tenant or occupier could also be an individual or a corporation but the way they receive the landlord's "commercial" approach may be felt as belittling their own importance

CONSIDER EMOTIONS, NEEDS AND EXPECTATIONS 3.10

The significance of the emotional impact on the disintegration of the pre existing relationship cannot be underestimated. Without the recognition that the actions of one party caused an emotional reaction in the other there can be no moving forward. This is not a question of being "touchy-feely" in commercial relationships but rather a realistic recognition that even in the commercial environment the emotional impact of a series of actions does need to be addressed. It is not just in personal relationships that parties may feel anger, disappointment and even betrayal and such an emotional response leads to a perception of the other party's position and thus ultimately translates into actions which may serve to exacerbate rather than improve the difficulties.

Whether the conflict is in a commercial or residential landlord and tenant setting or in a neighbour dispute a regular complaint is that the other side was "not listening" to what was being said. Whether this is real (in the sense that the recipient of the complaint was simply dismissing as unimportant the protestations) or whether the impact was not fully understood is not relevant. It is the "message" that is being received and the result is the person who is doing the complaining is left feeling (either justifiably or not) that they are (or at least their views are) less significant than those to whom the complaint is being made.

Accordingly, in any kind of relationship dispute the dynamic of the apology becomes very important. The catalyst that caused the dispute may (once the parties are talking and beginning to recognise each other's standpoint) be relatively easy to resolve but what may be crucial before any attempts to work together can be embarked upon is to deal with the issue of the apology. However, often the difficulty becomes that the party from whom the apology is being sought (because of the breakdown in communication) feels that they also have been wronged. Their standpoint is often that although the relationship may not have been perfect; although there may have been things that could have been dealt with in a different manner, the difficulties that arose did not entitle the complaining party to behave in the way that they did. Accordingly, no apology is warranted because whilst "we" may have been to some extent in the wrong the other party is too.

3.10.1 The experience of a mediation in a dispute referred by the Housing Ombudsman clearly identified this situation.

A tenant had been in occupation of premises for a period of 12 years, the first seven of which he was a "model" tenant, observed the regulations, paid the rent on time, was a helpful member of the community, and the relationship continued without difficulties.

The property in question was a maisonette. He occupied the upper part. After the first seven years a new tenant moved into the lower maisonette. Clearly they did not get on. The tenant of the upper maisonette complained about noise from below and coming and going and general difficulties in getting on. He felt that the new neighbour's behaviour impacted on his enjoyment of the property.

A particular problem was the shared use of the common entranceway and allegations were made of leaving rubbish, not closing the door properly and noises in the common parts.

The tenant of the ground floor denied all complaints and counter-complained about the behaviour of the first-floor tenant.

The landlord found itself in a difficult position. Allegations were being made by each tenant against the other and evidence was brought by each to support their own claims. It was quite apparent that as the relationship between the neighbours became worse and worse each did behave towards the other in a way which invoked criticism from the landlord.

The first-floor tenant then became ill and unable to work. Rent fell 3.10.2
into arrears and as the relationship deteriorated with the other tenant so the relationship deteriorated with the landlord.

The first-floor tenant felt that he had been a good tenant for seven years and that it was unreasonable that the Housing Association would simply not believe his version of events when it was only because of the "new" tenant that there were problems. From his perception it was clearly not his fault and he supported this by saying that there had never been problems in the past. The tenant perceived he was not being listened to, that he was somehow entitled to an enhanced level of respect because he had been a long-standing satisfactory tenant. He felt that the landlord was unsympathetic to his current physical situation (*i.e.* illness) which resulted in his current financial situation (*i.e.* being behind in paying his rent).

From the landlord's point of view this was one of thousands of properties that it controlled and owned. The hard-pressed officers responsible for the day-to-day management of the properties saw this as a "problem" case where there was a dispute between tenants and there was non-payment of rent. In addition the individual officers responsible changed regularly and thus there was no continuity from the landlord's side to recognise the historic relationship between the tenant and the Housing Association (at least in the mind of the tenant).

The nature of the allegations between the parties were also issues which needed to be addressed and were delicate and complex. This does identify how personal aspects can cause an impact on the relationship and create issues that need to be addressed. In this case the ground-floor tenant made claims of racism as well as allegations that the first-floor premises were being used for both illegal and immoral purposes.

MOVING ON FROM HERE 3.11

A number of points emerged when the matter came to mediation. Firstly however much the parties understand that a mediator's role is not to offer a determination or pass judgment that in circumstances where emotions are involved the party that sees themselves as the "wronged" party seeks confirmation and reassurance from the mediator that their position is "right". When such confirmation is not given and when the mediator refrains from condemning the other side's behaviour as being improper or inappropriate, this can result in the "wronged" party feeling further aggrieved. This expectation has to be carefully managed.

Secondly if the mediation is to succeed it is essential that the matter of the "apology" is addressed at an early stage. In this case the Housing Association officer felt no need to apologise for the actions taken (*i.e.* trying to ascertain the facts over who was right and who was wrong and ultimately issuing proceedings against the tenant for non-payment of rent). What became significant was the recognition that their actions were perceived by the tenant as hostile and partisan (even when they were not intended to be) and thus allowed the Association to proclaim that they "felt sorry" that their actions had made the tenant feel the way that he did. This is of course a little short of an apology but recognises the effect of their actions on the tenant. Such circumstances are not unique to residential property and you can imagine in a commercial setting similar actions by a landlord or a managing agent where they simply do not recognise the impact of their commercial decision on the day-to-day lives and operation of the premises on their tenant or occupier or neighbour.

Thirdly once the emotional impact of the parties' action is dealt with the parties can then begin to address the issues over which the original dispute arose. This can involve anything from reconfiguration of entranceways, laying down reasonable rules over the use of shared services, agreeing a phased implementation of a programme of works and ensuring that such works are carried out so as to cause as little disturbance and annoyance as possible (whilst having regard to the impact on cost to those carrying out the works, etc).

A fourth important issue and one which should be carefully addressed prior to drawing up the settlement agreement is the establishment of a channel of communication to deal with future disputes. This is fundamental in relationship disputes in particular, as it recognises that in any ongoing relationships there are to be disagreements and the way of avoiding these escalating into a dispute and thus eventual litigation is to have the opportunity of discussing these issues with a view to finding a solution. Furthermore, the opening of lines of communication ensures that the parties have a human face to whom they can address their issues. Landlords and tenants, neighbours, companies and partnerships do not exist as physical entities on their own, they are all run by human beings and it is not the bodies themselves that "fall out" with each other but rather the human beings that run them. Accordingly, if there is a channel of communication which recognises that there is a past, a present and a future to the relationship then the prejudices of both sides as to the standpoint of the other will be broken down.

If the mediation has achieved a resolution it is important that the relationship that will have developed through the mediation is not lost and is indeed built upon. In transactional disputes this may be desirable but ultimately does not really matter. In relationship disputes it is part of the mediator's role to ensure that there are channels of communication open so that the potential for future disputes is minimised. It is quite likely that the mediation process will have resulted in the parties gaining some respect for each other. Indeed, getting to a stage where the parties at least recognise the other side's position is likely to result in a (perhaps unexpressed) respect by one side that the other stood up for itself. This is very much the encapsulation of the idea of "win/win" where both parties emerge from the mediation with a sense of achievement and a sense they have been able to retain and perhaps even enhance their professional dignity. **3.11.1**

Mediation is unique in that as part of the settlement parties can agree to do things in the future and not just give compensation for things that were done (or not done) in the past. Thus a landlord's obligation to carry out repairs, to employ extra cleaning staff or to place a cap on service charges is something that can be encapsulated in an agreement for the future and this again emphasises the need for the laying down of the mechanism for future communication. So when the questions about what is to be done, when it is to be done and how it is to be done arise these can be addressed properly.

It is this unique position that makes mediation a favoured method of resolution of any property "relationship" disputes. There can be little doubt that it is this added dimension that makes it such a valuable tool in dealing with commercial property disputes and which will result in it becoming more widely used. **3.11.2**

Professional commercial landlords, be it of residential or business property, recognise the need for tenants and neighbours to share a sense of responsibility for the property that they own and occupy. At the beginning of the twenty-first century there will undoubtedly be further legislation that will seek to continue to find a balance where bargaining positions are perceived as being balanced unfairly.

The government's view of litigation in general, the changes in the CPR and the government's own adoption of mediation in commercial disputes with which they are involved will seek to encourage a consensual method of resolution of differences.

Commercial property disputes, be they "Transactions" or "Relationship" disputes, are well suited to mediation and the government, in furthering its desire to "unclog" the court system, may well now give consideration to compulsory mediation of certain types of disputes. Voluntary schemes for neighbour disputes set up by local authorities are beginning to take off. Mediation of inter-tenant disputes imposed by landlords could easily be written into a lease and tenancy agreement. There are a number of organisations that recommend modern mediation clauses for contractual agreements and there is no reason why a forward thinking property owner looking to encourage good relations would not agree to standard mediation clauses in commercial and residential agreements and leases.

There is no doubt that specialist mediators add value to the mediation process. They can challenge the strength of a party's case with confidence and assist in constructing a settlement from a viewpoint of understanding the practicalities of the ongoing relationship between the parties. The mediator will have in his skills bag a number of techniques including a sympathetic ear, the ability to ask illuminating questions and the experience to know when to challenge the parties with the "stick" of "what if you lose?" and the "carrot" of the "what would settlement enable you to achieve?" He will bring with him the ladder to allow the parties to climb down from the positions that they have assumed and if they have come to the mediations with a truly positive intent he will also be the hod carrier, bearing the bricks for both of the parties to build their own bridge over which they must travel to resolve their dispute.

Chapter 4

EMPLOYMENT DISPUTES

JOHN BOWERS Q.C AND MICHELE GILL

Introduction to ADR 4.1

Employment tribunals—the traditional route for resolving individual employment disputes—can be expensive, time-consuming, unpredictable, stressful and damaging to ongoing relationships. Dissatisfaction with the legal process in terms of the remedies offered there and its enormous cost in financial and human terms has meant that alternative forms of dispute resolution—known collectively as ADR—are finding an increasing role because of the different processes and different outcomes that they offer.

Alternative Dispute Resolution (ADR) is a broad term referring to the spectrum of dispute resolution processes that are alternatives to going to court. The ADR options for employment and workplace cases are essentially conciliation, arbitration and mediation. Central features of these processes are that they are voluntary, speedy, informal, private and independent from employment tribunals. ADR processes are distinct from litigation in their non-adversarial approach. The emphasis in ADR is not on winning but on settling. Proving facts, presenting evidence and making legal arguments are largely absent from most types of ADR and the focus shifts instead to exploring the issues and negotiating a settlement. The solutions available through ADR are not necessarily limited to the legal remedies.

What differentiates each of the ADR options is the degree of initiative taken by the third party and the degree to which the parties retain control of the settlement. This chapter explores the case for using ADR in general, and mediation in particular, for resolving employment and workplace disputes.

The ADR options 4.2

Conciliation

ACAS provides an independent and impartial service to resolve statutory employment disputes. The Advisory, Conciliation and 4.2.1

Arbitration Service ("ACAS") was established as an independent industrial relations organisation in 1974 and became a statutory body under the terms of the Employment Protection Act 1975. In its early days ACAS frequently made the headlines because of its involvement in conciliating a number of high-profile industrial disputes, particularly those in national industries and services.

In addition to conciliating collective disputes ACAS also provides conciliation for a wide range of individual employment disputes. Once a claim has been made to an employment tribunal a neutral and independent conciliation officer will make contact with the parties or their representatives. The role of the conciliation officer is to inform parties of their legal rights, examine the strengths and weaknesses of their case and explore the options open to them. The conciliation officer may facilitate some bargaining to take place and if settlement is reached it is the parties and not the conciliation officer who determine the settlement.

Cases which do not settle through conciliation proceed to a tribunal hearing. The conciliation process normally does not involve any face-to-face meetings between the parties. However, conciliation officers do relay the perspectives of one party to the other. Officers will not reveal information that one party wishes to keep from the other and information given to a conciliation officer in connection with conciliation is not admissible in evidence before a tribunal without the consent of the person who gave it. If conciliation does not resolve the dispute before the date fixed for the tribunal hearing, the matter will be decided by the employment tribunal.

In ACAS conciliation more than 40 per cent of claims are resolved without a tribunal hearing. Conciliation is also available prior to making a formal claim to a tribunal. If both sides agree then conciliation can proceed in the same way as if a formal claim had been made to a tribunal. If the case is not settled then the individual can take the complaint to a tribunal.

Arbitration

4.2.2 ACAS also has responsibility for an arbitration scheme under the Employment Rights (Dispute Resolution) Act 1998 as a means to resolve claims of unfair dismissal. The arbitrator hears from both sides and then makes a binding decision. The decision is therefore the arbitrator's and the parties lose their power over the settlement. The arbitrator's award is final and the case cannot then proceed to a tribunal. Parties therefore make a choice between arbitration and going to tribunal and thus far few have decided on the former option.

The ACAS arbitration scheme was set up to offer a distinct alternative to tribunals, and one of its key features is that it is designed to be free of legalism. Hearings are private and confidential, and inquisitorial rather than adversarial. No cross-examination is permitted and clarification or questioning is conducted through the arbitrator. The parties are given the opportunity to state their own cases and comment on the case of the other side. The arbitrator rules on procedural and evidential matters rather than points of law. The arbitrator can only make awards of compensation, reinstatement and re-engagement, so the settlements reached are limited to those provided by law.

In the arbitration scheme there is no appeal in respect to the arbitrator's award, except on grounds of serious irregularities. The scheme is voluntary so both parties will have to opt for it.

Mediation

Mediation is a process where an independent neutral third party assists disputing parties to reach a settlement. The mediator does not play the role of judge or arbitrator and will not seek to impose a solution. Mediation does not attempt to determine the rights and wrongs of the case but identify and focus on the real issues, and create "win/win" options for resolution that satisfy the needs of both parties. It is a process where the parties, not the mediator, decide the terms of the agreement, keeping the outcome of the dispute firmly in their hands. Like all ADR processes, mediation is voluntary, private and informal. The process involves bringing the parties together for at least one face-to-face meeting and the degree to which parties continue to meet in joint session will vary. Mediators may give an opinion or make suggestions for settlement. 4.2.3

Mediation may be used for a range of non-statutory workplace disputes, such as disputes between employees or between employer and employee, and where it exists, as a stage within an organisation's grievance or complaints procedure. Mediation is increasingly being considered for the resolution of statutory employment disputes, in particular harassment and discrimination cases, which are the most intractable of the statutory rights. Indeed, the Cambridge study on Reform of Discrimination Law chaired by Professor Hepple recommended that there should be a pilot project to examine the use of mediation for sexual harassment cases. The DTI Consultation Paper "Routes to Resolution: Improving Dispute Resolution" published in the summer of 2001 sought to encourage the development of alternatives to employment tribunal litigation as a means of resolving employment disputes and uses as case studies the Workplace Mediation Project and an ADR project within NAAFI.

One of the biggest obstacles to the use of mediation for resolving disputes is that many lawyers, advisers and other professionals are at present unable authoritatively to discuss mediation with their clients and some are positively hostile to it. It is important for any potential participants in mediation to be clear about what mediation is and what it is not. Mediation is a non-adversarial, interest-based approach with the emphasis on solving problems rather than winning points. The role of the mediator is to help parties explore what they want and the ways they can secure it. The central issues are not the legal arguments of the case but the practical issues that are important if the parties are to move forward. If legal arguments are discussed it is only in the context of assessing the likely results if the case proceeded to a tribunal.

Like all ADR processes, participation in mediation is voluntary: either party can decline mediation and the decision to take a case to mediation does not replace or supercede the right to register or proceed with a claim to a tribunal. Terms reached are binding only once the agreement is signed.

4.2.4 Mediation is a process that not only explores what has gone wrong in the past and what has brought them to the present dispute, it is also an opportunity to establish how parties will work together in the future and this is especially important in disputes where the parties are still in an employment relationship. Parties in dispute might find it difficult to talk to each other and have trouble moving towards any kind of agreement. A skilled mediator can help to uncover misunderstandings, expose the real issues in dispute and facilitate better workplace relationships above and beyond the dispute before them.

Mediation is thus flexible in terms of both process and outcomes and may be ideally suited for problems concerned with workplace relationships or behaviour. Mediated agreements can include protocols about future behaviour, a written apology, an explanation of what took place and decisions about what might happen in the future. None of these are within the power of an employment tribunal.

Mediated settlements can be achieved more quickly than tribunal decisions and as a result of time-saving can reduce legal and other costs. The only constraint is the availability of those who will attend, and a typical mediation lasts one, sometimes two, days. Preparation time is less time-consuming and expensive: there is no cross-examination of witnesses or formal presentation of evidence. The long wait for a tribunal hearing and the process of preparing for it can be especially nerve wracking, often makes attitudes harden further, and can lead to a further deterioration of the employment relationship. Mediation, in contrast, allows for the early and efficient resolution of disputes, reducing the financial and human costs of an ongoing dispute.

A major advantage of mediation over adjudication and arbitration is its potential for producing creative, "win/win" outcomes that satisfy parties' genuine needs. Judges or arbitrators often cannot offer creative solutions, as the remedies are limited. In mediation, parties are not constrained by legal rules and can solve problems by developing innovative and forward-looking solutions that satisfy the genuine needs of both sides.

4.2.5 Mediation may be particularly beneficial where the employee is still with the employer and all parties want to continue the relationship. Employment tribunal cases may last weeks and by the time the hearing is reached it is not uncommon for the employment relationship to have irretrievably broken down. The early resolution of problems coupled with the non-adversarial nature of mediation is more likely to restore and safeguard relationships.

In mediation the disputants resolve disputes themselves and identify their own solutions. Mediation thus keeps ownership of the problem and the settlement firmly with the parties.

Arbitration and conciliation provide little if any opportunity for parties to vent frustrations and to express their views to the other disputant. Venting emotions may be vital if the parties are to find a satisfactory outcome since parties may be unable to deal with the issues and explore solutions until they are satisfied that they have been listened to. Mediation provides a setting in which both parties can listen to and hear each other's point of view. It gives the parties an outlet to vent their frustrations and express feelings. In this respect in some cases mediation is more likely to provide a satisfying "day in court" than a day in court. The informality of the process means that parties can participate fully rather than through their advocates, and this is often vital to reaching a settlement.

Mediation as compared to litigation may provide for review after a period. Litigation is usually a once and for all outcome, and many employers to whom we have spoken have stated that often the worst problems arise after the litigation is over and people come back to work.

Finally: mediation works; the vast majority of cases settle either during mediation or soon afterwards.

WHAT ADR OFFERS IN CONTRAST TO LITIGATION 4.3

Compared to litigation ADR processes cost less, take less time to arrange, involve less preparation and fewer staff resources, and less time to conduct. The speedier resolution of claims means savings in cost and time to the parties as well as the tribunal system. ADR is also more user-friendly, offering a less intimidating and more accessible process than tribunals because of its informality. Another key advantage of ADR for the parties is that it is private. While the public forum of an employment tribunal may be important in some cases, parties may prefer the more supportive and private forum that ADR processes provide. Although the Employment Tribunal Rules provide that there may be no reporting of sexual harassment cases during their hearings, the press may report such cases after the decision is given, and there is no such restraint in other areas where embarrassing details may emerge.

Also, most ADR processes can offer a wider range of solutions than are available through tribunals. Tribunals can only award compensation, reinstatement and re-engagement or in limited circumstances in discrimination cases make a recommendation as to the future conduct of the employer.

The legal process is in some cases not only inadequate in the remedies it can offer, it is also unpredictable, and one of the attractions of ADR is that parties maintain control of the settlement.

4.4 ADR providers

Mediators may be selected through a mediation/ADR organisation or independently. Most mediation/ADR organisations will have a panel of trained mediators who mediate for the organisation on an as-needed basis. Some mediators can be contacted independently.

Many mediators in the U.K. will be CEDR-trained and -accredited. CEDR (The Centre for Dispute Resolution) provides mediation training and is a mediation provider for mainly commercial disputes. Other mediators will be trained through community mediation groups and this training is usually accredited by Mediation U.K., the umbrella organisation for community mediation groups in the U.K. Increasingly mediators working in the community setting are extending their services to the employment and workplace setting.

The Workplace Mediation Project has a pilot project with a major local authority which is currently being evaluated.

4.5 Advantages of mediation over other ADR processes

Despite falling under the classification of ADR, arbitration is perhaps more akin to litigation than mediation, and has fewer of the benefits of mediation. The advantages of arbitration in relation to litigation are that it offers a less formal, less adversarial, more private and speedier process than litigation. However, in contrast to mediation it is the third party that decides the terms of settlement and not the disputants, and the terms of the settlement are limited to the legal remedies. As in the tribunal process, arbitration results in a winner and a loser, and in choosing arbitration, parties forfeit their rights to take the claim to a tribunal. Arbitration is limited in the type of dispute it can settle: in employment disputes ACAS arbitration is only at present available for cases of unfair dismissal.

Conciliation is a term that is often used interchangeably with mediation. In the context of ADR for employment disputes, mediation and the conciliation service offered through ACAS are two distinct processes. One of the essential differences between mediation and ACAS conciliation lies in the degree of active intervention by the third party. Due to the high-volume of work that each ACAS conciliation officer handles each year the process is generally limited to a telephone conversation with each party. There is no face-to-face meeting between the parties, little time to explore the background to the dispute, and much of the work is not done with the parties directly but with their legal representatives. In mediation, the mediator works closely with the parties, bringing them together for a least one joint session, facilitating communication, exploring what people want and the reasons they want it, and examining settlement options. The success of mediation rests largely on the meeting of the two parties and the resultant progress that such contact—skillfully facilitated by the mediator—can have.

Mediation and conciliation also differ in the nature of the third party's involvement. In ACAS conciliation, while conciliation officers do not make judgments about the merits of the case or impose settlements, they may give advice to the parties and may recommend a particular settlement. Conciliation is largely an evaluative approach in which the conciliation officer helps both parties to evaluate the strengths and weaknesses of their case and frames the settlement process in the context of their rights. Mediation is primarily a facilitative process in which the mediator assists the parties in clarifying the issues and negotiating a settlement. In both processes the decisions around the terms of the agreement remain entirely with the parties.

Mediation is a dispute resolution process which may in many cases reach the heart of the problem, where key issues can be discussed and solutions reached that are likely to meet the needs of all those involved. As such, mediation can be an important tool for restoring relationships and moving people forward.

HOW MEDIATION WORKS 4.6

Handling the client

There are many misconceptions about mediation and the process 4.6.1 can be intimidating and somewhat cryptic to those with no experience of it. For clients to risk a process that they are at best unsure about, and at worst distrustful of, it is essential that clear explanations and reassurances are available. It is important that clients understand that the mediator is independent and will not take sides or give advice to them; that the process is entirely voluntary, and that they can leave at any time during the process and do not have to agree to anything against their will. Further, nothing said during mediation can be used against a party at a later time; the entire process is "without prejudice." If a satisfactory outcome is not reached through mediation, parties can still pursue a grievance or bring a claim to an employment tribunal (subject to time limits).

One of the common perceptions about mediation is that it is a soft option, and that it is second best to more formal processes. The offer of mediation is not to be taken as a sign of weakness. It may rather be a sign of strength if a party is willing to fully discuss the issues in the open and frank forum of a mediation. The credibility of the process is closely linked to a clear understanding of what mediation is and the degree to which mediation has been recognised and integrated into mainstream practice.

When to begin mediation

4.6.2 The general principle is the earlier the better, not least in order that the issue does not become more bitter as time goes on, but also because the cost and time savings are the greatest. However, part of the flexibility of mediation is that it can be used at any stage in a dispute and can run in parallel to a formal grievance or tribunal process. Sometimes, conversely, time is a healer and the best time to mediate will be some time after a case has been lodged and perhaps some interim stages are out of the way. If mediation is used prior to making a claim to a tribunal it is important to consider the time limits for issuing proceedings.

Making contact with the other parties—the approach

4.6.3 Persuading the other side to agree to mediation is one of the biggest obstacles for those wanting to use it and a party contemplating mediation must think very carefully before doing so, and about how best to put the proposition to the other side. Even when relations have not broken down, it is common for one party to respond negatively to another party's suggestion of mediation. In the context of traditional adversarial dispute resolution processes what is advantageous to one side is often considered disadvantageous by the other side.

If mediation is part of an organisation's internal grievance or complaints process then raising the mediation option is relatively easy. If a judge or tribunal recommends that mediation be attempted then the task of persuading the other side is considerably easier since it has been raised in a neutral way.

If mediation is neither part of an internal grievance process nor court-referred, the only way forward is to persuade the other side to try mediation. One party can approach the other party directly or indirectly. The direct approach is contact between the parties themselves or through their respective lawyers or representatives. The indirect approach to the other side is likely to be through a mediation organisation, which has the advantage of giving to the other party the opportunity to discuss any concerns and be informed about the process in more detail. Which approach to use will depend on the particular circumstances and personalities of each case. One way to facilitate the way to the mediation table is to offer to meet in order to discuss mediation and this can include a representative from a mediation organisation. The discussions can inform participants about the process and itself may create some momentum for further negotiations.

Selecting a mediator

Selecting a mediator is not always a straightforward process, particularly since both parties must agree to the selection. Often parties request a mediator who is a specialist in the area of the dispute. While the advantages of a specialist mediator lie in a familiarity with the jargon and knowledge of procedures, the disadvantage may lie in the difficulty the specialist mediator may have in remaining detached from the dispute. It can be strongly argued that too much importance is placed on specialist knowledge and too little importance on mediation process skills. In fact much of the specialist knowledge required in a mediation can be provided by the parties themselves and their respective advisers. The priority should be in selecting a mediator who is skilled and experienced in the mediation process. **4.6.4**

Parties may prefer to choose a mediator with a legal background, but should not assume that having legal training equates with being a skilled mediator. A mediator uses a different set of skills than that of a legal professional. Effective mediation involves building rapport and trust, facilitating clear and effective communication between the parties, and defusing emotions. An understanding of human psychology and behaviour is fundamental to mediation since the bulk of the process involves exploring and understanding what people want and why they want it. Also, a key role played by the mediator is that of the neutral negotiator, using negotiating skills to bring parties towards a resolution.

Regardless of whether a case involves declared issues regarding gender, race or other potential discrimination, the authors take the view that any mediator working in employment and workplace dispute resolution should have a minimum level of training in diversity and equalities awareness. This is important for heightening the mediator's awareness of diversity issues in general, their own personal prejudices, and the more subtle manifestations of prejudice and discrimination which may seep into any mediation process. While it is often logistically difficult, if not impossible, for the mediator or mediators to reflect the diversity of the parties, mediator providers should at the very least have a stated equal opportunities policy and endeavour to build a panel or network of mediators that reflect the diversity of the workforce. Two mediators may bring the combination of skills, personalities and other qualities that makes co-mediation an attractive alternative.

The mediation agreement

The terms on which the mediation is to take place are outlined in a short document that should be agreed by the parties and the mediator. The mediation agreement sets out the practical details of the mediation such as date, time, venue, selected mediator, etc. The agreement also establishes the legal features of the mediation such as "without prejudice", confidentiality, mediator immunity and **4.6.5** authority to settle. The document should be simple and straightforward so that all parties will be willing to sign it. A typical agreement is shown on p. 70, although it should be adjusted for the facts of each particular case.

Who should attend the mediation?

4.6.6 Ideally the mediation should be attended by those parties with first-hand knowledge of the issues and full authority to settle the dispute. Lawyers and other representatives can play a positive and constructive role in mediation, despite the view of some cynics! If lawyers or other representatives do attend the mediation with their clients it is important that they understand that their role is not to represent their client in the traditional sense, but rather to support them in seeking a solution going forward. Mediation does not deal with the case as defined by law but with the personal realities of the dispute as experienced by the parties. In this respect it is the clients and not their representatives who are the experts and therefore it is usually best that they take the lead role and their representatives a supporting role. Unrepresented parties may want to consider bringing a "friend" to the mediation, that is someone who can play a supportive and largely observational role. Union representatives may also have such a role.

What papers should be passed to the mediator prior to the mediation?

4.6.7 It is common for parties to submit to the mediator a brief summary of the dispute highlighting the key issues from each of their perspectives. This can help parties to focus on the real issues in dispute that they wish to address. In many disputes there will also be some relevant documentation that is appropriate for the mediator to see in advance. The case summaries and relevant documents are then exchanged between the parties and copied to the mediator, at an agreed date before the mediation. Parties may bring additional documents to the mediation for only the mediator to see.

Length of the mediation

4.6.8 Most mediations take no longer than one day. The length of a mediation depends on what parties feel comfortable with in terms of time and cost. Sometimes the mediator(s) will meet both parties separately prior to the mediation. This provides an opportunity for the mediator to become more familiar with the case, to establish rapport with both parties, and to address any concerns that they may have. Pre-mediation meetings have the advantage of freeing up more time on the day of the mediation since some of the exploratory stage will have taken place.

The venue

4.6.9 The venue should be somewhere neutral, and ideally somewhere pleasant and comfortable. There should be a room of appropriate size for the joint sessions, and two separate rooms for private (caucus) meetings. Flipcharts should be available, rooms should be adequately soundproofed and catering arrangements covered.

The cost of mediation

Fees are usually agreed in advance of the mediation. The fees are charged on the basis of any other professional fees, and most commonly on a daily rate to spare the participants from the added pressure of rising costs as the hours drift by. Mediations often only take one day so the costs are unlikely to be high. **4.6.10**

The fee for the mediation is usually negotiated to cover the case management fee, and separately any other costs such as room rental, refreshments, travel, etc. The fees are relatively small in comparison with the costs of a contested tribunal hearing.

The settlement agreement

At the conclusion of the mediation, the mediator will assist the parties to prepare a list of the points they have agreed upon. Once the agreement has been written it can be signed and formally typed up later. No agreement will be considered legally binding until it is written down and signed by the parties or their authorised representatives in the form of a compromise agreement or ACAS COT3 form. It is important to ensure that the settlement which comes out of an employment mediation meets the criteria of compromise agreements within the Employment Rights Act 1996 because otherwise they will not restrain the employee from taking the issue to an employment tribunal. The most important requirement is that the employee states that (s)he has been independently advised by a relevant adviser. **4.6.11**

Post settlement issues

An important feature of mediation is that it may provide for a review process, which is not possible in the once and for all circumstance of the tribunal. This may be important in cases of alleged sexual harassment where the result may be that the "harasser" is moved away from contact with the "victim" or a protocol is agreed for future behaviour. In such cases it is important to build in a review mechanism after say six months. **4.6.12**

Role of private meetings or caucuses

Private sessions between the mediator and the individual parties are an opportunity for open and confidential discussion of the issues and settlement options. They can be used for a variety of reasons, such as to privately examine the strengths and weaknesses of a particular proposal, to build more trust with each party, or to challenge positions and judgments. Private meetings (sometimes called caucuses) can be crucial to progress in a mediation, and the degree to which a **4.6.13** mediator will use them will depend on the mediator's preference and on the circumstances as they arise. A key aspect of the private meeting is its confidential nature and mediators should always check what can and cannot be conveyed to another party. The danger of using caucus meetings is that the mediator will become a shuttle negotiator, moving back and forth between the two parties until agreement is reached. Joint meetings are important for building relations between the parties and encouraging parties to see the process as one of working together to find a mutually acceptable agreement.

Preparation for mediation

4.6.14 Preparation for mediation begins with everyone being made clear about what mediation is and how the process works; this includes lawyers and professional advisers as well as the parties themselves. Most important is an understanding that the mediator will not act as an arbitrator or a judge and that mediation is a non-adversarial approach. Parties come together in mediation with a view to achieve a settlement and this factor alone contributes significantly to the mediation's success. It is also best that participants remain open to the possibility of different outcomes, rather than fixed on the outcomes they enter the mediation with.

Mediation is a process that exposes the assumptions, perceptions and feelings in a conflict as much as it explores the facts. It is about coming face-to-face with some of the difficult issues in a dispute and it can therefore be an emotionally challenging—and draining—process. It is important for parties to be aware that frustrations, anger, and other emotions can emerge and that the process is set up to manage this. Mediation also requires parties to be prepared to take responsibility for deciding the outcome themselves, rather than relying on a judge or arbitrator, and for some this can be the most challenging part. Lastly, the willingness of parties to be open to explore possibilities beyond the well-worn issues of the dispute can go a long way to achieving innovative solutions.

The practical preparation for mediation is different from preparing for litigation, but equally important. Remember: mediation is driven not by the intellectual or legal aspects of a dispute but by the concerns and the needs of the parties involved although these may be conditioned by the legal framework in which the issues arise. Be clear about what you want to achieve, what the main issues are, and why they are important to you. Ask yourself what you really want. It may be compensation; it may also be an apology, or improvements in your work circumstances. Also consider whether you want a future relationship with the other side.

In preparing for mediation it is important for each party to consider realistically the "what if" question, *i.e.* what happens if we don't settle today? What are the risks and costs of not settling? Consider the hard costs such as lawyers' fees, as well as the human costs of stress and reduced productivity that may result if the case continues to an employment tribunal. What is your BATNA (Best Alternative to a Negotiated Settlement) and what is your WATNA (Worst Alternative to a Negotiated Settlement)?

Before the start of the mediation it is important to be sure of the extent of your authority to reach agreement. Be very clear about what you can offer and the possibility of exceeding that offer. If you are negotiating on behalf of an organisation you may have a fixed amount you can offer and no more. It is a good idea to establish in advance who is available to contact on the day of the mediation if you need extra authority to settle.

When mediation is suitable, when it is not

Any type of employment dispute, in theory, can be mediated; but mediation is not always the best option for resolving a dispute. The suitability of a case for mediation is determined less by the type of case and more by the circumstances of the individual case at the particular timeframe when the mediation takes place. **4.6.15**

When there is a relationship to preserve mediation is a better option since it is non-adversarial process that unlike litigation or arbitration does not produce a winner and a loser but an acceptable settlement for both sides. Mediation is suitable when you want to save the time, money and stress of a protracted dispute. When you want to keep control of the outcome rather than accept a judge's or arbitrator's ruling and when you want to keep the matter in private, then mediation is a good option. Also when you are looking for remedies which a tribunal or an arbitrator cannot award then mediation is a good way to achieve them.

Certain cases should go to a tribunal hearing, such as when the parties want a public trial or are seeking a public vindication. When the establishment of right and wrong is important or when a fundamental point of principle is involved then the legal route is a good way to achieve it.

There are some cases where it is not clear cut whether mediation or a more formal process may be more appropriate. On the one hand, when in doubt, do not try mediation. On the other hand, most employment cases settle out of court and this one probably could too. When there is an imbalance in power or a history of violence, parties may feel particularly uncomfortable with a face-to-face and may even refuse to meet the other party. Shuttle mediation is an option: the parties do not have to meet in joint session and the mediator literally shuttles between the parties conveying their views and discussing settlement options. In considering the range of dispute resolution processes the choice should not only be appropriate to the dispute, but also likely to leave everyone satisfied with the process and the solutions reached.

4.7 APPENDIX TO CHAPTER 4

Sample Agreement to Mediate

This is an agreement between **[NAMES]** regarding the mediation service that we have requested from **[THE MEDIATION PROVIDER]** for the dispute concerning:

....

on the following terms and conditions:

Role of the mediator(s)

Your mediator(s) will be **[NAME(S)]**. The mediator will maintain impartiality with respect to your dispute at all times. His/her objective is to assist each of you in exploring your own interests, understanding the perspective of the other, and determining your situations. If you wish to proceed to an agreement s/he will assist you in reaching an agreement that you consider satisfactory. S/he will refrain from any attempt to influence the outcome of this matter. S/he will not act as an advocate for any of you nor will s/he provide legal representation, legal advice or legal services. S/he will use any professional knowledge or experience to help you fully understand the issues of your dispute. Nevertheless, as a mediator s/he will be bound to refrain from offering you professional advice. We recommend that you consult with others (such as your union representative) who might be helpful in providing professional or technical information about the relevant law, or about any other field of expertise that may be a part of the mediation.

Mediation fees and expenses

[To be added as agreed]

Your role

The mediation process is based on voluntary negotiations between you, the parties in this dispute. You therefore each agree to use your best endeavours to participate fully in the process and to provide full and complete disclosure of all information necessary to reach informed decisions and a fair agreement.

Mediation procedure

Those who will take part in the mediation are listed below as signatories of this agreement. It is understood by all of us that this list of participants includes all of the parties in the dispute and/or individuals who will represent the parties (union representatives and/or legal advisers) and will have authority to settle the dispute.

We agree that this mediation process is entirely voluntary. The mediation begins with this agreement and any party or the mediator may terminate it at any time. To formally end the mediation any party or the mediator must declare in writing that it has ended. The mediation process may include meetings, telephone conversations and correspondence. The terms of this mediation agreement will apply to the entire period of the mediation process and to whatever type of communication is used.

Confidentiality

During this mediation you will be making full disclosure about matters of a confidential nature. Because we believe that these confidential discussions will facilitate agreement on unresolved issues, we agree that the entire mediation will be kept confidential. We will keep confidential all statements and documentation relating to the mediation including any settlement agreement. However, this confidentiality agreement will not apply to any information necessary to implement and enforce any settlement agreement resulting from this mediation or to enforce the terms of this Agreement to Mediate. We agree that the entire process of the mediation including all documents, submissions and statements whether oral or written made or produced for the purposes of the mediation will not be used as evidence and will not be made available for use in any tribunal, arbitration, trial or similar proceedings except that evidence which is otherwise available as evidence shall not become unavailable by reason of its use in connection with this mediation.

No participant in the mediation, including parties and everyone who represents and/or accompanies them, may have access to the notes of the mediator, or of any of the staff or other participants of the [**THE MEDIATION PROVIDER**], or call the mediator or any of the staff or other participants of [**THE MEDIATION PROVIDER**] as a witness in any proceedings relating to any of the issues between them, and the opinion of the mediator or of any of the staff or other participants of [**THE MEDIATION PROVIDER**] will not be available as evidence in any subsequent proceedings which may take place between the participants concerning the subject matter of the mediation.

Settlement agreements

At the conclusion of the mediation, the mediator will prepare a list of points which you tell him/her you have agreed upon, and will provide the list to you for your use. Any formal written agreement will be prepared by you, or your union representatives and/or your legal advisers for your signature. No agreement about your dispute will be considered legally binding until it is written down and signed by you or your authorised representatives in the form of a compromise agreement or ACAS COT3 form.

Documentation

You (or you union/legal representative) may send your mediator a brief summary of your case in the form of a letter or using any existing documents that you believe will provide him/her with useful information about your situation. Please send any such documents directly to your mediator so that s/he receives them no later than [date]. Please limit any letter to five pages of text with any necessary supporting documentation. Documents sent to the mediator should be copied to the other party and his/her representatives. You may bring to the mediation meeting any supporting documents or other materials that you feel will aid you in clarifying your situation.

Choice of law

This agreement shall be governed by and construed in accordance with English law, under the jurisdiction of the English Courts.

Please carefully review this agreement and, if you agree with its terms and conditions, sign this copy.

____________________ ____________________

Name (Party A) Name (Party B)

____________________ ____________________

Signed (Party A) Signed (Party B)

____________________ ____________________

Date Date

____________________ ____________________

Mediator Mediator

____________________ ____________________

Signed Signed

____________________ ____________________

Date Date

CHAPTER 5

FRANCHISING DISPUTES

CLIVE FREEDMAN Q.C. AND PHILIP BARTLE

INTRODUCTION 5.1

Coco the Clown does magic tricks at children's parties. To the children, his clown's costume and bag of tricks are unique. But the parents know that there are several Cocos. However, what neither know is that the Coco the Clown business is a franchise. Each clown runs a business of his own as a franchisee of the Coco the Clown company. He uses the trade name and the uniform as well as the goodwill which attaches to it.

Typically, but not exclusively, franchises operate in retail outlets on the high street, *e.g.* fast food (hamburgers, ice cream, doughnuts, etc.), fast printing, car hire, estate agency and cosmetics. Many household services are performed by franchisees, *e.g.* cleaning services, drain cleaning and home improvements. Coco the Clown shows that franchising exists even where you least expect it.

Whilst franchising is used to describe a wide variety of business relationships such as licensing, distributorship and agency relationships, this chapter will consider ADR in relation to "business format franchising", that is the granting of a licence by one person (the franchisor) to another (the franchisee) which entitles the franchisee to trade under the trade mark/trade name of the franchisor. The package comprises all the elements necessary to establish a previously untrained person in the business and to run it with continual assistance on a predetermined basis.[1]

There is a useful definition of franchising in the European Code of Ethics for Franchising which has been adopted by the British Franchise Association as follows:

> "Franchising is a system of marketing goods and/or services and/or technology which is based upon a close and ongoing collaboration between legally and financially separate and independent undertakings, the franchisor and its individual franchisees, whereby the

[1] Derived from the definition of the British Franchise Association.

franchisor grants its individual franchisees the right and imposes the obligation to conduct a business in accordance with the franchisor's concept. The right entitles and compels the individual franchisee in exchange for a direct or indirect financial consideration to use the franchisor's trade name and/trade mark and/or service mark, know-how, business and technical methods, procedural system and other industrial and/or intellectual property rights, supported by continuing provision of commercial and technical assistance within the framework and for the term of a written franchise agreement, concluded between parties for this purpose."[2]

5.1.1 Franchising brings advantages to the franchisor and the franchisee. The franchisor is able to expand its business and the value of the trade mark/trade name on the back of independent businesses bound to follow the close and continuous control exercised by the franchisor. Whilst this imposes significant fetters, the franchisee is nonetheless able to establish its own business with significantly less risk of business failure than a new business without the umbrella of a large organisation. There is a perception both of franchisors and franchisees that the returns are such that a franchisee will be incentivised to work harder than a local employee manager.

The franchising relationship is long-term. The franchisee is typically making a very substantial investment paying an initial franchise fee to the franchisor and having significant start up expenses either in order to set up the retail premises according to the signage and trade mark of the franchisor or, in a business involving household services, to acquire and set up the van and the basic tools of the trade. Those expenses have to be amortised over a period of time. To that end, the agreement has to be for a minimum period of time, and there are usual clauses about renewals, providing the franchisee with an option for renewal subject to various conditions being observed by the franchisee.

There are usually provisions for early termination in the event of breaches by the franchisee including, typically, the failure of the franchisee to perform to required levels of performance. In recognition of the investment of the franchisee and the long term nature of the relationship, there are usually clauses (not dissimilar from leases) giving the franchisee the opportunity to put right remediable breaches. In a well-drafted agreement, there may be restrictive covenants not only preventing the use of the trade mark/trade name after termination (to protect and preserve the franchisor's ownership of these intellectual property rights), but also preventing the franchisee from trading in the same trade within an area of the retail premises concerned or in the context of other businesses from dealing with or soliciting customers of the business (to protect the goodwill of the business operated by the franchisee).

[2] Reprinted by permission of the British Franchise Association.

EFFECTIVE COMMUNICATION BETWEEN FRANCHISORS AND FRANCHISEES 5.2

The relationship between the franchisor and franchisee should be a close one and mutual co-operation is fundamental to its success. Usually, the parties realise that they obtain more benefit from the relationship if they perform their contractual obligations. The breakdown of a relationship leading to termination of the franchise can cause harm not only to the franchisee who loses its business but also to the franchisor who might spend many months looking for and training a new franchisee during which time the franchised outlet will be non-operational and competitors may secure permanent gains.

There is an imperative in the long-term relationship of franchising to have effective channels of communications available between the franchisor and the franchisee in order to limit the scope for conflict and to minimise disputes. An effective franchise network depends upon a preparedness for mutual accommodation. Thus, when disagreements arise, it is important that the parties can get together immediately to discuss and resolve potentially contentious matters. Franchisors have to be even-handed as between franchisees because much harm occurs when there is a perception of favouritism by a franchisor of some of its franchisees.

Negotiations can be carried out between the parties directly or with the assistance of professional advisers. It is always advisable that negotiations should be expressed to be "without prejudice" so that the parties are not inhibited by the prospect of any concession or admission being held against them in subsequent court proceedings in the event that negotiation does not settle a dispute. It is important that any settlement is recorded in a clear document so as to avoid the revival of the dispute.

The Code of Ethical Conduct of the British Franchising Association recognises the importance of using best endeavours to resolve individual disputes providing (cl. 2.4) that members:

> "Should resolve complaints, grievances and disputes with good faith and goodwill through fair and reasonable direct communication and negotiation".

The Code of Ethics arose in part due to a perception that the inequality of the relationship between many franchisors and franchisees was open to abuse. Some franchisees suggested that franchisors avoided conciliation in the knowledge that the complainant could not afford to pursue the matter through the courts. The British Franchise Association, which has about 200 franchisor members, emphasises the importance of direct negotiations as much from the perspective of the commercial interests of a franchisor as from any sense of ethical duty. Experience shows that the best run franchise operations are those where there is good communication and support between the franchisor and the franchisees. To this end, large franchise operations frequently have area or regional support managers whose function is to liaise with franchisees in relation to their concerns and to promote the future development plans of the franchisor.

5.3 Types of dispute

Nonetheless, the best intentions do not prevent disputes from arising. Sometimes, they are due to perceived lack of service by one party or the other. Sometimes, their source is a perceived unfairness in the operation of the franchise agreement because one party or the other appears to be doing well at the expense of the other. On occasions, disputes arise from agendas outside the scope of the franchise agreement. The franchisor may decide that it would prefer a managed outlet or to close the outlet and make the franchisee so uncomfortable by lack of co-operation so as to attempt to bring about the termination of the relationship. Alternatively, a franchisee, who is doing exceptionally well, may wish to remove itself from the fetters of the franchise but retain the customer base. To that end, the franchisee may take steps lawful or otherwise as part of a strategy to appropriate the franchised business to itself.

In the context of a long-term franchise relationship, disagreements will have to be resolved and the parties will have to continue to co-exist. Examples of such disputes are:

(a) that the franchisor has failed to fulfill the projections at the beginning of the relationship as to likely turnover and profits of the business;

(b) that the franchisor is not performing its contractual obligations as regards the quality of support and training, either by not providing services at all or not providing them to a reasonable standard, or that the franchisor has not innovated enough or has introduced changes which do not work;

(c) that the franchisor's advertising and promotion are ineffective and the franchisees are not enjoying any benefits from them;

(d) where there is supply of goods, that the franchisor is not supplying goods of the right quality;

(e) the construction of the franchisee's obligation to pay to the franchisor continuing fees referable to the turnover of the business;

(f) the scope of the franchisee's territory and related questions about the ability of the franchisor to compete with the franchisee or to appoint other franchisees in the vicinity or territory of the franchisee;

(g) questions relating to the exercise of the option of renewal of the term of the franchise;

(h) that the franchisee is not operating the system properly or is not reporting as required by the contract or is not maintaining the quality standards or is not marketing the business properly;

(i) that the franchisee is not paying all sums due under the agreement and/or is not devoting enough time to the business and/or will not update equipment or is not adequately maintaining the premises;

(j) that the franchisee has set up a competing business to which it is diverting business.

Disputes can also arise in the termination of the franchise agreement. Examples are:

(a) whether, in the events that have occurred, termination is justified;

(b) the state of the account between the parties on termination;

(c) issues relating to the giving up of the premises owned by the franchisor;

(d) what is to the happen to the fixtures and fittings of any property and the stock-in-trade of any franchise business taking into account expenditure by the franchisee and the intellectual property rights of the franchisor;

(e) the terms upon which the franchisee may sell or transfer the franchised business and any possible option to purchase by the franchisor;

(f) non-competition covenants.

The contractual rights of a franchisee are derived from an agreement between the franchisor and the individual franchisee. The relationship is frequently one of inequality because the franchisee's business and resources are limited relative to those of the franchisor. However, the interests of one franchisee are very likely to coincide or overlap with the interests of other franchisees. For example, the resolution of a dispute about the construction of a clause in a standard franchise agreement relating to the percentage of turnover payable by a franchisee to a franchisor will affect all of the franchisees. Similarly, there may be a common issue of construction regarding the option to renew a franchise and there may be commonality of interest about the enforceability of a post-termination non-competition covenant. Thus, it frequently occurs that the battleground is between the franchisor and a number of franchisees seeking to act collectively.

5.4 ROLE OF COURT

Where informal negotiations fail to result in a resolution of disputes, the court process remains the most used. Whilst there are serious shortcomings of the court process to resolving franchise disputes, the major perceived benefit is that it brings the issues between the parties to a determination which is binding on them. Further, where there is urgency, the court process is the only one to provide a remedy to the injured party either by way of injunction or declaration. Therefore, if the injured party has an intransigent opponent, he will have to apply to the court where he requires that relief. Also, where a party has an unassailable claim so that there is nothing about which to negotiate, the court process is frequently the most attractive one because it provides a summary process which should be a speedy and relatively economical resolution of the dispute.

Where the relationship between the parties is at an end and there is no question of one buying out the other, the court process will usually be the obvious starting point after the breakdown of any negotiations. This provides a focus within which the parties' case can be stated and their remedies sought. Crucially, it provides a method of extracting all relevant documents by compulsion through the disclosure process. Where parties are evasive about their case, they can by court order be forced to provide further information.

In some disputes, there has been very serious wrongdoing in the nature of or tantamount to fraud. As the mediation process depends on both parties acting in good faith, the only effective assistance in these cases is through the court which can impose what have been described as the nuclear weapons of law, namely search orders (for the preservation of documents) and freezing orders (the preservation of money and property) with the sanction of imprisonment for breach.

Many cases involve what is colloquially known as a "straight swear" where one party is telling the truth and the other is lying. Whist not excluding the possibility of mediation and other forms of ADR for those disputes, they do lend themselves peculiarly to the court process in which witnesses are tested by rigorous cross-examination in the light of documents which the "accused" party has had to disclose.

5.4.1 Where franchisees seek unilaterally to alter a distinctive feature of the franchise business, this is generally unacceptable and does not admit of compromise. Usually, a franchisor has to be very careful not to dilute his trade mark and the features distinctive of the business licensed to the franchisee. Thus, a franchisor of a pizza chain would generally view with horror a franchisee who claimed that it should be able to allow different ingredients to accommodate a local palate. Such a change might go to the heart of the business, affecting the implied promise to the public that its pizza in Newbury will taste the same as the pizza in Newcastle-upon-Tyne. The change may affect the ownership of the goodwill, in that a successful franchisee may argue on termination that the local success has been caused by the franchisee's unique ideas rather than the concept or method of the franchisor.

Similar problems might arise in relation to signage. Local problems can arise due to restrictions of planning authorities or landlords as to the use of the usual sign of the franchisor. In those instances, a franchisor might be willing to make its own modifications. However, if a franchisee were, at its own initiative, to permit that to occur, then the danger would be that the franchisor concept would be challenged.

Most franchisors would take the view that these matters, capable of diluting the franchise concept, must be non-negotiable because they affect the lifeblood of the franchised business. If one franchisee was able to make changes and this was permitted by some form of compromise, there would be the serious danger that other franchisees may follow. Most franchisors would recognise that a consistent message has to go out to all of its franchisees that this would not be permitted. In relation to such fundamental issues, the rigidity of the court process and its single solution to problems might be regarded as an advantage. Different considerations may exist if the problem was more complicated: for example, the point of the franchisee had some merit, or there was some inherent weakness in the standpoint of the franchisor such that the uniformity of its method could be challenged. There may be occasions when the dispute is symptomatic of a deeper problem for which there is more than a single solution, where mediation is likely to provide a much needed flexible way of resolving problems.

LIMITATIONS OF LITIGATION IN FRANCHISE CASES 5.5

Notwithstanding the above, the court process is frequently a blunt instrument in dispute resolution. It concentrates on all or nothing resolutions of disputes. Thus, in a dispute about a restrictive covenant, the court will decide whether the covenant is or is not enforceable, that is whether it is no wider than is necessary in order to protect the interests of the franchisor. The court is not permitted to provide a compromise by re-writing the covenant in a way which might accommodate the concerns of both the franchisor and the franchisee. That can only be achieved by the agreement of the parties.

Also, the court cannot take account of the exigencies and the dynamic of a continuing relationship of franchisor and franchisee. A winner takes all solution in court, with orders as to costs in favour of the winner, provides emotionally a difficult basis for the franchise relationship to continue

It is frequently the case that the issue before the court is only the sub-text of the real commercial agenda between the parties. For example, a franchisor may contend that the franchisee has lost his option to renew which is vigorously challenged by the franchisee. The parties may become locked in difficult issues of construction and fact. However, the real agenda may be that the franchisor wishes to buy out the franchisee but the parties cannot agree a price. If so, then better that it should be confronted by the parties outwith the court process than that there should be shadow boxing about unreal issues.

There are more general disadvantages of the court process. Save for summary and interim remedies, those are that it can involve huge expenditure of time and resources, it can polarise the parties to adopt extreme positions; and the parties lose control over their destiny by entering a trial where the evidence often emerges in a way not foreshadowed and which produces sometimes a surprising assessment of witnesses.

An example of this loss of control in franchising would be a dispute about the projection of turnover and profit. Such cases often descend into a morass of detail about the nature of the projection, the effectiveness of exclusion clauses, the cause of the lack of success of the business with allegations that the franchisee was incompetent and complicated, and detailed and expensive evidence of forensic accountants. Even after the Woolf reforms introduced in 1999, such a trial is likely to last for many days with oscillation about the prospects of success of the parties. Such cases can destroy businesses and the litigants behind them.

5.6 ARBITRATION

Advantages of arbitration

This is often the preferred option. The advantages of arbitration over the court process are that:

(a) The dispute can be kept outside the public arena. In an age where the trade press is more active than ever before, the risk of adverse publicity by dirty linen being washed in public is correspondingly greater. For the franchisor, this can affect the goodwill of the business as a whole.

(b) The dispute can be tried by specialists in the field. When a case comes to court, it is rare for the judge to have had substantial experience in franchising. By contrast, the arbitrator is selected for expertise in relation to franchising or commercial disputes.

(c) Arbitrations usually come to final hearings more quickly than court cases. Timetables are dictated solely by the time to take the preliminary preparatory steps to trial and the availability of the arbitrator, the witnesses, the parties and their representatives. In court cases, parties have to wait their place in the queue of litigants.

(d) The arbitrator is concerned solely to resolve the dispute between the parties without regard to the interests of other litigants. In court, the judge is obliged to consider restricting the amount of court time to take into account the court's obligations to try the cases of other litigants.

(e) The absence of public funding for parties in arbitrations can be a particular advantage to a franchisor. In court cases, where such funding is available, there is the risk that cases are pursued in the knowledge that usually there can be no effective order for costs against the unassisted party. There are also cases where the system is unfortunately abused where unmeritorious claims are pursued because they are publicly funded.

Disadvantages of arbitration

However, there are also serious disadvantages of arbitration, namely:

(a) Whereas after paying the court fees, the court and the judge are provided without further charge, the parties have to bear the expense of the arbitrator and of the arbitration room. The daily charge of the arbitrator (who must charge for reading time before the case and the cost of preparing the award after the oral hearing) and the arbitration room are a very considerable part of the costs of the arbitration as a whole.

(b) Although there is greater speed in arbitration, it still takes considerable time bearing in mind the usual need for Statements of Case, disclosure and witness statements. Whilst an arbitrator can take some short cuts with the agreement of the parties, it is usually the case that the oral hearings take as long as court cases.

(c) The criticism in relation to litigation being a blunt instrument applies equally to arbitration.

(d) Parties are dependent upon the views of the outsider: they are not in control of their own destiny.

(e) Where an individual litigant has limited resources, public funding is not available unlike for court cases.

The British Franchise Association has an arbitration scheme which includes not only the appointment of an arbitrator but, also, the appointment of one franchisor representative and one franchisee representative to advise the arbitrator in every arbitration. However, the sole power and authority to make any award is with the arbitrator. Its latest arbitration scheme was published in July 2001. The British Franchise Association has a panel of arbitrators for its arbitration scheme derived from experienced practitioners in the field. At the time of writing, the British Franchise Association is about to launch a New Mediation Scheme reflecting the considerable advantages to which reference is now made.

5.7 MEDIATION

In a mediation, a neutral third party (the mediator) assists the parties to come to an agreement settling their dispute on terms which each finds acceptable. The process is "facilitative". The mediator merely assists the parties to find their own way to a settlement. This is often achieved by assisting the parties to define and concentrate on the *real issues* and enabling them to arrive at a settlement. Mediation can also be "evaluative", that is where the mediator is asked to give an assessment of the strength of the parties' cases, whether as a matter of law or in relation to some technical or scientific issue.

There are advantages which mediation has over other processes which are common to all forms of disputes. These are that, in comparison with other dispute resolution processes:

(a) it is quicker because an early date is easier to arrange;

(b) it is simpler because neither the more stringent rules applicable in court or in an arbitration nor the obligation to disclose documents apply;

(c) it is cheaper because the amount of time spent in a mediation and preparation for it is very much less than the time that would be spent in a court case or in an arbitration;

(d) it is less stressful because it is neither adversarial nor antagonistic and it is very much less formal than other processes.

There are particular advantages of mediation for franchising disputes which are:

(a) a wider range of solutions;

(b) the involvement of numerous franchisees;

(c) avoiding public loss of face.

These will be considered separately.

A wider range of solutions

It has already been noted that a disadvantage of the court process is that it frequently involves all or nothing findings. Take the case of a non-competition covenant. If, at the termination of the franchise, a court is considering a covenant that the outgoing franchisee will not trade in a retail outlet in the same trade as the franchisee for a period of two years after termination and within a radius of five miles from the retail outlet of the franchise, it may be difficult to predict whether or not a court will uphold the covenant because of competing arguments as to whether the covenant is more than is necessary in order to protect the goodwill of the franchise. Consideration will have to be given as to whether or not there is a need for an area covenant at all, and if there is such a need, whether or not a period of two years or a radius of five miles is excessive. The court will decide only that the covenant is valid or that it is void and not whether it should be altered to a lesser restriction which may be valid. However, the parties may well be prepared to negotiate some intermediate restriction or there may be a readiness to negotiate a wider restriction on the basis that there is a purchase by one party of the other. All of this can be agreed as a one off with a confidentiality provision in a mediation, and may be regarded as much more beneficial than the court process. 5.7.1

Both parties in the court process may think that they have too much to lose. Apart from the expense, if a franchisee were to lose entirely, then the possibility of realistically starting again may be non-existent: his sole hope may be of trading in some way within the radius, which may be the only area where he or she has ever carried on business. Likewise, if the covenant is held to be void, a franchisor may be in danger of not only losing its presence within the radius concerned, but also of there being a precedent which will enable other outgoing franchisees to challenge their respective covenants.

The question of flexibility is not restricted to anti-competition covenants. There are frequently cases in which the real question, albeit not the one before the court, is whether or not one party ought to buy out and, if so, at what price. The dispute before the court may be apparently completely different. It may be whether or not there has been a valid termination of the franchise agreement by the franchisor: the franchisor may contend that there is a termination for breach, whereas the franchisee may contend that the termination was invalid and that the franchisee is entitled to remain trading as such. Alternatively, the franchisee may contend that there is an option to renew whereas the franchisor may contend that, as a matter of construction or, in the events which have occurred that there is no such right. In reality, in both cases, the disputed termination and the disputed option to renew, the franchisee may be ready to get out, but at a price which provides some compensation for the work in building up the franchise into a profitable unit. The question before the court about the validity of the termination and the concomitant examination of the conduct or performance of the franchisee may be a side issue relative to how much should be paid to the franchisee. Mediation, involving a greater flexibility, will offer the parties a more direct and, in the end, satisfactory route to the inevitable buy out.

Sometimes, the solution may be the other way because a franchisee or a group of franchisees are interested in having a buy out of all or a part of the business of the franchisor. The agenda before the court may be whether or not the intellectual property rights of the franchisor or the contract are such as to prevent the franchisees from carrying out their trade in a certain manner. Alternatively, there may be contentions that proper support is not being given or the argument may be about how much is payable to the franchisor. The reality may be that this is a dispute shadowing the real agenda, namely the desire to have the franchise equivalent of a management buy out of all or a part of the business. The choice may be between shadow boxing in court or a more direct approach in a mediation. The response of the determined franchisor may be to fight in court or to make an offer to buy out the franchisees or to sell to the franchisees. No doubt an ingenious mediator will work out more possible solutions in dispute resolution.

Involvement of numerous franchisees

5.7.2 A court dispute can only resolve the dispute between the parties before the court. Sometimes, disputes involve numerous parties, and there can be representative actions. A point of construction common to all franchise agreements may involve all franchisees equally so that they can be before the court. However, sometimes there will be issues with a common flavour, but where each case will be strictly separate on its own facts. The resolution of whether or not there was a misrepresentation may involve separate issues of precisely what representation was made and the extent of the reliance in respect of each franchisee. Sometimes, there will be a question as to whether or not an exclusion clause is valid notwithstanding the provisions of the Unfair Contract Terms Act 1977. This may appear to admit the same answer in each case, but if one franchisee is a retired and rich lawyer or chartered accountant dabbling in a limited business to amuse himself in his dotage, whereas another is a young uneducated person starting in life and having been enticed to the franchise by the franchisor, the answer may be completely different. The result is that each case may have to be considered separately unless franchisees are prepared to treat one case as representative. In the misrepresentation case, this will be very difficult indeed. However, in a mediation, it is possible to involve numerous parties. It is not necessary to treat one franchisee as representative. The mediation may settle the dispute of numerous franchisees, and it may settle the disputes of only some of them. There may be different interest groups which can be separately represented, so that some disputes may settle and others may not.

In a multi-party mediation, there may be many parties before the mediation, and there may be several mediators working as a team to effect settlements. So different from the courtroom, where the first instance judge is a solitary figure.

Where the issue is the purchase of a business, a neutral expert, capable of giving evaluative comments, may sit with a mediator and assist in bringing the parties closer to agreement. Alternatively, in circumstances where the purchase of a business is the issue, it may be that the parties wish to conduct the mediation in stages. In the first stage, the parties will try to reach a non-binding heads of agreement with a view to arranging formulae and terms to be considered with a view to reaching a final binding agreement. After that, the parties will then consult with their respective lawyers, accountants and expert valuers with a view to resolving the matter finally. It may be unnecessary to return to the mediator but, if there is a hiccough on the way, the mediator may be there to assist at a second stage. It may even be that the very fact that the support is available may bring the parties to a resolution of the dispute without the need to revert to the mediator.

Avoiding public loss of face

The mediation is confidential to the parties. Similarly, any settlement may be expressed to be confidential. It may be damaging to a franchise business to have allegations in a public forum showing that the retail chain of franchised outlets is not everything it may appear to be. A franchise priding itself on moral standards, and benefitting from the public perception that it lives up to such standards, may not relish a public loss of face which may arise in a court 5.7.3

battle (in the unlikely event that the reporter happens to turn up to court).

A court case can become a test case, *e.g.* the case of a restrictive covenant or a case about the construction of the exercise of an option. It may be attractive to a franchisor to avoid test cases, even if there is the risk that a franchisee may flout the confidentiality obligation. There may be more to lose from a court judgment, which may be a precedent about a clause in a contract, than a one off settlement, even if a party chooses to leak the settlement.

Sometimes, there are settlements which are made at mediation in order to bring to an end a dispute which may interfere with an intended buy out or an announcement to the Stock Exchange. Sometimes, it is the circumstances of the franchisee which are crucial. He may appear to have the resources to fight a case, but it may be an illusion. There may be health reasons which preclude a court case.

Why is the public loss of face consideration particularly important in a mediation? The answer is because the franchise network involves numerous people with a common interest, sometimes adverse to the franchisor. The danger of public defeat in a courtroom is the ripple effect on other franchisees. In many cases, a retailer may have no reason to fear a dispute against a wholesaler because each agreement with each wholesaler may be totally different. However, it is the common nature of each franchise agreement which gives rise to the ripple effect. Such effects may be reduced or mitigated in the event that a dispute is not resolved in a public domain, and (unlike in the case of an arbitration) without the possibility of judicial review or scrutiny.

However, mediation may not be effective in several circumstances. For example, if an urgent injunction is required in order to preserve the concept or the business of the franchisor, then immediate recourse to the courts may be appropriate but, once an interim remedy is in place, it may be appropriate to have a mediation, provided that the franchisee recognises from the start that which is non-negotiable. The dispute may be such that the franchisee is making challenges which go to the heart of the concept which is the subject of the franchise or that if there was a compromise with one franchisee, there would be a serious risk that it would have a knock-on effect as regards other franchisees. These are circumstances where many franchisors, if confident of their legal position, would regard mediation as inappropriate and sending out the wrong messages.

5.8 CHOICE OF MEDIATOR

Even if a mediator is not evaluative, but is the usual facilitative mediator, it is essential that the mediator must have knowledge of franchising: how it works in practice and some knowledge about the legal principles. Without this, a mediator may spend much of the day being informed about franchise law or practice without bringing to the table the extra dimensions which an able mediator is able to provide. The questions asked of the body organising the mediation about the experience of the mediator should be frank and direct. There is a forceful argument in Mackie in the second edition of the ADR Practice Guide[3] that there is a preoccupation about the mediator's expertise, when in fact more important is the process skills of the mediator in finding opportunities. In reality, and as is conceded by the authors, a combination of both sets of skills is required. The more specialist the area of dispute, the more vital some degree of specialisation and familiarity with the subject matter by the mediator.

VENUE OF MEDIATION 5.9

This may be very important in mediations where there is perceived inequality of the franchisee *vis-à-vis* the franchisor. In such cases, it will only exacerbate the tensions if the mediation takes place in the well-appointed boardroom of the head office of the franchisor or of the large city firm of solicitors which acts for the franchisor. Much better to go the mediator's premises or to find some other neutral venue.

INVOLVEMENT OF PROFESSIONAL ADVISERS 5.10

Whilst this is usually of value both in relation to legal disputes and in relation to financial disputes, it is important as far as possible to have equality of arms. A mediation is unlikely to be effective if one side by himself is drowned out by an array of professional advisers on the other side. If the decision is that counsel should attend, then this is more likely to work where there is counsel on both sides. It is helpful if the parties either directly or through the mediator are able to consider the appropriate attendees of the mediation. There are no rules, but sensitivity to the other party even before the mediation starts is likely to be valuable.

STAGGERED MEDIATION 5.11

This has been touched upon in the context of the different stages required in order to settle a franchising dispute. The first stage may

[3] Mackie and others in the second edition of the ADR Practice Guide pp. 165–166.

not require any valuations, but it may require lawyers who can assist in the process of formulating a way of resolving differences. A second stage may require the presence of valuers. A yet further stage may be required in the event of a complicated settlement when one party is buying the business of the other. It is to be hoped that the mediator may not be required at each stage, but it is possible that the mediator would be central at one stage, and on call to help at a later stage if required. This is another instance of the flexibility of mediation in dispute resolution. ADR will need to be taken seriously and will require the commitment of management time for the duration of the discussions. A day may be long enough to resolve many disputes but, if it takes longer, while progress is being made the time should be made available. According to CEDR, the largest mediation organisation in the U.K., 82 per cent of its cases were resolved in one day.

5.12 PREPARATION FOR THE MEDIATION

The following are the minimum preparatory steps which need to be taken prior to the mediation:

(a) By the time the parties agree to a mediation, the issues between them should be clear and it is advisable to try to agree formally what those issues are.

(b) A bundle of documents for the mediation should be agreed between the parties. This will consist only of the documents which the parties wish to rely on in the mediation. It may include the pleadings if there is ongoing litigation but this is not obligatory and, if the parties can agree a summary of the pleadings, it is likely that they can be omitted.

(c) Each party should prepare a brief written summary of the dispute, with an explanation of the position taken by that party.

(d) The representative of the party and the lawyers who are to attend should ensure that they are thoroughly prepared for the mediation. It is a grave mistake to think that, because a mediation is informal, detailed preparation is unnecessary.

(e) The representative of the party who is to attend must have authority to agree a settlement.

(f) Ascertain the costs incurred to date and an estimate of the costs which will be incurred if the dispute goes to trial or an arbitration hearing as the amount of costs is likely to be a crucial factor in the amount of any settlement.

(g) Make an assessment of the realistic options which are available in the event of a failure to agree a settlement with the other party.

STRUCTURE OF THE MEDIATION 5.13

The mediator is there to provide the framework in which the parties can negotiate their way to a settlement. A typical mediation will proceed as follows:

(a) The mediator will introduce himself to the parties and their representatives and take them to their private room where they will spend most of their time during the mediation process.

(b) When all parties are present, the mediator will bring them all together in open session where the mediator will explain the process and each party will then be invited to outline their position in relation to the dispute and the mediation itself.

(c) The parties will then retire to separate rooms where they will be visited (in turn) by the mediator and discussion will take place in confidence. The mediator can only reveal the contents of these discussions to the other parties with the consent of the party who has provided the information.

(d) The mediator "shuttles" between the parties to assist the parties to come to a settlement with which they are content.

(e) The parties will have signed a binding agreement. Until such time as they have agreed a binding settlement (in writing) there is no settlement and, if all attempts at settlement fail, the dispute will revert to more traditional dispute resolution, through the courts or by arbitration.

SETTLEMENT AGREEMENT 5.14

The settlement agreement of a franchising dispute may be extremely complicated if it is a buy-out of a business. Suddenly, commercial lawyers emerge centre stage as their litigation partners go to find their next case. In the pressure to settle a dispute, it is important to see the wood for the trees. It is not settlement at all costs, not least because any settlement must be capable of enduring and not leading to a whole new dispute. An agreement to sell a business is not something which can just be eked out on the back of a court order staying court proceedings. Such an agreement will usually require a travelling draft as complicated suggestions go between the various parties. In the context of a mediation, consideration should be given to the logistics of getting to such agreements, and the continued availability of the mediator to help at the sometimes difficult final stages.

5.15 Conclusions

There will be many occasions when litigation will be the appropriate way to resolving a dispute, not least when urgent injunctions are required. There will be matters of discipline so fundamental to the franchise relationship that mediation or compromise will send out the wrong message to the franchisees. However, the vast majority of disputes which result in litigation are resolved by settlement which is a clear indication that disputes can be resolved ultimately by discussions between the parties.

The particular attraction of mediation in franchising disputes is that, unlike litigation and arbitration, it offers the parties a far better chance of continuing with their relationship. They need have no fear that they will be subjected to a procedure which will result in an outcome which determines who is right and who is wrong.

The best run franchises have in-built procedures to ensure good communication between franchisor and franchisee: that includes being able to negotiate at an early stage to nip disputes in the bud. Mediation is an extension of this. A culture where parties are aware of mediation, perhaps including an ADR clause in a contract, which would make the courts the more inclined to send people to mediate, will be of benefit. The ability to resolve a dispute and move on shows maturity and recognition of mutual self interest. It is usually too lofty an ideal in the context of litigation, but in the new world of mediation, parties are helped to control their own destiny to such an extent that not only can they resolve their differences, but they can work on together and heal their divisions. In the context of the long-term relationship of franchising, this is invaluable.

CHAPTER 6

INSOLVENCY DISPUTES

CHRISTINE DERRETT

THE STATUTORY FRAMEWORK 6.1

The first question which has to be determined is whether an officeholder appointed under the Insolvency Act 1986 has the power to use mediation as a method for dealing with a dispute. The officeholder will be a licensed insolvency practitioner, usually a trained accountant, but sometimes a practising solicitor.

The powers of the officeholders are set out in the schedules to the 1986 Act and benefit from detailed consideration before moving on to consider the types of disputes in this area which are appropriate for mediation and the role of mediation in dealing with them.

If we look at the Insolvency Act 1986, what are the powers of the different types of officeholder?

Administrators

An administrator is appointed primarily for the benefit of the body 6.1.1
of creditors as a whole, he does not have an allegiance to any particular group of creditors and his proposals must be approved by the creditors at a properly summoned meeting. The overriding duty of the administrator will depend upon the reasons set out in the order by which he is appointed. It might be the survival of the business as a going concern (in whole or in part), or to facilitate a voluntary arrangement or scheme of arrangement with creditors, or to permit a more advantageous realisation of the company's assets than would be effected on an immediate winding-up. Administration has the benefit of the statutory moratorium which means that the company cannot be pursued for its outstanding debts once the administration order is made and the administrator must act in the best interest of the creditors as a body. The powers of the administrator are set out in Schedule 1 to the Insolvency Act 1986 and the powers which are of particular relevance in the context of mediation are:

Paragraph 14

Power to carry on business of the company.

Paragraph 18

Power to make any arrangement or compromise on behalf of the company.

Paragraph 23

Power to do all other things incidental to the exercise of the foregoing powers.

The Act, in effect, gives to administrators the power to make any arrangement or compromise on behalf of the company and to do all such things as may be necessary for the management of the affairs or business and property of the company.

Since one of the purposes of administration is to preserve the business, an administrator would clearly be acting properly if, in his view, mediation was an appropriate way to manage a dispute which arose in the course of the business of the company.

Administrative receivership

6.1.2 This is not an insolvency proceeding in the strict sense but the remedy of a secured creditor which allows for the realisation of assets which are subject to his security. The administrative receiver is conducting himself for the benefit of his secured creditor and unless they are overridden by the provisions of the debenture under which the administrative receiver is appointed, he has the same powers under the Insolvency Act 1986 as an administrator and is bound generally by Schedule 1 to the Act. Again he would have the powers in paragraphs 14, 18 and 23 as set out above, which means that he too would clearly be acting properly if, in his view, a mediation was the appropriate way to manage a dispute which arose in the course of his duties as far as the company is concerned. But remember he is always acting for the benefit of his secured creditor.

Liquidators

6.1.3 Liquidation is also known as winding-up and this is the procedure by which the assets of a company are realised by the officeholder and distributed to creditors in the order provided for in the Insolvency Act 1986. A winding-up can either be by way of a voluntary liquidation which occurs following a resolution of shareholders which may be converted into a creditor's voluntary liquidation by holding a subsequent creditors' meeting or a compulsory liquidation which occurs as a consequence of a court order. Once a liquidation has been concluded the company would be dissolved. During the course of the liquidation there is nothing to prevent a secured lender from appointing an administrative receiver, but there is a stay on the commencement or continuation of proceedings against the company without the leave of the court.

Schedule 4 to the Insolvency Act 1986 sets out the powers of a liquidator. It is divided into three parts: Part I deals with powers exercisable with sanction; Part II sets out powers exercisable without sanction in a voluntary winding-up but with sanction in a winding-up by the court; and Part III, powers exercisable without sanction in any winding-up.

The relevant powers of the liquidator in Schedule 4, Part I are:

Paragraph 2

Power to make any compromise or arrangement with creditors or persons claiming to be creditors, or having or alleging themselves to have any claim (present or future, certain or contingent, ascertained or sounding only in damages) against the company, or whereby the company may be rendered liable. **6.1.4**

Paragraph 3

Powers to compromise on such terms as may be agreed: **6.1.5**

(a) all calls and liabilities to calls, all debts and liabilities capable of resulting in debts and all claims (present or future, certain or contingent, ascertained or sounding only in damages) subsisting or supposed to subsist between the company and a contributory or alleged contributory or other debtor or person apprehending liability to the company; and

(b) all questions in any way relating to or affecting the assets or the winding up of the company;

and take any security for the discharge of any such call, debt, liability or claim and give a complete discharge in respect of it.

In other words, the liquidator has the power to make any compromise or arrangements with creditors or any person claiming to be a creditor or persons having a claim against the company and to give a complete discharge in respect of it. By *sanction* the Insolvency Act 1986 means the sanction of the court or the liquidation committee —see section 167 of the Insolvency Act 1986. The preference of the officeholder would be to operate with the sanction of a liquidation committee but, even if consent was not available from them, an application to approve a settlement could be made under section 168 of the Insolvency Act 1986. This section enables the liquidator to apply to the court for the court's sanction of his actions.

Schedule 4, Part III provides the liquidator with powers which are exercisable without sanction in any winding-up. Of particular relevance is the following:

Paragraph 13

6.1.6 Power to do all such things as may be necessary for winding up the company's affairs and distributing its assets.

This statutory power is wide enough to allow the liquidator to adopt mediation as the appropriate method for dealing with a dispute even if the settlement will ultimately require approval by either the court or the committee.

Provisional liquidator

6.1.7 From time to time it proves necessary to apply to the court after a winding-up petition has been presented but before an order made for the appointment of a provisional liquidator. The provisional liquidator is usually appointed because of some perceived concerns and his functions will be tailored to meet those concerns, his powers may be limited by the order appointing him. It is therefore necessary to consider ensuring that the order making the appointment is sufficiently widely drawn to enable him to achieve compromise by way of mediation.

The trustee in bankruptcy

6.1.8 An individual who becomes bankrupt is then subject to the control of his trustee. Schedule 5 to the Insolvency Act 1986 sets out the powers of a trustee. Part I deals with those powers which are exercisable with sanction, Part II sets out general powers and Part III, ancillary powers. Again the sanction required under Part I is that of the creditors' committee or the court. Schedule 5 gives the trustee the following powers:

Paragraph 6

6.1.9 Power to refer to arbitration or compromise on such terms as may be agreed on any debts, claims or liabilities subsisting or supposed to subsist between the bankrupt and any person who may have incurred any liability to the bankrupt.

Paragraph 7

6.1.10 Power to make such compromise or other arrangement as may be thought expedient with creditors, or persons claiming to be creditors, in respect of bankruptcy debt.

Paragraph 8

6.1.11 Power to make such compromise or other arrangement as may be thought expedient with respect to any claim arising out of or incidental to the bankrupt's estate made or capable of being made on the trustee by any person or by the trustee on any person. Here again we see that the trustee in bankruptcy has powers wide enough to encompass mediation albeit with the sanction of the court or creditors' committee.

Supervisor of a voluntary arrangement

Both individuals and corporate entities can reach a compromise with their creditors, thereby avoiding going into a more formal insolvency process. This is commonly known as a voluntary arrangement. The process has to be conducted by a third party, currently an insolvency practitioner, who will prepare the details of the proposed arrangement, liaise with the court, call and conduct the creditors' meeting. If the compromise is agreed then that person will become known as the supervisor and it is their responsibility to ensure the compromise is put into effect. **6.1.12**

The supervisor's powers are largely controlled by the terms of the arrangement but they are subject to court scrutiny. They will need to deal with any disputes which may arise and, if for no other reasons than cost, mediation should be an option which is given due consideration. They could not be criticised for trying to settle a dispute by using mediation.

The role of the creditors' committee

A number of the powers given to officeholders require sanction by either the court or the creditors' committee. Accordingly, it can be seen that the creditors' committee takes on a very important role in the context of mediation for, without their concurrence, the officeholder's hands may be tied and he will be prevented from adopting mediation as a method for resolving the dispute. To understand the role of the creditors' committee it is necessary to refer to the Insolvency Rules 1986 which need to be read in conjunction with the Insolvency Act 1986. **6.1.13**

In the case of administration and administrative receivership, rules 2.34 and 3.18 of the Insolvency Rules 1986 *require* the creditors' committee to *assist* the officeholder in discharging his functions so they should support any proposed mediation.

The emphasis for liquidators is somewhat different. Rule 4.184 of the Insolvency Rules "provides that the sanction of the committee, shall not be *a general permission* but shall relate to a particular proposed exercise of the liquidator's power in question". Accordingly, a liquidator should make any settlement conditional on obtaining the sanction of the creditors' committee.

Rule 4.155 imposes a duty on the liquidator to report to the committee *all matters* which appear to the liquidator to be of concern to the *committee* with respect to the winding-up. The position of a trustee in bankruptcy is similar—see section 314 of the Insolvency Act 1986 and Schedule 5. **6.1.14**

The costs in particular and the work of officeholders generally, have received a considerable amount of adverse publicity and criticism from the judiciary in recent years. It could be suggested therefore that nothing should be of any greater concern to a committee than costs and, in such circumstances, it can be argued that a liquidator or trustee has a *duty* to discuss alternative ways of resolving disputes with his committee, if he is to maximise realisations for distribution to the creditors as a whole. It would certainly be sensible for the trustee or liquidator to explain this in some detail to his committee at a very early stage in the process and to encourage them to buy into the process of mediation, possibly even to participate in the mediation itself, although that might be a bit extreme. This raises issues of confidentiality which are dealt with later in this chapter. What cannot be in doubt is that mediation is generally a much more cost-efficient method of resolving a dispute.

Also, it may be seen to be to the officeholder's advantage to argue at the mediation that the settlement has to be approved by the committee to demonstrate that it is reasonable, thereby giving the officeholder further protection. This could be seen to be a weapon in the officeholder's favour, giving him greater bargaining strength. Overall, it does mean that the officeholder should highlight and explain to the committee the advantages of mediation before embarking upon litigation if criticism is to be avoided.

6.2 TYPES OF DISPUTE

There is a common misunderstanding that simply because an officeholder, whether that be a liquidator, an administrator, an administrative receiver or a trustee in bankruptcy, has been appointed that the nature of a dispute changes: it does not. Officeholders will have to deal with all different types of contractual and tortious disputes. The Insolvency Act 1986 may impact upon the conduct of litigation, indeed, compulsory liquidation proceedings may not be commenced or continued without the leave of the court but it does not mean that any dispute which arises should not be dealt with by the said officeholder. Officeholders will commonly deal with the following types of disputes:

(a) disputes with landlords;

(b) disputes with tenants;

(c) disputes with former professional advisers;

(d) insurance claims;

(e) employment issues;

(f) product liability issues;

(g) disputes arising out of section 238 of the Insolvency Act 1986, preferences;

(h) disputes arising out of section 239 of the Insolvency Act 1986, transactions at an undervalue; and

(i) disputes over claims (including priority disputes).

Recovery of assets is obviously a priority for officeholders and to that extent they will have to deal with any disputes arising in relation thereto.

All such disputes are capable of resolution through use of alternative dispute procedures, mediation being one of the most obvious examples available. The alternative is for the officeholders to litigate, and this has historically been the approach they adopt on the basis that the officeholder cannot be accused of making a wrong decision or criticised if the court has determined the outcome of the dispute. However, as considered above, the power to compromise is contained within the Insolvency Act 1986 and so mediation is a viable alternative which should be given proper consideration by officeholders. It will provide a cheaper and quicker method of resolving a dispute, leaving the officeholder with more time to recover assets for the benefit of creditors and, perhaps most importantly, to ensure that money is not wasted on litigation costs but preserved for the benefit of creditors to whom it will ultimately be distributed or equally to be used to invest in the rescue or restructuring process itself.

Officeholders are often faced with multi-party disputes. For example, claims against professional advisers often involve litigating against a number of professional advisers at one time, or where there have been a significant number of investors in funds, it will be necessary to join those investors to proceedings in order to trace their funds into specific assets. Multi-party disputes are expensive to litigate and can often be more satisfactorily settled through mediation, although many mediators will admit that it often takes longer to negotiate the sharing agreement between the dissenting parties rather than the overall settlement itself.

The globalisation of business has resulted in an increase in global insolvencies and it is not uncommon for a multi-national company to find itself in different forms of insolvency process in different jurisdictions. Then the prospect arises of officeholders competing for the limited realisations for the benefit of their creditors within their own jurisdictions. In those circumstances, it can be virtually impossible to bring litigation to a successful conclusion as there will simply be non-co-operation by the various officeholders and so litigation is not a viable option. Therefore in order to address the competing concerns and needs of the officeholders and the creditors, mediation may become the only viable method of resolving the dispute. The parties then need only to agree on the law to be applied to the compromise. Although business and insolvency may be increasingly global, culture is not and cultural differences can be divisive. They can be far more easily addressed by mediation. The skill required by the officeholder is in the choice of mediator: they need to be someone sensitive to these issues rather than someone who necessarily understands the English law of insolvency. Mediation has a very important role to play in multi-jurisdictional disputes.

6.3 THE ROLE OF COURTS AND TRIBUNALS

The reforms introduced by Lord Woolf and the adoption of the Court Practice Rules mean that there is much more encouragement from the courts to persuade the parties to consider forms of alternative dispute resolution (ADR).

The Commercial Court has taken the lead in encouraging ADR, and the procedure seems to have worked well and been beneficial. We are seeing the High Court generally becoming much more pro-ADR. ADR is reviewed and considered at Case Management Conferences and pre-trial reviews, and sanctions in costs can result if the parties unreasonably refuse ADR or act unco-operatively in the course of ADR.

Insolvency matters are dealt with by the Chancery Division, in the Companies Court and in Bankruptcy. In the late 1990s the judiciary was very critical of the costs which officeholders incurred in pursuing litigation. The courts do have a particular role to play as regards officeholders. We have seen that the statutory framework requires the court's approval in many instances for settlement, they will also scrutinise an officeholder's conduct and issues such as officeholder's remuneration can and are subject to the overview of the courts. Indeed, Ferris J., in *Mirror Group Newspapers v. Kevin and Ian Maxwell and the Personal Representatives of Robert Maxwell (Deceased)* [1998] 1 B.C.L.C. 638 made some points of general application which are worthy of repetition:

(a) Any officeholder is a fiduciary with a duty to get in and, ultimately, pass on to others assets and property which belong not to the officeholder but to the creditors or beneficiaries of one or another kind. Officeholders have a fundamental obligation to account both for the way in which they exercise their powers and for the property with which they deal.

(b) Officeholders are trustees and the usual rule is that a trustee must not profit from his trust. That rule applies to all kinds of persons who are in a fiduciary position, hence the allowance of any remuneration at all represents an exception to this rule because there is a clear conflict between the interests of the fiduciary (the officeholder) and the interests of those to whom the fiduciary duties are owed (the creditors).

(c) The test to determine whether an officeholder has acted properly in undertaking particular tasks, including litigation, at a particular cost in expense or time spent, must be as follows:

> "Whether a reasonably prudent man, faced with the same circumstances in relation to his own affairs would lay out or hazard his own money in doing what the officeholders have done. it is not sufficient, in my view, for officeholders to say that what they have done is within the scope of the duties or powers conferred upon them."

Which ultimately means the courts will look very critically at the conduct of an officeholder if he has failed to consider mediation at all as a method of dispute resolution. Adopting the words of Lightman J. "The prudent businessman would regard litigation as the remedy of last resort . . ."

We see that the courts are encouraging mediation. As yet it is not mandatory, although for insolvency a strong case can be made out that it should be.

THE ROLE OF ADR GENERALLY AND IN PARTICULAR THE ADVANTAGES OF MEDIATION OVER OTHER FORMS OF ADR 6.4

As explained, ADR, particularly mediation, is becoming an increasingly accepted technique in insolvency cases particularly as costs have become a much more critical issue and officeholders should be very concerned about the costs and effectiveness of litigation.

Why mediation as opposed to other forms of ADR? We can look at other jurisdictions for examples of very successful mediation processes:

Australia

The territory of New South Wales has introduced the Farm Debt 6.4.1
Mediation Act which requires banks to mediate before taking action against farmers. The banking industry embraced the use of mediation as a mechanism for resolving disputes and encourages its use generally.

Canada

Since the mid-1980s there has been a programme of mandatory 6.4.2
mediation in farm foreclosure actions. Further mediation has now been adopted as a standard process in personal bankruptcies where a dispute centres around surplus income of the bankrupt and the timing of discharge from the bankruptcy. The Rules of Court in some Canadian Provinces require the parties to try to find a solution by using ADR before settling the matter down for trial.

United States

6.4.3 The United States has many examples of programmes involving mediation. The ADR Act of 1998 directs each U.S. district court to make some form of ADR available for all civil actions, including adversarial proceedings in bankruptcy. Mediation is the most commonly used form of ADR and is gaining increasing acceptance among insolvency lawyers and judges. There is no specific federal rule of bankruptcy procedure or provision in the Bankruptcy Code that governs or regularises the procedures for using ADR in bankruptcy cases. Local bankruptcy ADR rules do exist but they differ in content and scope so the ADR process is applied on quite an ad hoc basis depending on the court. Nevertheless, mediation has been introduced in Chapter 11 cases in order to achieve a more efficient resolution of disputes and to reconcile differing positions as to the provisions of a reorganisation plan. As the U.S. courts have embraced mediation, the courts of a number of bankruptcy districts have introduced standard or local rules creating mediation programmes for bankruptcy proceedings and the general view is that, particularly in relation to small to medium-sized bankruptcies, both personal and corporate mediation is a very useful tool of the insolvency trade.

England and Wales

6.4.4 In the jurisdiction of England and Wales, we have seen ADR being used very successfully. Perhaps one of the earliest examples of its success was its use in the case between the U.K. Government and Arthur Andersen arising out of the collapse of De Lorean. After 12 years of litigation, the presiding judge (Coleman J.) ordered the parties to use ADR to attempt to reach a settlement, which they did, somewhat to their own surprise, as neither party wanted to mediate.

The collapse of Atlantic Computers plc in 1990 brought down British & Commonwealth Holdings plc, the company that had taken it over, as well. There was an extensive DTI Investigation into Atlantic Computers plc after which B&C commenced proceedings against six parties, including: BZW who had been their advisers in the takeover; N. M. Rothschild, Atlantic's advisers; OC&C, strategy consultants in the takeover; Atlantic's former auditors; various Atlantic directors; and Atlantic itself. The claim was in excess of £850 million. The trial was estimated to last 15 to 20 months and scheduled to start in May 2000. The costs were to be tens of millions of pounds. Some of the parties decided to invite CEDR to advise and design a process capable of bringing this complex case to closure. Lord Griffiths (a retired Law Lord) and Jonathan Marks (a U.S. mediator) achieved a settlement over a 15-month period.

ADR takes many forms. The focus here is on facilitative mediation, in which a neutral third person, a mediator, helps the parties to reach a settlement. Sometimes the mediator is asked to perform an evaluative role. It is surprising how the presence of an independent mediator who has the respect of the parties can provide a catalyst for settlement.

We have seen the commercial court provide a lead in encouraging ADR and certain features of its court practice should encourage officeholders. The court considers that two types of cases are particularly suitable for ADR; first, those where costs are critical and, secondly, where litigation would not resolve all the issues between the parties. Certainly costs are a critical factor, particularly where the officeholder may have funding difficulties and the costs themselves may be disproportionate to the amount at stake. Also, it is often true that insolvencies give rise to a number of inter-connected issues which need to be resolved before funds can be distributed. Before starting proceedings, the officeholder should explore whether or not mediation is appropriate with both his creditors' committee and the other side.

The confidential nature of mediation is also an important factor. This brings us back to the creditors' committee whose role is important in mediation. The creditors' committee will usually have signed a confidentiality agreement which itself can be expanded to cover the fact of a mediation and the result. Such confidentiality may mean that the other side is more willing to settle on terms agreeable to the officeholder without the risk of losing face publicly. Certainly for an administrator there may be considerable advantages in dealing with a dispute by way of mediation as maintaining confidentiality may be vital if he is going to ensure that the business survives as a going concern. Matters relating to the reputation of the company and ongoing business relations with the debtor, or indeed, trade creditors may benefit greatly from the confidential aspects of mediation.

There may be other factors; mediation can provide a useful way out of the administration through a Creditor's Voluntary Arrangement (CVA) or a scheme of arrangement under the Companies Act. For example, such a scheme or CVA could be made conditional on a creditor voting in favour of the CVA or scheme, that could certainly not be achieved by court process. Equally, if an administrator is seeking to preserve the company as a going concern they may be able to capitalise on ongoing business arrangements through a settlement achieved by mediation. It cannot be denied that, compared to the other options, mediation is a quicker, cheaper and less confrontational method of resolving commercial disputes.

THE ROLE OF STRAIGHTFORWARD NEGOTIATION 6.5

Obviously the best, cheapest and most economical way of resolving any dispute is by negotiation. Insolvency practitioners are very experienced negotiators—for them it is an everyday activity which enables them to do their job. Some are better at it than others; face-to-face negotiation requires a level of communication, understanding the dispute and a willingness to compromise. Commonly, parties will adopt positional bargaining, a traditional strategy in negotiation. For many it is the only way they know how to negotiate. The tactic is to put forward your best, *i.e.* most extreme position on what you demand or offer. For example, if you are really willing to settle for £100 you would start off by asking for £1,000 and the other side would counter with £1.

Problems arise when, inevitably, the party has to justify their position, which usually results in them becoming entrenched in their first extreme offer or demand. A period of haggling, threatening, bullying or even lying will then occur in an effort to achieve movement or agreement from the other side. Ultimately concessions will be given by both sides and a settlement is usually achieved somewhere in the middle of the extreme position. Such settlements often occur at the door of the court.

There are tactics which can be adopted to improve the results of positional bargaining, for example, by withholding sensitive information such as a weakness in the case, making threats, engaging in bluff, walking out, standing your ground and conceding nothing.

An important factor is often whether the parties will meet again. If it is a one-off situation then the parties may become more extreme, there is no reason to be restrained or have any regard for the other side if they have less of an influence. Experienced negotiators will develop their own ritual behaviours, treating the whole exercise as a game, running the negotiations to their own script. It has to be said that many insolvency practitioners are very experienced at doing this. External factors can also influence positional bargaining, for example preserving reputation, target and ego.

6.5.1 As an alternative, one can adopt the strategy of principled negotiation. This is intended to be a much more co-operative problem-solving approach, thereby cutting out gamesmanship but, at the same time, ensuring that you are not exploited. Negotiation will be undertaken on the basis of principles and not conditions, an objective standard will be applied to support the decision-making process and the parties will be encouraged to solve the problem. The aim of the negotiator is to make a greater effort to establish their case on the basis of the best alternative to a negotiated agreement and to see how a deal can be established to achieve a fair outcome which will meet all the parties' real interests. So you need to be objective, to work on the problems together to encourage a co-operative approach and to focus on interest, not positions or needs or wants. An element of realism must enter into the discussions and there must be objective criteria and standards by which to measure the decision.

Looking at the wider issues and trying to find some mechanism for maintaining a relationship or providing an alternative form of gain are crucial in this process and this is largely the basis upon which the mediator will operate. The negotiation is seen to be truly a problem-solving opportunity which will provide an outcome which is satisfactory for both sides, more satisfactory than would be achieved by litigation or positional bargaining and hopefully achieved at less cost. It avoids a stalemate arising or an imbalance of power in which the bully wins.

For the insolvency practitioner this will probably be a one-off encounter and his hands may be tied to the extent that he has statutory obligations to the creditors. Although officeholders are able to reach a compromise subject to necessary approvals and that, in itself, may be of assistance in achieving a settlement, as they can always say the matter has to be referred back either to the creditors' committee or the court. It is, nevertheless, important for the insolvency practitioner to be capable of presenting their case and negotiating from the position of strength to ensure that they do not have unrealistic expectations, and to remain objective, which is largely compatible with their role.

THE ROLE OF MEDIATION 6.6

Handling the client

It is very important to sell the benefits of mediation to the client as the process can be treated by the inexperienced as a last resort. The first task is to convince the client of the value of the process. 6.6.1

Who is the client?

In an insolvency there may be a whole series of clients, each of whom has to be persuaded. For the legal adviser it will be the officeholder, but for the officeholder is it: 6.6.2

(a) the creditors as a whole?

(b) the secured creditor?

(c) the creditors' committee?

The benefits can be identified in general terms as preservation of relationships or reputation, confidentiality and the avoidance of loss of face, savings on costs, concentrating everybody's efforts on negotiating, introducing a fresh mind and objectivity in the form of a neutral third party, the ability to look at all the aspects of a dispute at one time rather than just focusing on identifying fault and apportioning blame, giving an opportunity to communicate with the other side in less hostile surroundings, thereby managing the process towards a settlement. The goal of mediation is to settle the case in a manner satisfactory to the client. It is helpful to consider certain factors with the client, including for example:

(a) What has prevented this case from settling? An analysis of the reasons from both sides is helpful.

(b) Do the parties have a relationship to be preserved?

(c) Is resolution important or will settlement suffice? The distinction being that resolution addresses all the parties' underlying business and/or personal needs whereas a settlement may not.

(d) What style of mediation is best for the dispute?

The approach of many mediators is strictly facilitative. But you can appoint someone who is directive or evaluative. The facilitative mediator will focus on the parties' interests rather than legal rights and will be more concerned with resolution than settlement. A directive or evaluative mediator will focus more on the parties' legal rights and would be more likely to suggest alternative approaches or challenge a party's legal analysis and to push the parties towards settlement, even if it does not result in resolution.

(a) Who should be present and how should the mediation be conducted? The requirement for lawyers to attend is not a pre-requisite although they do tend to participate in most commercial mediations, but sophisticated clients such as an officeholder may well choose to proceed without lawyers.

(b) Are the mediator's credentials important to the parties, and if so, what will make the mediator acceptable to the parties? A mediator who has the respect of the parties may increase their willingness to co-operate in the process or reach a settlement.

(c) Does the mediator need to be a lawyer? The answer may well be no. It may be more important to have an experienced mediator than an experienced lawyer, but there may be issues which will require the individual mediator's expertise to be tested. The mediator will not determine the outcome of a case at law, but a person who has specific legal expertise which is relevant may assist the parties when considering the strengths and weaknesses of their own case.

(d) Are costs important? Does it matter how much the mediator will charge?

(e) Is the venue important?

These questions should be considered before the mediation.

Prior to issuing proceedings, and after issuing proceedings

Mediation can be applied successfully at any stage of a case. 6.6.3
Before proceedings have been issued, or at any time thereafter, but issuing proceedings is not a pre-requisite. It may even be contemplated after judgment has been handed down where the parties wish to avoid wasting the time and costs of appealing that judgment.

Once proceedings have been issued the court may direct the parties to attempt ADR to resolve the dispute and in those circumstances a stay for a short period of time will be imposed to enable the parties to go away and try and settle between themselves. The parties' frustration with the court process and its slowness may instil a desire for mediation. It may become apparent to the parties that it is a way of avoiding their litigation lawyers posturing and incurring costs through tactical applications. Today many commercial contracts contain mediation clauses and there are industry schemes which require mediation to be adopted.

Whether or not a dispute goes to mediation is very much between the parties themselves. They need to want to achieve a resolution or settlement. They must decide that they want to mediate and once they do they are then in control of the process, with the guidance of the chosen mediator and subject to the terms of the mediation agreement which must be entered into.

There is no difference in the process whether it is embarked upon before or after proceedings have been issued. However, it might be felt that the act of issuing proceedings could inhibit the ability of a true resolution being achieved as the parties' minds will be focused on settlement. Matters may well proceed quite a long way down the road of litigation before mediation is considered as a viable option, usually that arises when the costs of proceeding by way of court process become apparent to the parties, particularly where the claim is quite small in relation to them. In an insolvency where you are dealing with a multi-jurisdictional dispute, mediation is more likely to be considered before proceedings are issued. This happens because it is impossible for the parties to agree in which jurisdiction proceedings should be commenced.

To determine whether the case is suitable for mediation if proceedings have already been issued, then it is necessary to ask whether the case could reach negotiated settlement before trial. If proceedings have not been issued, then the question should be whether the current negotiations are making limited progress. If the answer to these questions is yes, then mediation could add value to attempts at negotiating a settlement.

Making contact with the other parties—the approach

6.6.4 To assess whether a case is suitable for mediation and whether this is the right time to make the approach the following facts are worthy of consideration:

(a) Do you have enough information to negotiate effectively? If not, would this information be obtained more easily by litigation or a consensual exploration?

(b) Are the negotiations constructive? Or have we reached deadlock? If it is in deadlock, then what can you do to improve the negotiations? Would introducing an independent third party unlock that deadlock?

(c) Costs—consider the costs of the legal proceedings, compare them to the best and worst outcomes. What would be added to those costs or risks if you went to an unsuccessful mediation? How can you reduce such costs or risk?

(d) Would there be a benefit in getting together in a forum which is outside the restrictive confines of the law courts to enable a broader exploration of the issues and the parties' negotiating positions before taking further steps in the proceedings?

(e) What is the likely damage resulting from exploring the idea of mediation with the other party who then refuses to participate? Consider how you might offset that risk.

(f) Have you got much to lose by stating that it's your policy to try to settle cases at their appropriate level?

How do you approach the other side?

6.6.5 It can be very difficult to find the best point of communication. It may not be through the lawyers. It is very important to take time to consider how best to make the approach. All proposals for mediation should be made in a restrained but exploratory tone. It is not a sign of weakness to suggest mediation. If approached in the right way, it can demonstrate that you are confident in the strength of your case, but concerned about other issues which may be particularly costly in both money and time, which mean that you are interested in trying to explore an alternative means of resolving the dispute.

It is sensible to have available recommendations of appropriate mediators and be able to explain the process which you are proposing should be adopted. Be prepared to discuss these with the other side. It can be best to approach the suggestion of mediation as a mediation process in its own right. You should be prepared to take time over the process. An insolvency case involving a multi-jurisdictional mediation took some nine months to set up, largely because of cultural differences, tactical perspectives and a lack of understanding of the process on the part of some of the other parties. The proposed mediator was heavily involved in the process of encouraging the parties to formally meet to pursue a mediation, and this is one of the tactics which can be employed. It may be necessary to acknowledge that you have reached deadlock and so a third party involvement looks inevitable, then suggesting that it might be preferable that this is a mediator rather than a judge. Emphasise that you are interested in positive negotiation and your belief that the case you have is a valid one. Point out that the court may direct ADR in any event or refer to any contractual conditions which require ADR or imply using a neutral organisation or mediator to talk to both sides.

The type of mediator

If you have agreed to proceed to ADR on a private basis you have complete control over the choice of the mediator. If the court directs that mediation or ADR should take place, generally they allow the parties to choose a mediator by mutual agreement as this will ensure that the parties have confidence in the neutral third party. Also the whole process is begun with the parties reaching an agreement on that issue which is often a helpful starting point. Where the parties cannot agree, the court may choose for them and they will often choose from a list submitted by the parties or from a court roster of mediators. **6.6.6**

When choosing a mediator it is important to look at the track record of the individual. They should either be able to speak to their own track record or belong to an organisation who can supply references. A mediator who has a history of success in helping parties who are deeply entrenched in their position to achieve a resolution is positive. Do not assume it has to be a lawyer. Good mediators come from a whole range of backgrounds and it is often better to have an expert mediator rather than an expert as a mediator, although it is fair to say there may be circumstances when someone who does have expert knowledge can help the party to truly consider the strengths and weaknesses in their case.

In a particularly complex dispute, which insolvency disputes often are, it may be appropriate to have more than one mediator: one being an expert mediator and the other having expertise in either the subject matter or possibly the culture, where dealing with multi-jurisdictional disputes. Also remember it is jolly hard work for the mediator so it may be appropriate to have more than one, especially if there are a lot of parties. When choosing a mediator, try contacting an organisation with a track record; beauty parades are acceptable, face-to-face meetings with potential mediators are often to be advised and personal recommendations are obviously helpful in making your choice. Throughout this chapter reference has been made to the different types of mediator, so it is important to ensure that you adopt a mediator who is going to be most suited to address the issues arising in the dispute with which you are dealing.

The mediation agreement

6.6.7 Most organisations will have their own standard form, blueprint and guidelines for the mediation process, but in an international or multi-party case there may be a need to formally negotiate the mediation agreement.

Issues which must be addressed include:

Confidentiality

The confidential nature of the process of mediation is vital to the whole process. It is essential that each party to a mediation is satisfied and trusts that:

(a) the mediator will not disclose information to the other side at all, unless directed to do so; and

(b) all parties will preserve the confidentiality of communications made during the mediation.

There are jurisdictions that do not protect compromise negotiations from disclosure, therefore the parties should consider whether this fact prevents them from having the negotiations. The agreement should provide that all parties to the mediation agree:

(a) to treat statements made during the course of the mediation as confidential;

(b) that a statement made in the mediation should be privileged against use at any other trial relating to the dispute, even in cross-examination;

(c) to distinguish between documents created specifically for the mediation (which will be protected from later disclosure in legal proceedings) and those which are contemporaneous to the dispute (which evidence factual and technical issues) and will not thereby be protected.

If there is any doubt about the source of the document, then it should only be disclosed to the mediator and will thereby be projected under the general confidentiality of the mediation. In some jurisdictions it is appropriate to agree that notes must be destroyed at the conclusion of a mediation upon the document of final agreement being executed. Also, in some jurisdictions it is necessary to agree that the mediator will not be called as a witness or otherwise be involved in any ongoing litigation should settlement fail.

Choice of law

It may be necessary to stipulate this for the mediation agreement where either the original contract is governed by a different jurisdiction clause or the parties are multi-jurisdictional, but care must be taken to ensure that this does not have any unfortunate results in relation to confidentiality.

Settlement

The mediation agreement will normally provide that any settlement will not be legally binding unless it is reduced to writing and signed.

Termination of the mediation

The agreement should provide for the circumstances under which the mediation will be terminated.

Automatic stay of legal proceedings

The venue, time and duration

You may want it to address the length of the mediation day—most mediators will work until a mediation is concluded, but in multi-jurisdictional matters different cultural expectations may prevail.

Authority to settle

The parties should be very clear about the constraints on the decision-makers, preferably in advance of the mediation.

Who should attend the mediation?

This requires careful thought. It need not include the parties' lawyers, but it does need to include someone who is fully appraised of the facts and issues, understands what is at stake and knows what they actually want to achieve. It may include an expert, if it is felt there are issues which require expert knowledge, but of overriding importance is that it should include the person who actually has the authority to settle. Very often mediations fail to settle for the 6.6.8

simple reason that the person attending does not actually have the authority to sign the deal.

What paper should be passed to the mediator prior to the mediation?

6.6.9 Commonly, the mediator will contact both parties before the mediation and invite them to prepare a briefing note for the mediator and the other parties, which will include an exchange of a written summary and supporting documents. The parties should distinguish between documents created solely for the purpose of the mediation and documents which support their case.

Length and conduct of the mediation

6.6.10 Before the mediation takes place a significant amount of preliminary work is needed. The mediator will contact the parties or their advisers in order to set the scene and establish relationships and check that all the administrative arrangements are in place. He will also gently coach each team on the most productive approach to the mediation, focusing on opening presentations and the roles of the parties and advisers in the mediation.

At the mediation itself the mediator will usually meet the parties individually to introduce himself and have a preliminary discussion to ensure that the parties understand the process of the mediation before bringing them together to make a more formal opening statement. The seating arrangements, the setting up of the room and the availability of refreshments are all matters which are under the mediator's control and are very important for the process of mediation. The mediator will make a formal opening statement which, among other things, explains the process, emphasising the benefits and opportunities which the process provides for the parties. He should underline that it will be a long day and they may have to spend much time alone or among themselves and he will be concerned to establish whether there are constraints upon their time. The parties will also be encouraged to make recommendations in order to move the discussions forward and the mediator may wish to facilitate dialogue between selective members of each team rather than simply putting the teams together.

The mediator will take control of the process, stamping it with his authority in order to give the parties confidence that they are in experienced hands. Unless the parties have confidence in the mediator then settlement will not be achieved. The amount of work done prior to the mediation by both the mediator and the parties can have a significant impact on the length of the mediation itself.

6.6.11 The process usually continues with each party making a presentation, the mediator deciding who goes first. Opening presentations are generally relatively short, lasting for no more than 30 minutes, but it is important that they set the scene. The presentations should cover the range of issues facing the parties, not just legal issues but commercial, financial, political or even personal issues which may be relevant, and they should not concentrate solely on pleaded claims reiterating issues set out in litigation framework.

Once the presentations have been concluded, then the mediator will usually send the parties to their separate rooms and try to open up discussions by holding separate caucuses. It is important for the mediator to explore the issues which concern the parties to try and open up a dialogue and encourage a broader discussion. At appropriate stages the mediator may bring the teams back together or put individuals together to try any alternative to see whether deadlock can be broken. The overriding responsibility of the mediator is to give the parties confidence that the procedure is properly controlled to inject trust, energy and a sense of structure into the search for a solution.

In the caucus or private sessions the mediator should at the outset try to give some indication of how long he proposes to be with each group so that there is a sort of timetable for the day. He may give tasks to the groups he has not seen straight away, but it depends on whether issues have emerged from the opening session which require useful exploration.

The exploration phase is then undertaken. The mediator will visit 6.6.12
each team to try to develop an interactive process of case review. He should also gauge the parties' reactions to what they have heard. It is important for the parties to open up in the private meetings, as this gives the mediator clues as to how best he can facilitate productive discussions. The process cannot be rushed, it takes time for the mediator to explore how best to proceed with the negotiations. Hopefully there will be a time when the parties move at least a degree closer and settlement begins to look a distinct possibility. It has to be remembered that mediators cannot impose settlement and should never bully the parties, but firm handling of difficult situations is very much what they should be doing. Good mediators will maintain optimism even if an end point seems impossible.

Commonly, for smaller disputes a maximum of a day is allocated; the day may be as long or as short as is necessary to achieve a settlement. Many mediations appear to take quite a while to get going, but then settle fairly rapidly once four o'clock in the afternoon is reached. There should be no fixed deadline. Sometimes it is impossible to achieve a settlement in a day and it is necessary to go away and come back again at a later stage. The length of the mediation will vary depending on the number of parties, the complexity of the issues and whether there are different jurisdictions involved.

The venue

6.6.13 A convenient venue for all the parties is obviously sensible, but often it is felt preferable to hold the mediation in what is seen as a neutral environment which may involve all the parties travelling some distance to the mediation venue. In multi-jurisdictional mediations it may not be possible to identify a convenient mutual venue and so the parties may require to meet in the country of one of the groups to the mediation.

The cost of the mediation

6.6.14 This should be clearly set out in the mediation agreement and it should be borne equally by the parties.

The settlement agreement

6.6.15 On the basis that settlement is achieved, then this should be reduced to writing at the mediation and signed by the parties. It is not necessarily the mediator who will write out the settlement agreement. It is often preferable for the parties to draft the agreement. If the agreement is going to take hours to design and the parties are tired, then it does make sense to allow enough time in the mediation planning to enable them to get the agreement right. If they have truly reached agreement, then putting together the right framework should not be too difficult and it is preferable always to reduce an agreement to writing as soon as possible. It may be appropriate to finalise an agreement incorporating the main terms including provision for agreeing a draft court order or further agreement.

It is important to distinguish between the two aspects of the mediation process. The process itself is non-binding, but an agreement achieved through that process can and will have the status of a legally binding contract. The settlement can take the form of either being a binding contract or could be a consent award or court order. The question of legal enforcement is perhaps less important than whether an agreement is workable. If the parties have confidence in the agreement then it will work. It is easy to try and rush the stage of concluding the settlement and the mediator should examine with each party the best way to structure the agreement so that it stands a real chance of working.

Post-settlement issues

6.6.16 In insolvency matters it may be necessary for the officeholder to have the settlement agreement sanctioned by either the court or the creditors' committee. This has been dealt with at some length in the earlier part of this chapter. Beyond that it is obviously necessary for the parties to work together to actually implement the settlement itself and that may require the drafting of additional documents, the filing of orders with the court, settling any litigation proceedings or the transfer of assets of distribution of money to creditors.

CONCLUSION 6.7

There is scope for mediation in the context of insolvency because it is likely to achieve settlement quickly and cost-effectively, coupled with the fact that the officeholder operates as a trustee. Also, there is the public interest aspect to consider. Insolvency is a form of accountability, and in large insolvencies the public interest can be very important. Finally, with the increasing globalisation of commerce, it may be the only viable method of resolving a multi-jurisdictional dispute.

CHAPTER 7

INSURANCE RELATED DISPUTES (INCLUDING REINSURANCE AND PROFESSIONAL INDEMNITY)

MICHAEL WOOD

The purpose of this chapter is to give the reader practical guidance for use in the mediation of insurance related claims. These include claims against insurers, reinsurance disputes and claims involving professional indemnity underwriters. The reader may glean assistance also in respect of those claims where no underwriter's name appears on the claim form but where an underwriter will be paying, or contributing to, the claim's settlement.

The format of the chapter is as follows:

1. Introduction;
2. Mediation of claims;
3. Mediation and reinsurance disputes; and
4. Mediation and professional indemnity claims.

In keeping with the central purpose of giving practical help, in the mediation of claims section, I have adopted a question and answer approach, posing the questions that a claimant and his legal adviser will have to answer when faced with the prospect of mediation, whether proposed by the opponents or imposed (by strong recommendation[1]) by a judge. The mediation of claims section is of general relevance and is followed by specific remarks regarding reinsurance and professional indemnity claims. I have included two hypothetical case studies as examples of what may be experienced in the mediation of insurance related claims.

7.1 INTRODUCTION

The concept of insurance goes back to antiquity, and reinsurance, at least, to the fifteenth century. Those whose occupation obliges them to make use of the external lifts on the Lloyd's building in

[1] Or, indeed, order—See *Kinstreet Ltd. v. Balmargo Corporation Ltd.* [1999] C.L.Y. 322 *per* Arden J.

London know by heart the words painted on the windows on the opposite side of Leadenhall Street—"Monte Dei Paschi Di Siena Bank established 1472". Thus, while in England, the Wars of the Roses were being fought, commercial men (in what would become Italy some 400 years later) were developing the tools of their trade, including letters of credit, double entry book-keeping and reinsurance.

Although insurance and reinsurance are of great age and, now, great sophistication, the methods of resolving disputes arising in these industries have been limited, until relatively recently, to litigation in the courts and private arbitration if the parties agreed to that course. Indeed, in the case of reinsurance, it is only in the last quarter of a century or so that disputes have seen the light of day. Prior to this, most disputes in the reinsurance world were settled by negotiation, sometimes during or at the end of a long lunch, or by arbitration. A negotiated settlement or arbitration award having been achieved, the parties returned to the more fruitful ways of their reinsurance business. However, at the same time as reinsurance litigation has blossomed in the Commercial Court in London, alternative dispute resolution (ADR) has arrived from the U.S. as the third portfolio of techniques for resolution of disputes.[2]

MEDIATION OF CLAIMS 7.2

This section approaches mediation from the perspective of a legal adviser to a claimant and answers the various questions that are posed in relation to a proposed mediation.

Your client is suing, or intending to sue, and the court or your opponent invites you to agree to a mediation.

Should I agree to mediate?

Almost certainly, the answer is "yes". You are probably in dispute 7.2.1
regarding a one-off claim and the prospect of lengthy, expensive, and uncertain litigation is not one to be faced with equanimity. Notwithstanding the introduction of the Civil Procedure Rules in April 1999, and the prospect of salami slicing of costs at the end of the trial (pursuant to CPR 44) you are to a great extent risking all on the outcome of the trial at which your client will have the unenviable duty to give evidence in support of the claim.

What are the risks associated with a mediation?

Often in litigation, the defendant will have the backing of an in- 7.2.2
surance company or Lloyd's underwriters. Sometimes these

2 Strictly, ADR encompasses a variety of DR techniques but this chapter will focus on mediation.

entities will themselves be defendants. Although insurance companies and underwriters in the Lloyd's market are becoming increasingly familiar with mediation, some sections of the industry (and their legal advisers) appear not really to welcome mediation as a method of resolving disputes. Sometimes, there is no genuine wish to compromise the claim (which, of course, should be the purpose of a bona fide mediation). In these cases, the defendants want your client to lose his claim (or to be ground down to such an extent that he is prepared to settle late in the day for a trifle) and will adopt the usual litigation strategies to bring this end about, *i.e.* delay, long winded correspondence and spoiling interlocutory applications (although the risk of this is reduced by CPR 44—the court's power to order immediate payment of interlocutory costs). Their aim is to force a claimant of average financial resource to expend large sums of money on fighting the litigation in the hope that the risks of going to court and losing become unbearable, forcing the claimant to settle on terms favourable to insurers. Accordingly:

(a) **Risk 1:** the defendants do not genuinely wish to compromise and, being experienced in mediation, will be better placed to resist the mediator's attempts to bring the parties together and walk away without coming to a settlement agreement.

(b) **Risk 2:** the defendant will use the mediation as a fishing expedition. At the mediation, it is best practice for the parties to be present in person, and have settlement authority on both sides, and, if the mediator thinks it appropriate, he may invite the principals to negotiate face to face, possibly in the absence of their legal advisers. You must ask yourself, *in advance*, do you want your opponents to see and hear your client and, possibly, his principal witness? Is your client going to make a good impression and satisfy the opponents that he will come across well at trial?

Because insurers are well aware that, for the most part, judges are in favour of ADR, they will not wish to be seen to be obstructing a court proposed method of resolving the dispute. For this reason, the fact that an insurer has agreed, apparently freely, to mediate, does not mean that he is genuinely interested in settling the claim. Accordingly, at the mediation you must be alert for signs which indicate the insurer does not truly wish to compromise the matter but sees the mediation as a useful device to find out more, possibly at an earlier stage than usual, about the strengths and weaknesses of your case.

What if my client does not want to mediate?

The judges in the Commercial Court and the Chancery Division in London are, by and large, greatly in favour of ADR as a method of dispute resolution. You cannot say to these judges, without explanation, that you do not wish to mediate. Section G1.2 of the Commercial Court Guide 1999 explains why the judges have this approach: 7.2.3

> ". . . the view of the Commercial Court is that the settlement of disputes by means of ADR:
>
> (a) significantly helps litigants to save costs;
> (b) saves litigants the delay of litigation in reaching finality in their disputes;
> (c) enables litigants to achieve settlement of their disputes while preserving their existing commercial relationships and market reputations;
> (d) provides litigants with a wider range of solutions than those offered by litigation;
> (e) is likely to make a substantial contribution to the more efficient use of judicial resources."

Apart from perhaps (e), and, the introduction of the words "can" or "might" at the beginning of each of the other propositions, the Commercial Court's view is undoubtedly correct. Section G of the Commercial Court Guide 1999 continues at G1.3 to the effect that "the Commercial Judges will, in appropriate cases, invite the parties to consider whether their dispute, or particular issues in it, could be resolved through ADR . . ."

Although the guide refers to "appropriate cases", in fact, in nearly every case in the Commercial Court, at the first Case Management Conference, or even earlier, the parties will be asked if they have considered ADR. The Commercial Judge will not be amused to be told either that they have not, or, alternatively, that they have but that they have rejected it as a possible way of resolving the dispute without first having given it due consideration.

In contrast with certain states in the U.S. and Australia, the Commercial Court does not formally have the power to order parties to mediate (but see the *Kinstreet* case referred to earlier). However, it does have the power to adjourn the case for a specified period of time to "encourage and enable" the parties to use ADR.[3] Further, a draft ADR order is at Appendix 7 of the Guide. 7.2.4

One way to deal with a judge who is being difficult on the question of ADR is to tell him that while your client would be perfectly happy to mediate at an appropriate stage, mediation is

[3] Commercial Court Guide 1999—G1.7.

inappropriate at this stage of the matter because you need (a) Statements of Case to be completed and/or (b) full disclosure of documentation by both sides and/or (c) exchange of witness statements and/or (d) exchange of expert evidence. This is a tactic well known to insurers and their legal advisers. Indeed, in one case, the solicitors in question agreed to a mediation but only on the basis that the mediation would take place *one week* before the trial date. This proposition is unlikely to impress the judge but judges will listen to sensible argument to the effect that the circumstances of the case are such that an early mediation is not necessarily the best way forward. You should invite the judge to order that the question of ADR be reviewed at a later "natural break" in the proceedings.

Timing of the mediation

7.2.5 Most litigators have experience of cases that, at their beginning, looked poor but, as the litigation developed, appeared to have better prospects of success and, on the contrary, and far more upsetting, cases that started out looking gilt edged but changed (perhaps, after disclosure) into a more sorry state. Typically, these latter cases are the high value, document heavy, international cases where the relevant evidence covers a number of years, the personnel involved have changed over those years, and the relevant documents have long since been put in boxes, stored and forgotten. However, certain types of case, where the facts are not seriously disputed, or where the amount of relevant documentation is modest and uncontroversial, are ones for which early mediation may seem to be appropriate. In any event, you must address the question of whether an early mediation is the right way to proceed, having regard to your assessments of the merits of the case, the approach of the parties in the early stages of the matter and the prospects for a changed outlook nearer to a trial date. Do not forget that the imminence of a trial date may lessen the enthusiasm to mediate.

If litigation is already in train, it is usually helpful for the parties to have at least exchanged their statements of case before any mediation takes place. This process should identify the issues; the extent to which there are disputed facts; whether or not expert evidence will assist; the likely length of time before which the matter will be ready for trial; and how long the trial is likely to take. In short, by completion of the delivery of statements of case, the parties should be able to make a reasonable estimate of the cost of taking the dispute to a completed trial. Subject to the questions of whether disclosure and expert evidence are necessary, a mediation may now be appropriate. At this point, let us consider the first case study.

Case Study No. 1

The occupier of an agricultural property has a claim in negligence against his solicitor for failing to ensure the renewal of his lease under the Landlord and Tenant Act 1954. 7.2.6

The solicitor's PI insurers, on his behalf, appoint one of its panel firms to represent the firm. The solicitors appointed by insurers advance various arguments intended to show that the damages suffered by the claimant are, in truth, little more than nominal and make a "nuisance value" without prejudice offer of £10,000. The claimant's solicitors deem this "derisory" since they assess the damages at in excess of £100,000. It seems that the argument on liability is not one which will be pursued, if the matter goes to trial, with any vigour.

Eventually, with each party claiming the "credit" for having proposed a mediation, a sole mediator is agreed and a date fixed for mediation to take place at the offices of the solicitors for the claimant. Sometimes there can be considerable argument over each of the minute details of the mediation, including where the mediation should take place.

Prior to the mediation, the claimant's solicitors send the mediator a position statement setting out the legal basis for the claim, citing appropriate authorities, together with a schedule of damages. The mediator has indicated that it can be useful for the parties to send him "for his eyes only" their position statements. However, in this case, since the claimant is trying to convince the defendants' insurers' solicitors (and not the defendant) of the correctness of their legal argument, a copy of the position statement is supplied to the PI insurers' solicitors.

The defendant's solicitors provide no position statement. At the mediation the claimant is present together with his principal witness, and two representatives from his solicitors. No representative attends from the insurers but, in response to a specific enquiry from the mediator, the solicitor for the defendants confirms that he has authority to settle. 7.2.7

The solicitor for the claimant briefly outlines the claimant's case and produces for the benefit of those present a sketch plan showing the property. The solicitor for the defendant makes a brief remark to the effect that the defendants wish to settle but that they see no need to go into the detail of their legal argument at this stage. Thereafter the parties move to separate rooms and the mediator has the first private session with the claimant's team.

Since the claimant is at the mediation in person, his solicitor suggests that he does most of the talking and explaining to the mediator. This has the dual benefits of allowing the claimant to develop confidence in explaining his case to a third party and, also, his solicitor can get a feel for how he will perform in the more strenuous atmosphere of a court trial. In this case, wisely, the mediator has imposed an informal deadline of seven hours for the completion of the mediation; also, he has said that the parties should be talking figures before lunch. His style is robust as opposed to touchy-feely.

Inevitably, the mediation requires the parties to prepare to a certain extent as if for a trial and the exchanges of information which take place result in the parties having a much better understanding of what each of them can produce to support the claim. At the claimant's solicitor's request, the defendant's solicitor produces a copy of an authority on which he says they place great reliance. The claimant's solicitor considers this while his client explains the case to the mediator.

7.2.8 It is clear from the exchanges conducted through the mediator that the defendant considers the claimant will have great difficulty proving the extent of his losses at trial (because of an absence of contemporary records of income and expenses). Also it is clear that there is a yawning chasm between the parties as to what is the correct legal analysis to apply to the calculation of the losses.

By about 1.00 p.m., the parties are indeed talking figures, as the mediator has asked them to do. However, the defendant has advanced to only £30,000 and the claimant has informed the mediator for his private information only that he will accept £90,000. The claimant's team have always had their doubts about the willingness of the defendant's team to take a constructive approach to the mediation and these doubts appear to be justified when the solicitor for the defendant says (through the mediator) that he must take instructions from insurers if the mediation is to advance.

The claimant's team become frustrated at the lack of progress and consider that, to a degree, they have been "conned" by the defendant's team. Although by the early afternoon the defendant has advanced to £45,000 and the claimant has indicated a willingness to settle at a much lower figure than previously indicated (now down to £80,000), at about 4.00 p.m. the claimant's team walk out of the mediation, having first informed the mediator of their intention to do so.

Some weeks later, the parties settle the matter.

Points to note: The absence of one of the parties from the mediation is almost always unhelpful. It will be rare for a party's solicitor to have unlimited authority to settle a dispute. If, in the absence of a party, his solicitor says he has authority to settle, press him to confirm the extent of that authority.

The parties have agreed to mediate: who should the mediator be?

7.2.9 It is paramount that the mediator be a trained mediator. In certain states in the U.S. the only necessary qualification to be a mediator is that the mediator be legally qualified. In the U.K. there is no necessary qualification to mediate a dispute and the parties can, although this is inadvisable, appoint a person to mediate who has no training in, or experience of, the mediation of disputes. In the U.K., the principal mediation organisations are the ADR Group (based in Bristol but able to offer accredited mediators throughout Great Britain, Channel Islands and the Isle of Man and with links to mediation organisations in Europe) and CEDR, the Centre for Dispute Resolution (based in London but, again, able to provide accredited mediators and assistance). Apart from these organisations there are other groups who can identify potential mediators. The majority of mediators are legally trained, both solicitors and barristers; if you are using a mediator to try to resolve a dispute, it is usually sensible to engage a legally trained mediator.

Mediators with particular skills and experience, such as accountancy, computing, or engineering, may be of value where their profession is the same as the subject matter of the dispute. Some people believe that the mediator does not need to have an understanding of the industry out of which any particular dispute arises, nor, possibly, the laws applying to it. This is a proposition with which I disagree. The parties at a mediation need to have confidence in the mediator and will be less likely to have the necessary confidence if the mediator does not understand the language of the dispute.

Retired judges, and Queen's Counsel, can often make good mediators, particularly in disputes involving a high legal content and in which the views of the mediator on the merits of the cases (not that these views will necessarily be indicated directly) will carry added weight. One factor to have in mind when instructing a retired individual is the possibility that they can be over-dominant in the process (possibly talk too much) and, also, they may lack the necessary stamina to see out a heavyweight mediation, which may last several days.

Preparation for the mediation

You will be asked to sign a mediation agreement and pay one half of the mediator's fees in advance. The mediation agreement should be relatively uncontroversial and a specimen mediation agreement appears at the end of this chapter.[4] The fees of the mediator are usually based on the premise that the mediation will last a full day and involve prior preparation by the mediator. In particularly complex mediations, or where there are several parties, it may be agreed in advance that the parties should allow two or even three days for the mediation, but this is unusual. You should expect to 7.2.10

[4] I am grateful to Stephen Ruttle Q.C. for supplying this draft.

pay anything between £500 to £5,000 as your contribution to the mediator's fees, some mediators charging a fixed fee and others charging on a time spent basis. Some mediation schemes are cheap. That administered by the Central London County Court involves fees of only a few hundred pounds although the parties are restricted to mediator time of three hours from 4.30 to 7.30 p.m. The Court of Appeal administered mediator scheme is presently pro bono although it is unclear why this should be so.

(a) *The position paper*—you may be asked by the mediator to provide in advance of the mediation a so-called "position paper" setting out, as succintly as possible, a statement of your position in respect of this dispute. Some mediators suggest that this is sent to them in confidence. Others propose exchange of papers prior to the mediation. Remember that, in contrast to a skeleton argument prepared for a court hearing, the position paper is not designed to persuade the mediator of the correctness at law of your client's position but, rather, to persuade the other side of the strength of your case, both legally and evidentially. Remember to mark your position paper "without prejudice: prepared for a mediation on [date]". The central message of the position papers is, usually, "I am going to win this case, for the following reasons; the opponent would be well advised to settle at the generous discount that I am prepared to agree".

(b) Advise your client carefully on what will happen on the mediation day (about which—see below).

(c) Should I instruct a barrister to attend the mediation on my client's behalf? In a two-party mediation, it is probably not necessary to instruct a barrister unless you feel that the complexities of the case (legal or otherwise) are such that you cannot do them justice. This applies even if the opponent has decided to instruct a barrister to appear for them at the mediation (unless you don't intend to make a settlement). However, if you are involved in a multi-party mediation, and all the other parties have instructed barristers to appear, you are probably well advised to instruct a barrister also, notwithstanding that, of course, this will add to the costs of the mediation.

(d) Should I take my expert to the mediation? Usually, the answer is "no". As all good defence lawyers know, expert evidence can be an excellent weapon for the purposes of causing delay, confusion, and added costs, but this is not necessary at a mediation. More often than not, it is best to have your expert available at the end of a telephone rather than have him with you at the mediation throughout the day. Apart from anything else, this saves costs.

(e) Decide in advance what is your "bottom line". One of the startling features of the mediation process is the extent to which, as if by magic, the parties will modify, particularly towards the end of the mediation day, negotiating positions which, earlier in the day, had been set in stone. A graphic example of this is given by Philip Naughton Q.C. in his article "Mega mediation—a case history".[5] In the case he describes, the parties changed position and narrowed the gap (between the morning of day one and the afternoon of day two) so that an initial divide of £15 million was reduced by the following afternoon to "only" £1.3 million. It is best to go into the mediation with a precise strategy of giving up points, abandoning side issues as the day progresses, and, hopefully, arriving at your true bottom line towards the end of the mediation process. Do not underestimate the extent to which, as the day wears on, you and your client will wilt and express a willingness to consider offers that, previously, were said to be completely out of the question.

The mediation

Most mediators will contact the parties before the day fixed for the mediation process. The purpose of this prior contact is to explain what will happen in the mediation and deal with any queries any of the parties may have. On the day itself, it is likely that the mediator will speak briefly and privately to each of the parties to remind them of the procedure to be followed and answer questions. Thereafter, he will bring the parties together for the opening joint session. **7.2.11**

At the beginning of the first joint session, the mediator will remind the parties that the process is voluntary, non-binding, confidential and without prejudice. The first three of these four propositions are uncontroversial but you should think closely about the phrase "without prejudice". Of course, by using that phrase, the mediator means that what is said and done at the mediation is not to be described or referred to in any present or future court proceedings, or elsewhere. However, the fact remains that the parties and their advisers cannot obliterate from their minds what they have seen and heard during the mediation process. To the extent that they can do so, they will use what they have seen and heard to their best advantage in any subsequent court process that may follow. This is a point to keep firmly in mind throughout the mediation.

The mediator will ask each of the parties whether they wish to

[5] See Arbitration and Dispute Resolution Law Journal 1996, 3 (Sep), 215–217.

make an opening statement, with, usually, the claimant going first. Should you make an opening statement? You are not obliged to but, almost certainly, the answer is yes. This applies even more so if your opponent has indicated that they will be making an opening statement to the mediator. Who should make the statement? If you have retained a barrister to appear, he or she is the obvious, but not the inevitable, choice. If you have a confident and articulate client who will express to the mediator much more strongly than any advocate could his strength of feeling and will to pursue his claim, let him make the opening statement. The mediator will have warned the parties that opening statements are to be delivered without interruption. Do not forget that the other side will be sizing up your client since he will be the principal witness at trial. Hopefully, they will come quickly to the conclusion that they do not want to see him giving evidence against them in the witness box at trial. However, any opening statement made by you must be carefully planned in advance. You must stick to the position statement and any other remarks agreed in advance to be made to the mediator and must not stray from it. Although the factual situations will vary hugely, central themes of a claimant's opening statement will include (a) I am right on the facts (b) I am right on the law (c) I am prepared to negotiate (d) we are here today to settle and to put the differences between the parties behind us. After the parties have made their opening statements, the mediator will direct them to their private rooms.

Should you offer an immediate discount in the opening statement? No.

Handling the mediator

7.2.12 As a mediator, one of the difficulties of mediating disputes is the continuing obligation to be even handed and impartial in one's dealings with the parties. During the course of the day, it is difficult not to come to the view that one of the parties is more likely to succeed at trial than the other: equally, it is often the case that one team are more congenial than another so that, instinctively, the mediator may empathise more with that particular party. Having in mind the psychology of the process, the so-called "group dynamics", your role should be to ensure that the mediator (even if he does not appear to show it) is more sympathetic to your argument than that of the opponents and, also, thinks you are more pleasant to deal with than the opponents.

How honest should you be with the mediator? My perception is that most parties keep something up their sleeve and do not, at least at the beginning of the process, disclose to the mediator (even though the disclosure is private and confidential) their true final settlement position. I have never attended a mediation where the claimant has indicated at an early stage a willingness to take a modest fraction of their claim.

The mediator will remind you that everything you say to him during that private meeting is confidential and that he will only disclose to the other side matters that you authorise specifically for disclosure. An English trained mediator will not make overt, positive criticisms of your case nor offer opinions as to your likely prospects of success. English mediation is "non-evaluative" and it is only by close attention to the mediator's questions during the private session that you may get a feel for his thinking as to your prospects. Remember that the mediator does not attend the mediation to give legal advice and, indeed, the mediation agreement may record expressly that the mediator will not at any time give any legal advice to any party.

You should expect the first private session to last between 30 **7.2.13** minutes to one hour after which the mediator will meet the defence team privately. When the mediator has conducted the first private session with the defence team privately, he will return to the claimant to take the process forward. Obviously, at this stage, the mediator will have some idea of the gulf between the parties and the extent to which bridge building and creative thinking will have to take place to enable the parties to come to a settlement. This process of "shuttle diplomacy" will continue until such time as the mediator forms the view that a further joint meeting of the parties may be productive. Be prepared for the possibility that the mediator will invite the parties to meet together privately in the absence of their legal advisers.

Assuming that the second joint session (usually not happening until the afternoon) does not produce a settlement, the mediator is likely to revert to private meetings to see if further progress can be made. The process being voluntary, any of the parties, and the mediator, can determine the process at any time, if it is felt that no benefit is being achieved. Although it is common for mediations to continue into the late evening, or even the early hours of the following morning, there is no obvious reason why such a procedure should be adopted by the mediator. The better course is for the mediator to impose a deadline and discuss with the parties whether they wish to continue the following day or at some other convenient time or whether they wish to abandon the process at the expiry of the deadline. It is well known that "failed mediations" are often followed by settlements within a matter of days or a few weeks.

Settlement

The majority of mediations result in a compromise agreement made **7.2.14** on the day. The mediator will insist the agreement is reduced to writing and signed by the parties before they leave the mediation.

On occasion, the mediator may be prepared to assist in the drafting of the settlement agreement, although whether he is wise to do so is debatable, since this raises the possibility that he may be blamed for any drafting errors. I now turn to the second case study.

CASE STUDY NO. 2

7.2.15 A factory in the Midlands owned by A Company Limited has suffered structural problems for some time, including a leaking roof, which has caused substantial damage. It blames contractors, B Company Limited, who were engaged to repair the roof. B engaged subcontractors, C Company Limited, specialist roofing repairers, to carry out the repairs to the roof.

A has claims against B for sums exceeding £1 million and these claims have been commenced in the Technology and Construction Court in London. In these proceedings, B has joined as Part 20 defendants the subcontractors, C.

B has made claims against its professional indemnity underwriters X Company Limited under its indemnity cover, but their claim for indemnity has been rejected by X on the grounds of alleged material non-disclosure. In consequence, B has asserted a formal claim against its Lloyd's underwriters X as well as against their Lloyd's brokers, Y Company Limited. No proceedings have yet been commenced involving X or Y.

C has notified its company insurers, Z Company Limited, of a claim under their professional indemnity cover.

It will be seen that the dispute involves six parties. Nevertheless, following "guidance" from the TCC Judge, the parties have agreed to an ad hoc mediation at which the mediator will be a Q.C. appointed by agreement of all parties involved in the dispute and each one of the parties (save for Z) has instructed a barrister to attend the mediation on the agreed date.

7.2.16 At first sight, the prospect of five barristers arguing the matter in mediation appears unpromising. Nevertheless, the mediation takes place. At the first meeting involving all parties, only the barristers instructed on behalf of A, B and C make representations. Inevitably, since X and Y are present, A is aware of the possibility that there may be an issue on liability as between B and its underwriters. X's attendance at the mediation, as between it and B, is without prejudice to its contention that it is under no liability to B to indemnify B in any event. Similarly, the attendance of Y at the mediation is without prejudice to its contention that there has been no default on the part of the brokers so that their attendance is, essentially, to try to assist (as between their client and the underwriters) in seeking amicable resolution of the matter.

Inevitably, the opening stages of the mediation focus on the primary dispute and the strengths of A's claim against B. Inevitably, also, the mediator cannot afford to spend too long with each party in the private meetings since this will result in considerable down-time throughout the day. This is a case where a co-mediator should perhaps have been considered with a view to speeding up the process.

The mediator has been asked to facilitate the settlement of not one but four claims. In theory, this should make his task a great deal more difficult. However, following a series of private sessions throughout the day and into the early evening, the parties eventually are able to come to an overall compromise whereby all claims are resolved. The savings in legal fees, looked at in the round, are enormous. The dispute between A and B was essentially a factual dispute: the dispute between B and X and Y was essentially a legal dispute. Nevertheless, all matters were resolved within a period of about 12 hours (albeit, of course, there was substantial preparation by all concerned for the mediation). **7.2.17**

This example shows what can be achieved, even in cases which at first sight appear most unpromising for mediation.

Mediation "surprises"

Flexibility is one of the key features of the mediation process and you should be prepared for unusual and, at times, excessively creative solutions being mooted by the mediator to bring the dispute to an end. Apart from this, the mediator may have a number of problems to contend with that would not be encountered by a judge or an arbitrator: **7.2.18**

(a) The parties will not sit together in the same room. An unusual problem for the mediator but not unheard of.

(b) The mediator may be requested by one of the parties to offer an opinion on the law to both parties. Mediators don't like to do it but, if asked, preferably in advance of the mediation day, it is something that they may be prepared to do. Obviously, if you consider you have a strong case, you will be content to agree to a request being made to the mediator to offer an opinion. The reverse will apply if you consider your case to be weak. However, unless both parties consent, the mediator should not give any opinion to the parties jointly.

(c) One party agrees to buy the other. Not what either party was expecting at the beginning of the day but it has happened.

(d) A party which had indicated previously that it has authority to settle the dispute, announces that it needs to telephone the Chairman or Managing Director to obtain the necessary authority. Although hugely frustrating, and assuming that it is not yet 1.30 a.m. the following day, it is probably wiser to resist the temptation to walk out and allow the delinquent party to make the call.

Dissatisfaction with the mediator

7.2.19 It is rare for the parties at a mediation to be unhappy with the conduct of the mediator.[6] A well drafted mediation agreement will exclude any liability on the part of the mediator in negligence. In the absence of such a clause, one's first reaction is that a claim in negligence might lie against a mediator who had demonstrably failed to conduct the mediation to the standard of reasonably competent and skilled mediators. Apart from claiming back the fee paid to the mediator, a party might be able to expand the claim if, for example, it could be shown that the mediator had failed in his duty to maintain the confidentiality of the private sessions. The unauthorised disclosure of confidential information to the opponent could tip the scales dramatically in subsequent litigation between the parties. The fear of inadvertent disclosure of confidential information is probably the mediator's greatest fear when it comes to the risk of any allegation of professional misconduct.

There is no single regulatory body in the U.K. to whom a complaint might be made which has the power to investigate the mediator's conduct and, if appropriate, impose some form of penalty or compensation. However, if the mediator has been provided by one of the established mediation bodies, there is no doubt that they would take any complaint seriously and investigate it in a professional way.

Whether the complaint was made in the courts in negligence, or to a regulatory body, the complainant would have practical difficulties in advancing a claim against a mediator. The mediation, by definition, is private, confidential and without prejudice. Presumably, the question of calling the opponent to give evidence would not arise and, if it did, it might well be that the opponent would not agree with the suggestion that the mediator had been incompetent or negligent. What would constitute negligence? The mediator is not present to advise either of the parties on the law and does not act as advocate for either of the parties. U.K. trained mediators generally adopt a non-evaluative approach so any suggestion that a mediator had given negligent legal advice would face obvious difficulties. The suggestion (more likely in practice than an allegation of giving poor legal advice) that a mediator had broken a duty of

[6] But see the response of the British Insurance Law Association to the Lord Chancellor's Department Discussion Paper: November 19, 1999. In their response, BILA suggest that the two principal reasons why mediations do not produce a mediated settlement are: (1) the mediation takes place at the wrong time; and (2) the mediator is "inappropriate".

confidentiality might be incapable of proof, even to the lower standard of the balance of probabilities.

MEDIATION AND REINSURANCE DISPUTES

What I have written in the previous section applies to parties to reinsurance agreements (and retrocessions) facing the possibility of mediation. However, there are certain other significant matters, which I consider in this section. 7.3

Generally, the parties to reinsurance disputes, both the legal advisers and the players, are specialist practitioners familiar with the laws that apply to reinsurance and, often, with mediation practice. As mentioned earlier, reinsurance litigation has boomed in London in the last 25 years or so, not least because of the dynamics of the global reinsurance industry and the relentless pressure to maximise profits. However, there is no reason in principle why mediation (or indeed other ADR techniques) should not be used to settle reinsurance claims.

Direct claim—reinsurance cover

The crucial point for an underwriter, who is being sued by an assured, to have in mind is what effect a mediated settlement will have on the right to recover under his reinsurance(s). The basic principle is that the reinsured must prove his loss.[7] In this case, the Court of Appeal held that, in the absence of a follow the settlements clause, Commercial Union had to demonstrate that they were legally liable to their assured (Exxon) before they could recover from their excess of loss reinsurers. They were unable to do so and the Court of Appeal dismissed their claim. The straightforward answer to this predicament is to obtain reinsurers' prior agreement to the proposed course of action *viz*. a mediation with the assured to explore the possibilities of settlement of the direct claim. 7.3.1

The reinsurer is entitled to know how the underlying settlement was arrived at.[8] If there is a claims control clause in the reinsurance contract, the reinsurer must be involved in the decision to proceed by way of mediation. If there is a follow the settlements clause, the usual test applies, *i.e.* the reinsurer will be liable if the claim falls within the risks covered by the reinsurance agreement and the mediated settlement was made "in a businesslike fashion".[9] The onus of proof is on the reinsurer to show that the insurer did not act in a businesslike manner.

[7] *Commercial Union Co. v. NRG Victory Reinsurance Ltd.*, March 16, 1998, CA (1998) 1 Lloyd's Rep. 80.

[8] *Charman v. Guardian Royal Exchange Assurance Plc* (1992) 2 Lloyd's Rep. 607.

[9] *Insurance Co. of Africa v. Scor (U.K.) Reinsurance Co. Ltd* (1985) 1 Lloyd's Rep. 312.

If the position is that there is neither a claims control clause nor a follow the settlements clause in the reinsurance cover, the direct insurer must involve the reinsurer in the decision whether or not to try to mediate the claim. As always, the agreement of the reinsurer and what it is that he has agreed to, must be recorded in writing.

Practical points

7.3.2 The more complicated and esoteric the dispute is, the more important it becomes to appoint a mediator with knowledge of the industry, from which the dispute has come. The mediator does not need to be legally qualified but if the dispute involves consideration of difficult legal argument, it makes obvious sense to appoint a legally qualified mediator, whether a solicitor, barrister or retired judge. Indeed, an option available with a senior figure from the legal profession, or the bench, is, in the event of continuing deadlock, to invite the mediator to give an informal evaluation on one or more of the points in issue. The mediator may be reluctant to do this, and, indeed, it carries an obvious risk (that the scales will be tilted, possibly sharply, in one party's favour) but it is something to consider if the mediation appears to be becoming stalled and you have positive legal advice in which you are confident.

It is sometimes said that high value, multi-party claims are more difficult to resolve by mediation than "simple" claims involving only a few thousand pounds. I disagree (as does Philip Naughton Q.C.).[10] However, different techniques may be required. A preliminary meeting of the parties to agree "directions" for the mediation can be of great value. If a large sum of money is at stake, the parties cannot reasonably be expected to meet cold on day one and go away at the end of the day having agreed to forego or to pay an enormous amount in settlement of a dispute that may have been rumbling for years. Although a mediation in stages is more expensive, the costs, when compared with the amounts in issue, and the legal fees associated with the claims and counterclaims, are modest, a fraction of the costs of taking the issues to trial.

Having regard to the amounts likely to be in issue, and the significance of the legal argument to the outcome of the dispute, you will probably want to instruct Counsel to attend the mediation.

Co-mediation

7.3.3 Because of the high value at stake, the parties may be prepared to agree to engage two mediators. Although this will double the cost, the down time is reduced since each mediator can be working with a party throughout the process.

[10] See his article in the Irish Insurance Law Review—Vol. 3 No. 2—1999.

PROFESSIONAL INDEMNITY CLAIMS 7.4

As with reinsurance disputes, the number of professional indemnity claims coming to the courts in recent years has escalated. The growth in PI claims has gone hand and hand with the growth of the compensation culture and there is no reason to believe that the rate of growth will diminish significantly. Accountants, barristers, dentists, doctors, engineers, solicitors, surveyors, all have PI cover and, increasingly, they are giving notice to their brokers of facts that may give rise to a claim.

Although there is no obvious explanation, it seems that a large part of the defence side of the PI industry (especially, perhaps, the solicitors) do not view mediation with particular favour. Whether this is due to a perception of self-interest or a lack of pro-active involvement by the PI underwriters, or a combination of both, is unclear. However, what is clear is that, as with reinsurance, there is no good reason why mediation should not at least be considered as a method of resolving PI claims.

However, there are some straws in the wind. The (PI) market ADR commitment was launched at the London Underwriting Centre in November 1998. It is an undertaking by a significant number of insurers to attempt mediation to resolve disputes. Notwithstanding, the rate of growth of mediation in this area is slow. It is particularly surprising that a very low percentage of straightforward personal injury and motor accident claims are mediated, and even more surprising that the number of mediations of clinical negligence claims is minute. The explanation of the low take up of mediation for personal injury and motor accident cases is perhaps due to a combination of:

(a) limited awareness of mediation on the part of the smaller law firms that prosecute these types of claim;

(b) restricted or no legal aid funding for mediation; and

(c) reluctance of insurers to mediate and their sticking to the "traditional" defence tactics of delay and obfuscation.[11]

In clinical negligence cases, the strategy of the NHS Litigation Authority and Hospital Trusts appears to be to fight all the way to trial and then, if so advised, settle at the court door. It must be doubtful that, looked at in the round, this makes financial sense. The report from the National Audit Office published in early May 2001 shows that the number of claims made and success rates since 1995 have increased. In 1997–1998, claims settled totalled

[11] No criticism is intended: under the old Rules of the Supreme Court, that was how defendants behaved in litigation.

£50 million, in 1998–1999 the figure was £107 million and in 1999–2000, the figure was £386 million. Interestingly, for claims up to £55,000, the costs involved exceeded the settlements in 65 per cent of the cases.

What makes the response to mediation of PI professionals all the more surprising is that one would expect most professionals being pursued in negligence to welcome the possibility of a private and confidential method (employed at a relatively early stage in the claims process) to get rid of a claim which calls into question their professional ability and judgment.

Notwithstanding this unpromising background, the likelihood must be that the take up of mediation for resolution of PI claims will increase. The Pre-Action Protocol for Professional Negligence Claims[12] has a section dealing with ADR as a method of resolving a claim.[13] However, the section dealing with this records only that "The parties can agree at any stage to take the dispute to mediation . . ." and the Protocol acknowledges that no party can be forced to mediate. It is suggested that this section could be "beefed up" to, at least, "If either party requests the other to mediate the dispute, that other party will agree to the mediation request, save where it considers in good faith that mediation is inappropriate in which case it will give written reasons for its refusal to mediate to the requesting party".

Although the take up of mediation by the PI industry has so far been low, it is highly probable that it will make increasing use of mediation as a method to settle claims. There are positive advantages—not least the saving of costs—and as knowledge of mediation (and confidence in it) spreads, its use will become more widespread.

APPENDIX TO CHAPTER 7

MEDIATION AGREEMENT

7.5 **DATED:**

PARTIES:

(1)
(2)

(Jointly the Parties)

[12] For use in claims against professionals, other than construction professionals and healthcare providers.

[13] Curiously, though, the Pre-Action Protocol for personal injury claims does not.

(3)
("the mediator")

(4)
(The Pupil Mediator/Mediator's Adviser)

IT IS AGREED THAT

The Mediation

1. In this agreement "the dispute" means the issues the subject matter between the above named parties. **7.5.1**

2. The parties will attempt to settle the dispute by Mediation. The parties undertake to participate in the Mediation in good faith in an attempt to resolve the dispute. All documents and conversations prepared or taking place for the purpose of the Mediation shall be without prejudice.

3. The Mediation will take place at .... on .... beginning at ....

4. Representatives of the parties [and their advisers] and the mediator will attend at the Mediation. The parties' representatives **must** have the necessary authority to settle the dispute and shall immediately inform the mediator if it becomes apparent, prior to or during the Mediation hearing, that a restriction or limit on their authority might reasonably be expected adversely to affect the mediation.

5. *The representatives* **7.5.2**

The parties will be represented at the Mediation as follows:

(a) For .... advised by ....
(b) For .... advised by ....

The parties will inform each other and the mediator immediately if there shall be any change in their representation at the Mediation.

6. *The mediator* **7.5.3**

The mediator:

(a) will attend any meeting with any or all of the parties preceding the Mediation if requested or if the mediator decides this is appropriate;

(b) will read before the Mediation each summary and all the documents sent to him in accordance with paragraph 9 below;

(c) will determine the procedure at the mediation after consultation with the parties and their advisers;

(d) will seek to assist the parties in compromising and settling the dispute by a process of conciliation and discussion during the course of the mediation;

(e) will assist, if so requested, in drawing up any written settlement agreement;

(f) will not during the currency of this agreement, or at any time thereafter, act for any of the parties in any capacity in relation to any aspect of the dispute;

(g) will maintain and respect the confidentiality of all information provided to him by the Parties.

7. The Parties accept that in relation to the dispute the mediator is not acting as agent of, or otherwise acting in any capacity on behalf of, any of the Parties.

8. The Parties and mediator will seek to agree, in advance of the Mediation, the basis and rate upon which the mediator's fees will be charged. In default of such agreement the mediator shall be entitled to charge reasonable fees for the work that he performs. These fees shall be payable within 14 days of receipt by the Parties of the mediator's invoice. Each party shall be liable for an equal share of these fees.

9. Exchange of information

7.5.4 Each party will exchange with the other and send to the mediator at least one week before the Mediation or such other date as may be agreed between the parties:

(a) a concise summary ("the Summary") stating its case in the dispute;

(b) a bundle of supporting documents to which it refers in the summary and to which it intends to refer in the mediation;

(c) in addition, each party may send to the mediator and/or bring to the Mediation further documentation which it wishes to disclose in confidence to the mediator but not to any other party clearly stating in writing that such documentation is confidential to the mediator.

10. The Parties will seek to agree the maximum number of pages of each Summary and of the documents and will, in any event, keep the Summary as succinct, and the documents as brief, as they

reasonably can. In default of agreement the mediator may make an appropriate ruling.

11. The Mediation

No formal record or transcript of the Mediation shall be made. **7.5.5**

12. The mediator shall have the overall conduct of the Mediation and shall be entitled to make such direction about the procedure to be followed at the Mediation as he thinks appropriate.

13. The mediator shall be entitled but **not** obliged, at any stage in the Mediation, to express his view on the reasonableness or otherwise of any settlement proposal made by any of the parties.

14. If the parties are unable to reach a settlement during the course of the mediation then, if all the representatives so request and the mediator agrees, the mediator shall provide a non-binding written recommendation on terms of settlement. The Mediator shall be free to take into account all such matters and issues as he shall think appropriate and reasonable in all the circumstances and will not be required to anticipate or be limited by what a court might order in resolution of the dispute.

15. All documents (which include anything upon which evidence is recorded including tapes and computer disks) or other information produced for, or arising in relation to, the Mediation will be privileged and will not be admissible as evidence and will not be disclosable in any litigation or arbitration connected with the dispute unless such documents or information would in any event be admissible or disclosable in such proceedings.

16. Every person involved in the mediation will keep confidential and will not use for any collateral or ulterior purpose:

(a) the fact that the Mediation is to take place or has taken place; and

(b) all information (whether given orally, or in writing or otherwise) produced for or arising in relation to the Mediation including the Settlement Agreement (if any) arising out of it

save as may be necessary to implement and enforce any such Settlement Agreement.

17. Any settlement reached in the Mediation will not be legally binding unless and until it has been reduced to writing and has been signed by or on behalf of the Parties.

18. Each representative when signing this agreement is signing on behalf of the party whom he or she represents and on behalf of all individuals representing, advising, or attending the Mediation on behalf of, that party.

19. None of the Parties will call the mediator, or seek to procure the attendance of the mediator, as a witness in any litigation or arbitration in relation to the dispute. Nor shall any of the Parties call or appoint the mediator as a consultant, arbitrator or expert in any such litigation. The mediator agrees that he will not give any such evidence and will not voluntarily act in any such capacity without the written agreement of all the Parties.

Termination of Mediation

7.5.6 20. The Mediation shall terminate when any of the following events occurs:

(a) a party withdraws from the Mediation by giving written notice of withdrawal to the mediator and each of the other Parties;

(b) a written Settlement Agreement is signed by the Parties;

(c) the mediator decides that continuing the Mediation is unlikely to result in a settlement or that it is undesirable or inappropriate for any other reason to continue with the Mediation;

(d) the mediator decides that he should retire for any reason;

(e) the time set aside for the Mediation expires and any one of the Parties gives notice to the mediator and to the other Parties that it wishes the Mediation to come to an end. In such event the remaining Parties may agree that the Mediation shall continue without the involvement of the party giving notice.

21. Each party shall pay its own costs and expenses arising out of the Mediation.

22. This Agreement shall be governed by English law and the courts of England shall have exclusive jurisdiction to settle any claim, dispute or difference which may arise out of or in connection with the Mediation.

23. Neither this agreement, nor the Mediation, will affect or impair the rights of the Parties under the Human Rights Act or under the European Convention of Human Rights. Should the dispute not be settled by Mediation the Parties' rights to a fair trial remain unaffected.

24. The mediator shall not be liable to the Parties for any act or omission in connection with the services provided by him or in relation to the Mediation unless the act or omission is fraudulent or involves wilful misconduct.

Signed: ....
For & on behalf of

Signed: ....
For & on behalf of

Signed: ....

Date: ....

Chapter 8

IT DISPUTES

TIM HARDY

8.1 Introduction

In November 1999 the Home Office admitted that three-quarters of its IT projects were running late and over budget. An examination of the projects conducted by the Committee of Public Accounts and the Comptroller and Auditor General[1] had revealed that 13 out of 17 projects were involved in expensive delays at a cost to the taxpayer of over £50 million.

(a) **The Passport Agency**[2]—In the summer of 1999 thousands of people had to queue outside the Agency's London headquarters after a new computer system, developed at a cost of £77 million to speed up the process of issuing new passports, had accumulated a backlog of 565,000 applications.

(b) **Civil Aviation Authority**[3]—millions of passengers face delays because the £623 million air traffic control centre has failed to open due to the need for further modifications.

(c) **Inland Revenue**[4]—computerisation is set to cost £2.4 billion, more than £1 billion more than originally planned and reported to have "lost" five million tax records.[5]

(d) **Contributions Agency**[6]—some 172,000 pensioners received short payments as the computer system for managing national insurance accounts could not cope with the volume of data.

[1] First Report of the House of Commons Select Committee on Public Accounts "Improving the Delivery of Government IT Projects" HC 65 ISBN 0102047006 January 5, 2000.

[2] *Ibid.*

[3] *Ibid.*

[4] *Ibid.*

[5] *Computer Weekly* July 27, 2000.

[6] First Report of the House of Commons Select Committee on Public Accounts "Improving the Delivery of Government IT Projects" HC 65 ISBN 0102047006 January 5, 2000.

(e) **Immigration Directorate**[7]—failures of the system designed to handle applications of immigrants and asylum seekers resulted in a backlog of 219,000 cases.

(f) **Ministry of Defence**[8]—abandoned project TRAWLERMAN without it ever being used resulting in a loss of £40 million.

And these problems continue. In June 2001 the government announced that the PFI project LIBRA, intended to speed up the criminal justice system, which was supposed to be ready for acceptance in July 2001 had been postponed indefinitely, amid spiralling costs and serious technical problems. The original cost announced at the award of the contract had been £183 million but had risen to £319 million plus an internal allocation of £26 million by the Lord Chancellor's Department for internal costs.[9]

This paints an alarming picture of failures of projects managed by civil servants but it would be a mistake to conclude that this is a problem peculiar to government infrastructure projects. Because these projects are subject to public scrutiny and accountability, their failings are very much in the public eye whereas the private sector tends to keep its problems confidential. Occasionally these private sector failures do become public, either because the private business involved is itself open to public scrutiny or the customer sues and the dispute eventually gets to a hearing in open court. For example:

(a) the London Stock Exchange's first attempt at computerised settlement with TALISMAN, followed by the equally disastrous TAURUS, were very much public affairs estimated to have cost the Exchange's members up to £200 million.[10]

(b) In February 2000 building products supplier Pegler Limited[11] was awarded £9 million plus costs in a claim against Wang (U.K.) Ltd in respect of an IT project commissioned in 1991.

(c) In June 2000 Kwik Fit Insurance Services Ltd[12] issued proceedings against Bull Information Systems Ltd claiming damages in excess of £17 million. The claim was disputed and settled before trial.

These are just a few of the numerous disputes which are endemic in the process of acquiring IT and it is not a problem peculiar to the

7 *Ibid.*
8 *Ibid.*
9 *Computer Weekly* June 28, 2001.
10 *Independent on Sunday* April 9, 2000.
11 *Pegler Ltd v. Wang (U.K.) Ltd* (No. 1) [2000] B.L.R. 218.
12 *Kwik Fit Insurance Services Ltd v. Bull Information Systems Ltd*, unreported, T&C Court, June 23, 2000.

U.K. Research by the Standish Group[13] in the U.S. in 1995 showed that U.S. corporations spent more than $250 billion every year on IT application development at an average cost of $2,322,000. Of those projects 31 per cent were cancelled before delivery was completed and 53 per cent cost nearly double their original budget. Only 16 per cent were considered to have been completed successfully.

8.2 TYPES OF IT DISPUTES

Understanding the reasons for the peculiar susceptibility of IT projects to these problems ought to help to avoid repetition of these problems and assist in the process of resolving the disputes which typically emerge. The Standish Group looked at this following the survey conducted in 1995 and identified the 10 most influential factors in determining whether a project was likely to succeed or fail.[14]

The Ten Most Influential Factors on Success in order of importance were:

1. User Involvement;
2. Executive Management Support;
3. Developing Clear Statements of Requirements;
4. Proper Planning;
5. Setting Realistic Expectations;
6. Small Project Milestones;
7. Competent Staff;
8. Project Ownership;
9. Clear Vision and Objectives;
10. Hard Working, Focused Staff.

Select Committee on Public Accounts

8.2.1 In November 1999 the Select Committee on Public Accounts produced a report with a similar objective entitled *Improving the Delivery of Government IT Projects*.[15] This usefully identified the cause of disputes based on a review of 25 government projects from the 1990s. The lessons to be learnt can be equally applied to

[13] The Standish Group "Chaos Chronicles" 1995. Website only at http://standishgroup.com/visitor/chaos.htm.

[14] *Ibid*.

[15] First Report "Improving the Delivery of Government IT Projects" HC 65 ISBN 0102047006 January 5, 2000.

any large IT project and it is no surprise that the cause of the failures was the mirror image of the Standish Group's list of 10 most influential factors on success. The following likely causes of disputes were identified in the Report.

Inception and design

- Failure to analyse and understand fully the implications of the introduction of new systems for the business and its customers. **8.2.2**
- Lack of analysis of the implications of implementing the proposed new system.
- Lack of understanding of what the business really needs in the context of wider changes to the business environment.
- Failure to take into account the business needs of the organisation and the requirements of users in sufficient detail in the Project Specification resulting in the delivery of an end product which is not what was intended, or is not user-friendly, or which has slow response times which results in staff not using the system as planned or even maintaining parallel manual systems.
- Failure to anticipate future changes to the business which coincide with the introduction of the new system.
- Being too ambitious at the outset can be fatal as excessive scale and complexity are major factors contributing to failure.
- Setting unrealistic timetables and budgets without a proper appreciation of the fact that they will benefit neither employer nor contractor in the long run.
- A "big bang" approach without incremental stages which themselves deliver auditable business benefit.

Delays in implementation

- Delays risk the project being overtaken by technological and business changes. **8.2.3**
- Lack of flexibility in project plans which would have allowed for the insertion of technological advances and business changes.
- Failure to build into the contract enough high level reviews to ensure it is not allowed to continue when changing circumstances mean that the business benefit is no longer going to be achieved cost effectively.

Managing projects

8.2.4
- Senior Management failure to appoint someone with real authority and IT experience to take responsibility for the success can have a profound effect on the project.
- Failure to support the project by proceeding without developing high quality project management skills and experience.
- Lack of clarity about the aims and objectives, failure to set clear criteria against which the success of a project can be judged.

Management of risk and contingency plans

8.2.5
- Risk and contingency planning is often not given sufficient attention such that the impact of failure is far greater than it need be.
- Failure to make decisions on a soundly based rigorous assessment of costs and benefits, together with a realistic assessment of risks.
- Lack of a risk management framework with individuals empowered to make decisions as the costs, risks and costs change during the project's life.

Relationships with suppliers

8.2.6
- Relying to too great an extent on the assurances of the contractor, particularly if the contractor has not got a sufficiently clear understanding of what is expected and required.
- Failure to precisely document the roles and responsibilities of the parties.
- Allowing contractors to sub-contract without ensuring the prime supplier's arrangements for managing the sub-contracts are consistent with the requirements of the main contract.
- Lack of clarity or debatable interpretation in a contract can lead to expensive misunderstandings.
- Leaving key issues to be resolved later is clearly undesirable.

Problems continue

8.2.7 These lists illustrate that just about every aspect of an IT project can be a source of a dispute and there are plenty of opportunities to argue that responsibility lies elsewhere. The report contains useful guidance for both claimants and defendants as to best practice. Despite all of this careful analysis and recommendations as to best practice, these problems persist in many projects.

Alfred Spector, president of Transarc Corporation tried to explain why IT projects were so prone to disputes by comparing software development contracts to bridge building. Bridges are usually built on time, within budget and work. The converse being true for software projects. His theory being that before building a bridge the design, right down to the last nut and bolt, is fixed whereas with software the design is fluid and uncertain. Certainly this goes a long way to explain the root cause of many problems but then again many more complex building contracts suffer from exactly the same problems as IT contracts. There are many similarities between IT and construction disputes so much can be learnt from observing how the management of construction disputes has evolved.

In the construction industry disputes are also endemic, so much so that many believe conflict is inevitable.[16] In the 1970s and 1980s these disputes were invariably litigated in the High Court but dissatisfaction with the time this took, together with the expense, led to arbitration being strongly preferred by many in the industry. However, this too lost favour as arbitration became increasing like court actions with all the attendant costs and delays. As dissatisfaction grew increasingly the parties turned to contractual adjudication, expert determination and ADR. In May 1998 the Housing Grants, Construction and Regeneration Act 1996 introduced a scheme of statutory adjudication into most of the main building and engineering standard forms. When invoked the Act aims to provide an equitable and swift resolution of any dispute within a matter of weeks. The adjudication's decision is final and binding unless or until the dispute is finally determined by litigation, arbitration or agreement between the parties.

Although many within the industry were not happy with the scheme when it was introduced it is generally accepted to have achieved its objective of resolving disputes quickly and reducing the amount of litigation and arbitration which was adding needless cost to the construction industry. Disputes in IT projects are just as frequent as disputes in construction contracts but there is as yet no demand to introduce a form of statutory regulation for IT disputes probably because few get to trial, the majority being settled through some form of ADR.

ROLE OF COURTS AND TRIBUNALS 8.3

The Technology and Construction Court

In the 1970s and 1980s the High Court sought to address perceived shortcomings in its ability to handle complex construction disputes 8.3.1

16 *ADR and Adjudication in Construction Disputes*, Hibberd & Newman (Blackwell Science, 1999).

by appointing judges who were specialised in handling construction disputes whilst at the bar to the Official Referees' Court and requiring cases involving technical and scientific issues to be heard before it. Since then the court's business evolved to include IT disputes and as a consequence in 1998 it was renamed the Technology and Construction Court (T&CC).

Construction disputes remain the principal business of the court but the judges acquire a degree of knowledge and experience of IT disputes as a consequence of hearing the IT disputes which make it to trial. The emphasis on construction disputes is reflected in the fact that the T&CC only has a Pre-Action Protocol for Construction and Engineering Disputes. However, a specialist Technology Protocol is being drafted by the Society for Computers and Law.

The cost of litigating IT disputes in the High Court can be enormous because of the formality of the process and the detailed forensic investigation into the rights and wrongs of all the parties' behaviour over a number of years. This invariably involves highly technical issues requiring skilled expert witnesses to delve into the interstices of both the history and the system itself in order to give evidence. It is therefore not surprising that litigants are often keen to find alternative ways of resolving these disputes. The judges are converts to the mediation cause and encourage the parties to give it proper consideration at every opportunity.

The existing T&CC Pre-Action Protocol provides that after an exchange of letters spelling out their respective positions the parties should normally meet. The aims of the meeting include consideration "whether and if so how, the issues might be resolved without recourse to litigation".[17]

8.3.2 The Technology and Construction Court Solicitors Association (TeCSA) has drafted an ADR Protocol and Mediation Procedure Rules suitable for use in both Technology and Construction Disputes. The Protocol is extremely practical and suggests the appointment of an independent chairman for any Pre-Action Meeting required under any Court Protocol, typically a practising solicitor specialising in T&CC work with more than 10 years' experience. TeCSA also volunteer to provide names of suitable chairmen on request.

If despite all of this encouragement the parties to an IT dispute cannot resolve their differences, a trial in the T&CC will be handled by a judge with a degree of experience in the likely issues and law. They will also be familiar with grappling with detailed technical evidence. Statistics[18] from the Lord Chancellor's Department suggest that the new emphasis on ADR is having a dramatic effect, reducing significantly the court's business.

17 Pre-Action Protocol for Construction and Engineering Disputes, August 2000 edition, para. 5.2.

18 Lord Chancellor's Civil Justice Reform Evaluation, March 2001.

Since the introduction of the Civil Procedure Rules in April 1999 implementing Lord Woolf's reforms, the business of the T&CC has fallen more dramatically than any other court. In addition a Government Best Practice Statement[19] encourages the use of ADR where a government department is party to a computer contract dispute and the Lord Chancellor's announcement[20] that in future government departments and agencies, the source of many IT disputes, will settle cases by ADR techniques wherever possible and only go to court as a last resort. All of this is likely to depress the T&CC's case load still further and result in speeding up the process considerably for those unable to resolve their dispute through ADR.

Arbitration

As arbitration has developed so as to be in many respects a mirror image of court proceedings with formal pleadings, disclosure and exchange of evidence, the perceived advantages of costs and time savings have disappeared. One of the principal remaining advantage over litigation is that the parties can chose to appoint as arbitrator an industry expert as opposed to a lawyer. However, many lawyers shy away from the appointment of arbitrators without a legal background as interpretation of the contract and weighing the relative merits of conflicting evidence can be crucial to the outcome of a case. Although arbitration before an industry expert may be quicker and cheaper it is still very expensive and can take as long. Regardless of the choice of arbitrator the process like litigation involves an investigation into the surrounding facts, followed by the application of the law to those facts in order to establish the legal rights and obligations of both parties. It takes a great deal of time to complete this exercise in complex IT disputes where the facts and law are hotly contested. **8.3.3**

Whether before a court or an arbitrator the parties to an IT dispute are likely to consider mediation at an early stage for a variety of reasons.

(a) The contract may specify it and despite ruling that such a clause may not be enforceable, being no more than an agreement to agree,[21] the court of Appeal[22] has made it clear that a party who chooses to ignore an ADR clause may well be penalised on costs when the issue comes before the court.

[19] HM Treasury Central Unit on Pronouncement, Disputes Resolution, CUP No. 50.

[20] Lord Chancellor's Department, Press Release, March 23, 2001.

[21] *Walford v. Miles* [1992] 1 All E.R. 453.

[22] *Dyson and Field (Executors of Lawrence Twohey deceased) v. Leeds City Council*, [2000] C.P. Rep. 42.

(b) The court or arbitrator may direct the parties to consider ADR.

(c) One of the parties may press for ADR.

Arbitration is still favoured by some, in particular those who want to keep any dispute confidential or in international contracts where there is a concern of local prejudice influencing the result. For many years it was the preferred resolution process specified in the majority of IT contracts and it will continue to be specified as first choice in many contracts.

All of the major arbitration providers can provide names of lawyers and/or industry experts who are qualified arbitrators and experienced in handling IT disputes. None of the providers have particular rules designed for IT disputes relying instead on their standard rules.

Dispute escalation clauses

8.3.4 As ADR has slowly gained acceptance as a valid and satisfactory method of resolving disputes the dispute escalation clause has become more popular. These tend to be idiosyncratically drafted to suit the particular circumstances of each case combining a mix of dispute resolution methods. Essentially these clauses enable the parties to choose whether to use mediation, expert determination or arbitration but in the event of a failure to agree any of these then the dispute will have to go to a specified court.

Example of dispute escalation clause

1.1 Disputes Escalation Clause

8.3.5 All and any disputes or differences arising out of or connected with this agreement, or the breach, termination or invalidity thereof ("Disputes") shall be resolved and finally settled in the manner provided for in this clause.

1.2 Disputes Committee

8.3.6 Disputes shall be referred by either party to a disputes committee ("the Disputes Committee") drawn from the senior management of the parties to this Agreement. If Disputes cannot be resolved by the Disputes Committee within [] days they shall be referred to the CEO of [the Contractor] and the CEO of [the Employer] for resolution.

1.3 Escalation Procedure

8.3.7 If the parties' representatives nominated under paragraph 1.2 above are unable to resolve the Disputes within [ ] days then:

1.3.1 All Disputes should be referred to Mediation in accordance with paragraph 1.4;

1.3.2 Disputes of a technical nature or expressed by this Agreement to be subject to expert determination may, by agreement between the parties, be referred for final determination to an expert ("the Expert") acting as an expert not an arbitrator in accordance with paragraph 1.5;

1.3.3 Disputes expressed by this Agreement to be subject to arbitration may, by agreement between the parties, be referred to arbitration in accordance with paragraph 1.6;

1.3.4 If the parties cannot agree, or fail, to resolve Disputes in accordance with clauses 1.3.1, 1.3.2, or 1.3.3 the parties irrevocably agree that the courts of England and Wales shall have [*non-*] exclusive jurisdiction to settle all Disputes and agree to submit to the jurisdiction of such courts.

1.4 Mediation

The parties agree to attempt to settle all Disputes by Mediation in 8.3.8
accordance with the [*insert choice of mediation rules*] ("the Mediation"). To initiate the Mediation a party must give notice in writing ("ADR Notice") to the other party requesting the Mediation in accordance with this clause. The Mediation will start not later than [. . .] days after the date of the ADR notice.

1.5 Expert Determination

Disputes to be resolved pursuant to this clause shall be finally 8.3.9
determined by the Expert to be appointed by agreement between the parties, or failing such an agreement, by the [insert choice of appointing authority].

1.6 Arbitration

Disputes to be resolved pursuant to this clause shall be finally 8.3.10
settled by arbitration in accordance with the [*insert choice of arbitration rules*]. The arbitrator shall be selected by mutual agreement or, failing agreement, within [ ] days after a request by one party to the other shall be chosen by [*insert choice*].

ROLE OF ADR GENERALLY—ADVANTAGES OF MEDIATION OR OTHER FORMS OF ADR 8.4

ADR methods can be divided into two categories, consensual and adjudicative. The principal adjudicative methods are arbitration and expert determination. Mini-trials or early neutral evaluation (ENE) can also be adjudicative, if the parties agree in advance that the outcome should be binding. The essential difference between adjudicative and consensual dispute resolution is that in the former the parties agree to accept the decision of a third party as determinative of the dispute and in the latter the outcome is not binding, unless the parties agree otherwise. It is that element of finality which parties are reluctant to accept in large IT disputes which makes the adjudicative methods of ADR less attractive. However, for small, discrete technical IT issues, where the decision does not have such large financial consequences, they are frequently preferred.

Expert determination

8.4.1 Like other adjudicative methods this has the advantage of producing a final and binding decision which cannot be challenged by either party. This is both its strength and its weakness. It is ideally suited to relatively small claims where the parties have a continuing relationship, such as a short and relatively unimportant delay in a staged delivery of a software package. It can also be very effective for resolving disputes during an IT development project, such as valuing work done or interpreting responsibilities.

It is seldom chosen as the method for resolving major disputes where a contract has failed or resulted in substantial costs overruns. This would seem to be because most parties, or possibly their lawyers, consider the dispute is unlikely to be resolved justly in line with the merits of their case and the relevant law by an expert. Experts are usually chosen for their particular industry skill and knowledge. In order to be a true expert they will be working in the industry, not sitting as an adjudicator listening to conflicting expert and factual evidence, carefully judging the weight to be attributed to each and applying complex legal principles. The outcome of such a process is difficult to predict and the parties are often reluctant to resolve their disputes in this fashion once a dispute has actually emerged, unless the contract already specifically provides that disputes of that nature can only be resolved by expert determination.

Facilitated negotiation

8.4.2 This is a form of ADR most suited to attempts to resolve disputes between parties who need each other, either because of a continuing commercial relationship or because they are locked into a contract where the terms are adversely affecting one party and need to be renegotiated. Both of these circumstances frequently happen in IT contracts where the employer is locked into a relationship with the contractor delivering bespoke software and/or the contractor has made a bad bargain to win the contract but cannot afford to continue developing the system it has contracted to supply.

The role of the facilitator is akin to that of a mediator but from the outset the emphasis is on keeping the parties together rather than resolving the dispute even if it means ending the relationship.

Early neutral evaluation

This is a much under-utilised form of ADR. The low take up is due to the fear that if the evaluation goes against one party the other will become more confident and entrenched in its position, thereby reducing significantly the prospects for settlement later in the case. It involves the appointment of a respected third party to whom each party makes representations about its case and the evaluator expresses an opinion, without prejudice and non-binding, as to likely outcome of the case were it litigated. **8.4.3**

Mini-trial

Typically, this involves senior representatives of all the parties involved in the dispute observing a formal, but short, presentation of each party's case in front of a respected, independent third party who helps the parties assess the likely outcome if the dispute were litigated. The third party, using its knowledge and experience, assists the parties to negotiate a settlement and will, if asked, express non-binding opinions on specific points to progress the negotiations. The principal disadvantages of this form of ADR are the cost and time associated with preparing for what can be a lengthy process. It works best where senior executives with no involvement in the dispute, or the management of the dispute, participate as the observers but most executives are reluctant to expose their disputes to such intense scrutiny by their superiors. **8.4.4**

Mediation

As demonstrated in the Introduction, computer contracts are particularly susceptible to disputes and this is not a new phenomenon. These disputes tend to be extremely complex so litigating them is very costly and time consuming. The majority of IT disputes settled without going to court before mediation became so popular. The principal benefit of mediation in this context is that it is leading to settlements earlier in the dispute resolution process. In view of the high success rate and suitability of mediation for IT disputes there is relatively little to be lost by using it and a great deal to be gained. **8.4.5**

The statistics from the Centre for Effective Dispute Resolution showed six per cent[23] of its mediation in 1999 were IT related and seven per cent[24] in 2000. Mediation is the most popular form of ADR for large IT disputes. This is partly due to its flexibility but largely because it affords the parties more control over the method of resolution and the resolution itself. The rules of all the major ADR agencies provide a basic template for the conduct of the mediation and they are not prescriptive. This flexibility is particularly helpful in

[23] Centre for Effective Dispute Resolution, Press Release April 26, 1999.
[24] Centre for Effective Dispute Resolution, 2000 Statistics.

large IT disputes which typically involve a number of parties, masses of documentation, highly technical issues, a complicated history and detailed expert evidence.

This was illustrated by the manner in which mediation was used in the high profile dispute between IBM and Fujitsu. IBM commenced arbitration proceedings complaining that Fujitsu had developed its systems software using IBM's proprietary material. The dispute was finally resolved by a decision in the arbitration but mediation techniques were used to great effect during the course of the arbitration to reduce the issues in dispute and to agree a formula for calculating the sum of $800 million to be paid by Fujitsu for past and future use of IBM.

In addition to the TeCSA Protocol referred to above there are a number of mediation schemes set up specifically for IT disputes.

(a) The Computing Services and Software Association (CSSA) in conjunction with CEDR has a scheme available where one party to a dispute is a member.

(b) The British Computing Society will nominate a mediator free of charge

(c) The Academy of experts has a list of IT experts who are experienced mediators.

(d) The Society for Computers and Law is drafting ADR procedures.

(e) The Chartered Institute of Arbitrators has developed The Rules of the Computer Software for Solicitors Arbitrators Scheme.

Role of straightforward negotiations

8.4.6 A number of sceptics have argued that ADR is just another form of without prejudice negotiations and they do not need the intervention of a third party to resolve their dispute. Martin Simmons Q.C. argued in *The Lawyer*[25] that lawyers possess the skills necessary to facilitate a structured discussion between themselves, their client and the other parties without requiring the invention of a mediator to reach a compromise.

While it is true that cases have settled, and will continue to settle, before court without the use of ADR, the intervention of a mediator has resolved many cases where the parties have failed to negotiate a settlement between themselves. This is in part because the process involves each party in exposing more of its case, more of its strengths and weaknesses, than usually happens in unassisted

[25] *The Lawyer* March 13, 2000.

party and party negotiation. Additionally, the magic ingredient in mediation is that it mimics the pressure the parties' senior executives responsible for the dispute will experience at the courtroom door and in the courtroom itself. The senior executives have to endure the presentation of their case to the other party and an experienced independent third party in a forum where it can and will be very publicly criticised.

(a) Each party will expend great effort exposing the other party's weaknesses.

(b) If personally involved, the executives will observe their own conduct being severely questioned.

(c) The risks of losing will be examined together with all of the costs implications.

These pressures, although present throughout any dispute resolution process, are not as manifest in an unaided party and party negotiation. Of course, straightforward negotiations have a role to play and many cases will settle without a mediator's intervention, so negotiation still has a very important role to play. Further negotiation is frequently used prior to mediation to sound out and lower the other party's demand position. It also frequently continues if a dispute is not resolved at the mediation itself and many cases settle a few days or weeks later as a consequence of unaided party and party negotiation.

THE ROLE OF MEDIATION 8.5

Handling the client

Avoiding surprises is key. If the client has never been involved in a 8.5.1
mediation before, great care should be taken to educate the client about what to expect.

Start with the mechanics of the process, the openings, the public sessions and the private sessions. Explain the rules relating to information given to the mediation in confidence. Warn that it is common to be left alone for long periods while the mediator works with the other party. This can be frustrating and lead to misunderstandings if not anticipated. Explain "reality testing", a process used by many mediators where they put the party's case under the microscope focusing on its weaknesses.

Explain the law relating to your case and examine its weaknesses. A weakness exposed for the first time in the mediation, perhaps previously perceived but not discussed so frankly with the client, can have a devastating effect on the mediation. It can undermine the client's confident in its own lawyer or, if the lawyer refuses to recognise the weakness, confidence in the mediation. This can be so serious as to cause the mediation to fail completely.

Complete a risk assessment and examine it in detail with the client. This leads on naturally to the development of objectives and strategy.

If possible, familiarity with the chosen mediator is ideal so that the solicitor can anticipate and warn the client of the mediator's particular style and idiosyncrasies. Indeed, the particular characteristics may well effect the choice of mediator in the first place. With a tough negotiator on the other side of a dispute who uses bullying tactics, it may be crucial to have a mediator who is equally resolute and will not be bullied. While the choice is made for very valid reasons it would be a mistake not to have explained all of this to the client at the time of making the selection.

The more dialogue with the client about these issues the better as mediation can be a very intense and at times uncomfortable experience. One of the benefits of using ADR providers such as CEDR or ADR Group is that they can provide guidance on the styles of the mediators they propose. This is a very important aspect of the selection process.

Warn the client that mediation is not an easy option. The reaction of the representative of one party to a major IT mediation sums it up: "I would not underestimate the stress involved in ADR: it is probably one of the most stressful things I have ever done."[26] It requires just as much preparation as a court hearing. As it will cover all aspects of a dispute, the work involved can seem overwhelming, but there is no room for short cuts. It is also crucial that the client is involved in the sessions where objectives and strategy are set so that it can participate fully in the process without unwittingly compromising the strategy. The client will also have valuable input when trying to identify the other party's interests and likely negotiating style. Both of these are important ingredients in determining the best negotiation strategy. Also, the client's input is invaluable when trying to identify imaginative options for solving the dispute.

Prior to the issue of proceedings

8.5.2 Mediation can take place at any time in a dispute. The earlier it takes place the more legal costs and valuable time will be saved. Against this must be weighed the chance that facts and arguments not yet exposed by the legal process might produce a better result. However, it is not necessary to know every detail before mediating, so delay is only really justified if there is crucial information yet to be exchanged.

In complex IT disputes there is an increased risk that an attempt

[26] *Computing* June 8, 1995.

at early mediation will be used by one party purely to gain information. It is important to guard against this by slowly building confidence in each party's goodwill through the opening exchanges. This can be done through the reciprocal exchange of small amounts of sensitive information in advance of the mediation itself.

The Woolf reforms promote full and frank disclosure of each party's case at the very outset so this should be seen as part of that process and not be allowed to hinder a willingness to discuss the merits of each party's position. A request for wide ranging disclosure should be resisted at this stage as it indicates the requesting party's intention to use the process as a fishing expedition and does not bode well for the successful outcome of the mediation. On the other hand, mutual requests for documents or documents relating to specific issues should be complied with as part of the process of building confidence in each other's intention to honour the process and discuss the merits of each other's case in an open and frank manner.

In IT disputes, which are likely to involve significant issues turning on highly technical expert evidence, it is extremely difficult to gauge what the final outcome may be in the early stages of a dispute. It is often argued by lawyers that mediation cannot be attempted until some step in the legal process has been completed: pleadings closed, disclosure and inspection completed, witness statements exchanged, expert witness reports exchanged, experts have met, quantum reports exchanged, etc. This may be an excuse to avoid a process the party does not understand or trust. Alternatively, it may be based on a belief that the only way to extract its client's just deserts, or avoid paying too much, is to fight the case all the way to trial. Handled properly, even with justifiable concerns, the client should not be disadvantaged by mediation. The client should in any event be told the risks and advantages of proceeding or settling at any stage.

After issuing proceedings

One of the most difficult times to reach an agreement to mediate an IT dispute is immediately after the issue of proceedings. The defendant will be under pressure to sort out its defence in a wide range of technical and legal issues and is likely to feel aggrieved and offended by the nature of the allegations made. An approach for ADR is unlikely to succeed and is best left until after the initial flurry of activity has died down. **8.5.3**

As discussed above, many are of the opinion that mediation has a better chance of success if conducted late in the litigation process when the parties have completed the disclosures of their case required prior to trial. Some have even expounded the theory that a dispute will not be "ripe" for mediation until the parties have suffered through the litigation process and only then are they sufficiently motivated to settle. It is true that a mediation of an IT dispute at a later stage is more likely to achieve a settlement which more closely reflects the merits of each party's case. But in many cases the parties would prefer to be rid of the dispute, worry and costs by concluding a commercial settlement at a much earlier stage of the process. If the project has been a complete failure, the contractor is likely to wish to defend its performance and attempt to reduce the employer's expectations as to what it might recover, attributing blame to the employer's behaviour, characterised as unreasonable and constantly changing demands. These conflicting pressures make mediation at an early stage of an IT dispute particularly difficult but not impossible.

In IT disputes in particular it is therefore important to keep an open mind on this issue and discuss the alternatives with the client. If there is no commercial relationship to be maintained, or if the paying party is defending through insurers, the prospect of achieving a commercial settlement will not be good as those controlling the purse strings of the paying party are likely to hold the view that they will pay less by driving the other party to the door of the court before settling.

The most important factor in determining the optimum timing for mediation is both parties' willingness to settle and, conversely, their willingness to litigate. Willingness to settle is more likely to exist at an early stage of a dispute if both parties have a commercial interest in a continuing relationship. This mutual interest frequently exists with the supply of an IT system which will require continued maintenance and service after delivery from those who developed it. Conversely, if the project has been abandoned as a complete failure, a willingness to litigate is more likely to exist than a willingness to compromise.

Making contact with the other parties—the approach

8.5.4 One of the most frequently cited reasons for not mediating is fear that being the first to mention mediation will be seen as a sign of weakness. An in-house lawyer summed it up "It is not that my mind is closed to mediation, but I approach this on a tactical basis. If you think you have a good case, then tactically it is not right to go to a mediation. It could be seen as a sign of weakness".[27]

The Woolf reforms have introduced many measures which ought to have dispelled these fears and besides many IT contracts will now contain some form of ADR clause. In addition to the Pre-Action Protocols referred to above within 14 days of the earlier of either the defendant acknowledging service, or the service of a Defence, the

[27] See "Beyond Disputes", *Legal Week* June 28, 2001.

T&CC's Practice Direction Supplementing CPR Part 49 provides that the claimant must issue an application for directions. When the court notifies the parties of the appointment for the directions hearing it will send the parties a "Case Management Questionnaire" which has to be completed, exchanged with the other party and returned to the court two days before the appointment. The very first question is "Do you wish there to be a stay to attempt to settle the case by negotiations or by any other form of alternative dispute resolution? If yes, at what stage and for how long? If no please give reasons." In the light of this clear direction from the court that the parties should consider ADR, being the first to mention it can be used to signal confidence and a willingness to get to the truth quickly with all of the attendant benefits of costs and time savings. Also it can be used to give a clear signal that although mediation is being considered, if unsuccessful the next step will be the issue of proceedings.

If a corporation still fears adverse inferences being drawn it should consider making its 'Corporate Policy' to consider ADR and use it wherever possible to resolve disputes. The opposing party could not assume that implementing that policy evidenced any sign of weakness.

Having decided when to broach the subject of ADR with the opposing party it is important to try and anticipate what objections may be raised in response. Expect the opposing party to be resistant, at least at first, fearful that they may be disadvantaged. Have a clear and reasonable plan as to who, how and where the mediation should take place recognising that you have to make those proposals attractive to the other party. If the parties' executives are still speaking, it is a natural topic for them to discuss but make sure the client has first been fully briefed as to the process. It is sensible, however, to leave the negotiation concerning the detailed arrangements for the mediation to the lawyers if they are going to be heavily involved, as is most likely in a large IT dispute.

The type of mediator

Parties to an IT dispute who have agreed to mediation frequently run into disagreement over the choice of mediator, particularly whether the mediator requires IT expertise. Although some embedded ADR clauses will have addressed the choice of mediator it is more usual for this to be left for negotiation once a dispute has arisen. 8.5.5

Sources of experts who are accredited mediators include:

(a) The Academy of Experts' panel of accredited mediators includes a number of IT experts.

(b) The British Computer Society appoints mediators free of charge and usefully also publishes a Register of Expert

Witnesses amongst whom are accredited mediators.[28] The experts on its panel include expertise in system development, modification, supply, licensing and project management.

(c) The Chartered Institute of Arbitrators has a specialist set of conciliation and arbitration rules for computer software disputes. It also has a panel of IT experts with qualifications as mediators and arbitrators.

(d) The Computer Services and Software Association (CSSA) in conjunction with CEDR has a mediation scheme.

In IT contracts the contractor is likely to want a mediator with an IT industry background who will have first hand experience of the problems routinely associated with a major project. This is in the belief that having that knowledge will make that mediator more sympathetic and understanding of the contractor's position. It also strongly suggests they are looking to the mediator to use his expertise to favour that party. Conversely, the employer is likely to feel disadvantaged by such an appointment as it may fear the mediator is being chosen to delve into the technical aspects of the dispute. Consequently, the employers tend to prefer to appoint mediators from a legal background as they will more readily understand the underlying law and be better trained in forensic skills.

Mediators with expertise believe it is crucial. "Although the typical issues in computer disputes are not usually related to leading-edge technology", Mr Michael Turner, a CEDR accredited mediator with an IT background, considers ". . . it is absolutely essential that the mediator of a computer contract dispute has sufficient understanding of the technical issues and a deep understanding of the parties' expectations and of computer industry practice". He concedes that a "technical" mediator in an IT dispute should also have "some understanding of general contract law, and a detailed knowledge of computer contract caselaw".[29]

It is quite understandable that a lawyer trying to recommend a mediator to a client, and the client when considering that recommendation, will both see benefits in the appointment of a mediator who is at least conversant with the subject matter of the dispute. They perceive that it eliminates the need for some lengthy explanations necessary to educate the non-expert mediator. It also allays concerns that the mediator will not understand the technical aspects of this case or the industry's accepted standards of behaviour.

8.5.6 Commonly those without IT expertise argue that expertise in the

[28] website http://www.bcs.org.uk.

[29] See "Dispute Resolution", *Legal Week* July 5, 2001.

process of mediation is what is required and not expertise in the subject matter of the dispute. Mr David Shapiro, one of the most experienced CEDR accredited mediators practising in London, argues "Insistence on a mediator with subject matter expertise reflects most litigators' preoccupation with finding a legal or factual answer to a specific question".[30] If a party wants the expert mediator to express opinions based on that expertise in order to encourage settlement, there is a substantial risk of destroying the mediator's impartiality and thereby put the mediator himself at risk. "The more expert the mediator is in the subject matter the more difficult the problem of impartiality becomes. For the temptation of the mediator to substitute his expertise for that of the parties is often overwhelming".[31]

The bottom line is that the mediator must be neutral and must have, and maintain, the confidence of all parties. Above all else the outcome is most likely to be influenced by the skill of the mediator as a mediator, and his suitability for the characteristics of that particular dispute.

Faced by intransigence on both sides, a solution which is becoming increasingly popular is a co-mediation. This involves the use of two mediators, typically one with a legal background and the other with experience in the subject matter. This should satisfy the typical conflicting attitudes of employer and contractor in IT supply contracts identified above. It can bring benefits of time saving where there are a number of parties as the mediators can work separately with different parties. However, it does require a high level of communication between the mediators. Although it will add to the cost, the extra mediator's fees are a small expense in the light of the sums involved in the dispute, particularly bearing in mind the potential cost-saving if the matter settles. Preferably the co-mediators will have worked together, or at least be familiar with each other, and do not have styles which will conflict.

The mediation agreement

The dispute resolution agencies have standard forms of mediation **8.5.7**
agreement which cover the essential ground whereby the parties consent to mediate and appoint the chosen mediator/s to conduct the mediation. Issues typically covered by a mediation agreement include:

(a) all discussions are without prejudice and confidential;
(b) the non-binding nature of the process pending the execution of a written settlement agreement;

[30] David Shapiro, "Expert mediators–not experts as mediators", *Resolutions* 16.
[31] *ibid*.

(c) the appointment of the mediator and remuneration;

(d) the venue, duration of the mediation and termination;

(e) costs sharing arrangements;

(f) commitment to the process;

(g) attendance by representatives with authority to settle;

(h) any procedural issues already agreed.

If the parties choose to appoint a mediator direct, the mediator should insist on a formal written agreement signed by both parties covering these issues.

Additional items which it is advisable, but not essential, to try and agree at the time of the appointment are:

Mutual exchange of submissions and the timing

8.5.8 It is surprising how often parties to a mediation cannot agree to a mutual exchange of position papers. Such tactics have been defended on the basis that one party wants to be free to put into their submission information for the mediator which the other party should not see. If there is any such information it should be included in a separate briefing paper and not allowed to obstruct a crucial part of the process. Similarly, objections are sometimes made to simultaneous exchange, the defendant sometimes seeking sequential exchange. This reflects a preoccupation with the strict legal analysis of the dispute and can result in a stilted unhelpful submission from the defendant which concentrates on refuting every issue in the claimant's submission with which it disagrees, rather than addressing the mediator on the strength of its own case.

One of the principal reasons for mediations failing is that one or more of the parties has not worked out precisely what their case is and/or a failure to spell it out clearly and brief the mediator so that the mediator and other party know what they are dealing with. Helping one party formulate its case may be a very useful exercise but it is not good use of the mediator's time. It is also likely to mean that the other party has not had time to consider and respond fully to the new case that emerges during the mediation.

Accordingly, agreement that each party spells out its case in a submission to be exchanged with the other parties in advance of the meeting with the mediator is advisable. In large IT disputes with many complex issues the mediator must be given sufficient time to consider the submissions and the parties are likely to want to put in responses. If this sounds too much like formal pleadings, nothing could be further from the intent of the process. The submissions must be informative and each party can be expected to make them persuasive.

Agreed bundles of documents

Inundating the mediator with duplicates of tenders, contracts, subcontracts and specifications can easily be avoided by sensible discussion and planning by the parties. Avoiding duplication of correspondence, minutes of meetings and supporting documents is more difficult but probably more important. Mediators are typically instructed late in the day and often on a limited budget. It is a waste of their valuable time if they have to sift through two similar bundles of documents but it is remarkable how frequently this happens. **8.5.9**

Responses and the timing

With complex IT disputes where submissions are exchanged simultaneously all parties are likely to want an opportunity to respond in writing before the mediation. Again, time must be given to enable the mediator to absorb all of this information, so care must be taken to set a sensible timetable at the outset and for all parties to stick to it. **8.5.10**

Pre-action document requests

Some ADR contracts provide that the parties agree to conduct the mediation in good faith and with a view to concluding a settlement of the dispute. In CEDR's Standard Mediation Agreement the parties agree to use their best endeavours to resolve the dispute. These agreements also frequently provide that the parties should co-operate with requests for disclosure of information whether in documents, witness statements or expert reports. One of the biggest problems when mediating IT disputes at an early stage is that one of the parties enters the process with no intention of compromising, using the process instead to see what additional information they can glean. Requests for wide-ranging disclosure are indicative of such a strategy and should be countered by offers to disclose specific documents or information related to specific identified events or issues. **8.5.11**

Who should attend the mediation?

It is not possible to be prescriptive on this. The choice will depend on a number of issues including the size and importance of the dispute, as well as the identities and strengths, or weaknesses, of the management team responsible for the project. **8.5.12**

Good mediators take particular care to ensure that the senior representatives of each party have complete authority to settle the dispute, including authority to sign any settlement agreement. Experience shows that it is advisable to record any settlement in writing signed by the parties before the meeting ends as agreements subject to senior management approval are likely to unravel before the parties can get pen to paper. In reality, it is often the case that despite assurances as to authority being given those attending in fact only have limited authority. That may be inconvenient but it should not be fatal, provided the representative present has a direct line of communication to those with the requisite authority. Care should be taken by the mediator to get these issues resolved in advance.

It is also advisable where there is a continuing relationship to involve those responsible for the future management of that relationship to attend as they will have practical knowledge of what is achievable. This will impact on the negotiations and any settlement agreement. They may also produce novel solutions which others would not spot.

What papers should be sent to the mediator prior to the mediation?

8.5.13 Remember that there is often a limit to the amount of material that the mediator can read because of time constraints imposed by the parties in an effort to save costs. This is a false economy but assuming that there are such constraints the parties should show sympathy to the mediator and avoid inundating him with every document.

Different considerations will apply in each case but here are some rules of thumb for consideration:

Detailed written submissions

8.5.14 As explained above, it is crucially important to the likelihood of success that the parties have spelt out their respective positions very clearly in submissions prior to the mediation meeting. This does not require a thorough explanation of every issue but rather a clear short explanation of the fundamental issues. As well as a statement of facts it is very helpful to include a statement of the legal argument. Also explain the relevance of attached documents or do not bother to attach them.

Pleadings

8.5.15 Where court or arbitration proceedings have been running for some time the parties invariably provide the mediator with a copious bundle of pleadings much of which is intractable. It is important to remember that the mediators do not fulfill the role of a judge. They need to see the contractual documents but not necessarily all the pleadings, which are often unhelpful when it comes to trying to understand what the parties' respective cases are on the core issues.

Witness statements

As with pleadings, witness statements are likely to contain a great deal of information much of which mediators do not need to know or which they can more usefully pick up, and understand the significance of, in a summary of a few paragraphs or possibly extracts. **8.5.16**

Expert evidence

If as invariably happens some of the core issues turn on issues involving expert evidence, even if the mediator is an expert in his own right, it is very helpful to let the mediator see any expert reports that have been exchanged. If it is too early in the proceedings for reports to have been exchanged, each party will greatly help the mediator understand their case if they include in their submission a summary of the expert evidence they will be seeking to adduce. **8.5.17**

Contracts and sub-contracts

In IT contracts the precise wording of many of the provisions will be in issue including lengthy exclusion, termination and warranty clauses. The mediator will need to have copies of all of the contracts and sub-contracts as the interpretation of key clauses is likely to be critical to all of the parties' respective positions. Many of the submissions and arguments will be lost on the mediator if he does not have a good understanding of what is in the contract. **8.5.18**

Tenders, pre-contractual representations and specifications

Depending on the nature of the claims, the specification may be relevant and in the majority of cases one of the parties will refer to it. As with much of the documentation it is likely to be voluminous with only a few passages which are relevant. The mediator will be most appreciative if the relevant passages are extracted in a separate document for ease of reference. **8.5.19**

Documents evidencing the progress of the contract

Unless the dispute is purely legal the volume of documentation involved in IT disputes tends to be immense but much of it is irrelevant to a mediation. Only some of it will be crucial. Identifying the crucial documents takes time but distilling it down to the core documents will pay dividends in saving everybody's time. **8.5.20**

Party and party correspondence since the dispute arose

Correspondence which spells out a party's position on an issue can be helpful, particularly the opening exchange of correspondence in a dispute where proceedings have not yet been issued. However, with respect to all litigators, much of this correspondence is **8.5.21** irrelevant to the mediation. Remember, the mediator does not need to be concerned with, and cannot be expected to know, every nuance of the case. Work out what is really important and only include that.

A chronology

8.5.22 A chronology of events in a simple list is very helpful but do not forget the value of spelling out the history of the dispute in the written submissions. It never ceases to amaze how often the parties expect the mediator to pick this up from reading the papers. Of course, the mediator can do that but it is so much more helpful if the submissions tell a story, with an explanation of the importance of the events as they occur. It will speed the process by ensuring the mediator understands your case and does not waste valuable time in the meeting. It enables the mediator to concentrate on finding a solution instead of trying to understand what has taken place.

Length of the mediation

8.5.23 If the parties want to give the mediation the best chance of reaching a settlement then sufficient time must be allowed to complete the mediation. If any phase is rushed resentment may be felt by a party that time has not been given to considering their case. This can lead to loss of confidence in, and collapse of, the process. On the other hand, if the parties are not given any time constraints there is an increased risk that they will continue stonewalling in the belief that the other party will tire and make concessions.

Assuming an exchange of clear submissions and responses, with an agreed bundle of core documents in advance of the mediation, each of the parties should come fully briefed so, even a complex IT dispute should get through the process in two or three days. Recognising that one of the parties may seek to indulge in stonewalling tactics late into the night, the parties can agree to an earlier cut off with the option of a limited extension if the gap between them is small. These issues should be agreed before the mediation starts and are likely to reduce stonewalling tactics.

The venue

8.5.24 Space, comfort, catering facilities into the early hours and several bottles of chilled champagne, just in case, are all advisable. A desire for a neutral venue is understandable but can add considerable expense and inconvenience to all parties. Access to masses of underlying documentation is useful as, even with well prepared cases, new issues or misunderstandings arise such that either party may wish to find some document which they believe will settle an issue beyond doubt. Accordingly, if disclosure has taken place it makes sense to use one of the offices of one party's solicitors.

The cost of the mediation

Usually the sums involved in IT disputes are so large and the legal representation so expensive that the hire of one of the more experienced, and therefore expensive mediators, is a wholly justifiable and sensible expense. The cost of the mediator should be shared together with the costs associate with the venue. Most disputes involve discussion as to how much the paying party is going to pay towards the winning party's costs and this is of course entirely negotiable. There is no reason why the cost of the mediation should not be included in that negotiation. **8.5.25**

The settlement agreement

It is sensible to give this issue some thought before the mediation itself, even if only to look out and take with you a copy of your standard settlement agreement. Having a precedent to work from after a gruelling session will pay dividends. In a highly complex dispute the settlement agreement is also likely to be highly complex, in which case great care must be taken to make sure it properly reflects the parties' agreement and is enforceable. Involving those who are going to have to implement the agreement in the drafting can help anticipate potential problems. If the parties have agreed a continuing relationship on new terms, those new terms may require a lengthy contract yet to be negotiated in which case signing a Heads of Agreement may be the only alternative to being locked in the mediation for a number of days. Even though expressed to be binding, Heads of Agreement are difficult to rely on. If they do not contain sufficient detail, they will only amount to an unenforceable agreement to agree. **8.5.26**

Recording the terms of settlement in a document signed by both parties before they leave the meeting should be everybody's goal. It may not always be achievable in which case the parties should be told of the risks associated with allowing any period of reflection or cooling off. Essentially, responsibility for recording the terms falls on the parties' solicitors, although the mediator is likely to get involved to the extent that the finer detail is still being worked out and it is the mediator's responsibility to ensure it will not unravel. This process can itself take many hours but do not drop your guard and get casual however late it may be.

Post settlement issues

If the dispute did not settle on the day there remains a good chance that the progress made may yet bring the parties to a settlement. Good mediators follow up the parties to see whether there is **8.5.27** anything else they can offer to help close the gap and frequently this is successful.

If the dispute was settled at the mediation there are usually a number of tasks that have to be performed before the case can be said to be closed. Make certain the clients complete these tasks as soon as possible and do not forget to notify the court that the case has settled.

8.6 TEN KEY POINTS TO REMEMBER

(1) Disputes are endemic in IT projects and they are notoriously expensive to litigate, so mediation is worth an attempt. There is nothing to lose.

(2) Do not be concerned that being the first to suggest mediation is a sign of weakness. Use it as a sign of strength and confidence in your case.

(3) Choose a mediator with the skill set you consider most appropriate for each particular case. In IT disputes an IT expert is not necessarily the best choice of mediator. Co-mediation may be a sensible compromise.

(4) The mediator is not a judge and does not need to burdened with all the pleadings, witness statements and party and party correspondence.

(5) The more complex the history of the IT project the greater the care that should be taken to present it clearly and succinctly.

(6) The huge learning curve involved in getting to grips with the history of a complex IT dispute is made much easier if the submissions tell the mediator a story.

(7) Exchange of clear submissions well in advance of the mediation meeting, including a section detailing any expert evidence relied upon, will provide the parties and the mediator with the best opportunity to settle the dispute.

(8) Educate your client thoroughly as to what to expect including in particular, preparation for a close examination of the weaknesses in your case.

(9) Do not allow the other party to dictate who should or should not attend the mediation meeting.

(10) If at all possible commit any settlement to a signed agreement before the mediation breaks up.

Chapter 9

LANDLORD AND TENANT DISPUTES

JONATHAN ARKUSH

Introduction 9.1

Disputes between landlords and tenants are peculiarly well suited for resolution by ADR. At first sight this seems to be an unlikely proposition, as many envisage that such disputes centre on the landlord's attempts to obtain possession and the tenant's determination to resist it. Thus, the argument runs, there is an 'all or nothing' quality about their disputes which make them resistant to ADR. However, even arguments about possession can be addressed by the ADR process. In fact, as this chapter sets out to demonstrate, landlord and tenant disputes range over a far wider field and ADR has a well-defined role to play in resolving them.

The types of landlord and tenant disputes amenable to ADR 9.2

The following is a summary of the main areas of conflict that are amenable to ADR. It is intended to be illustrative rather than exhaustive.

Breach of covenant by tenant

Allegations that the tenant has breached his covenants under the lease most commonly centre on the tenant's obligations with regard to: 9.2.1

(a) keeping the property in repair;

(b) using the property for the purposes specified in the lease;

(c) the restrictions on parting with or sharing possession.

A landlord's remedies for breach of these obligations comprise forfeiture of the lease and repossession together with or alternatively damages. In turn, the tenant is likely to seek relief from forfeiture, which will give rise to issues about the terms upon which relief should be granted, if it is to be granted at all.

Repairing and decorating covenants

9.2.2 Most leases contain covenants requiring the tenant to keep the exterior and interior of the property in a specified state of repair and decoration. Experience suggests that these obligations are a fertile source of argument and thus work for surveyors and others in preparing schedules of dilapidations and giving expert evidence. The *standard* of repair is often as controversial as the *extent* of the work that the landlord claims is required. In general, a property in Battersea would not have to be put in the same standard of repair as one in Mayfair. The difference of well qualified views as to what constitutes the appropriate standard in any given case may be considerable. The almost invariable need for expert evidence is likely to increase the cost of court proceedings while at the same time makes the outcome hard to predict. The sums at stake are usually sizeable. There is limited scope for the courts to take into account circumstances such as the tenant being financially hard up.

All these facts make ADR into an attractive option for resolving disputes over repairing and decorating covenants, in particular owing to its relative cheapness and flexibility.

User covenants and applications for change of user

9.2.3 Modern leases generally contain provision for the specified user to be varied on application to the landlord, whose consent is not to be unreasonably withheld. The nature of mediation is that it concentrates on the parties' *interests* rather than *rights*. Mediation is thus well suited to reaching a solution that meets the needs of the parties more flexibly than might be possible in court. For example, the parties may agree upon a variation of the user clause being personal to the tenant applicant, or being temporary, or for a limited time.

Restrictions on parting with or sharing possession

9.2.4 Landlords are understandably concerned to control who enters on their property and the purpose of these restrictions is to prevent them being saddled with an occupant of whom they do not approve. A tenant who breaches them has committed a "once and for all" breach that is too late to remedy and thus puts himself at risk of a forfeiture order without relief. However, in a suitable case, mediation may arrive at a flexible solution tailor-made for the parties' essential interests. Elements of this may include, for example, the unwanted newcomer being given permission to remain at the property for a limited time, or on stringent terms such as the payment of additional rent or the provision of security.

Breach of covenant by landlord

The landlord's usual covenants include obligations to keep in repair the structure of the property and to permit the tenant to have quiet enjoyment of the property without disturbance by him or others claiming through him. The tenant's remedies for breach include damages and, in a suitable case, an injunction. Damages can be the subject of mediation in the same way as any other money claim. While a mediator cannot grant an injunction, a settlement reached by mediation can certainly include provision for the parties to consent to an order made by the court in specified terms, including injunctive or other relief. **9.2.5**

Assignments

Modern leases generally impose an absolute bar against assigning part only of the property, but a qualified covenant that the tenant will not assign the property as a whole without the consent of the landlord, *such consent not to be unreasonably withheld*.[1] Disputes over the withholding of consent—usually in regard to terms that the landlord seeks to impose as a condition for granting consent—are commonplace. Statute has again intervened, in the shape of the Landlord and Tenant Act 1988, which imposes duties on the landlord to give consent, except where it is reasonable not to do so, to specify any conditions for giving consent and, where consent is withheld, the reasons. The burden of proof has also been reversed, so that it is for the landlord to show that he gave the consent within a reasonable time, that any condition imposed for giving consent was reasonable and that any refusal of consent was reasonable. **9.2.6**

A prime advantage of mediation over court process in this area is its speed. The parties generally need to know where they stand almost immediately when an assignment is decided upon. Prospective assignees cannot be expected to wait for months while the dispute proceeds by stages through the courts; their assignees likewise have to know whether or not the proposed assignment can safely be agreed upon. A mediation to address these issues can be set up very quickly. If it succeeds in resolving the dispute, the parties can agree the terms in writing (without the need for any court order if no proceedings have begun). If it fails, little time has been lost to the parties in taking the matter to the courts.

[1] Where the italicised words are absent, they will be deemed to apply by virtue of s. 19(1) of the Landlord and Tenant Act 1927. However, in the case of tenancies entered into after January 1, 1996, the parties are free to specify circumstances in which the landlord may refuse consent to an assignment: s. 19(1A), inserted by the Landlord and Tenant (Covenants) Act 1995.

Claims for rent arrears

9.2.7 In a straightforward case the landlord would be best advised to issue court proceedings and apply for summary judgment under CPR 24. If goods of a sufficient value are on the premises, the landlord may be entitled to distrain for them. If the landlord intends to bring the lease to an end, he can claim forfeiture and possession in addition to the arrears. It will then be for the tenant to apply for relief from forfeiture. Such applications are also liable to be decided summarily (in general the tenant will be obliged to pay the arrears and costs of the action as a condition of obtaining relief).[2]

Thus, if there is no realistic defence to the claim for rent arrears, the matter will almost certainly be settled in court and mediation offers no advantages.

In cases where the tenant has a defence with a realistic prospect of success, such as a claim for a set-off arising out of breach of covenant by the landlord, the parties should be encouraged to view mediation as a potential means of resolving their dispute before it escalates further.

Claims against guarantors

9.2.8 Claims for arrears of rent, or damages for breach of covenant, may also lie against any guarantors for the tenant under the lease. In a straightforward case the landlord is likely to prefer court process and seek summary judgment. However, disputes may arise that involve the liability of the tenant and hence the guarantor, or where the efficacy of the guarantee is in issue. If these cannot be resolved by the court without a trial, mediation becomes a useful option for attempting to resolve the issues.

Service charges

9.2.9 Charges made by the landlord for the tenant's proportionate share of expenses such as repairs and insurance are a fertile source of disagreement. Where the lease is of residential property, statute has intervened to impose conditions on the landlord's ability to recover service charges, including a requirement that the charges are reasonable.[3] Commercial leases are not subject to statutory control in this regard. Primarily, the position is governed by the provisions of the lease, which in some (but certainly not all) cases contain protections for the tenant such as a requirement that estimates must be submitted to him for approval before the work is carried out. Where such provisions are absent, there is likely to be implied at common law a basic condition that the service charge

[2] Supreme Court Act 1981, s. 38, County Courts Act 1984, ss. 138, 139.
[3] Landlord and Tenant Act 1985, ss. 18–20.

must be fair and reasonable.[4] However, the costs of insurance are a notable exception, as the courts have shown that they will not imply any requirement of reasonableness.[5] Even where a term as to reasonableness is implied, there is almost invariably room for disagreement whether any particular charge satisfies the requirement.

Disputes over service charges are thus likely to have the following features: (1) uncertainty of outcome, (2) a mass of detailed issues, (3) a requirement for expert evidence, and consequently (4) they will be expensive to resolve. These factors make mediation an attractive option over court process. If the dispute was adjudicated in court, each issue will have to be decided separately. A firm answer will be obtained, but at the price of considerable court time and thus expense to the parties. In mediation the parties will be encouraged to adopt a give and take approach directed to arriving at a settlement much more quickly and cheaply.

Rent review

Modern leases of commercial property invariably contain rent review clauses that are designed to ensure that the rent keeps pace with market rental values. Most involve fairly elaborate machinery for the process and method of ascertaining the reviewed rent. Disputes involving the machinery are probably more common than differences over what the reviewed rent should be! Disputes over process generally involve questions of principle such as whether an effective notice was served to trigger the review, or whether the time limits in the timetable are of the essence. The answer is usually "all or nothing", *i.e.* it favours either one side or the other. Given that the sums at stake can be very large, there is no obvious route to compromise these issues. By contrast, if there are differences as to what the reviewed rent should be, the issue will be left to experts, between whom there is generally a large measure of agreement. **9.2.10**

If the parties or their experts cannot agree, most leases provide for the appointment of a third party to determine the rent. The most common provision by far is that the appointment is to be made by the President of the Royal Institution of Chartered Surveyors. The lease will normally specify whether the appointee will act as an expert or as an arbitrator. In the vast majority of cases his decision either cannot or will not be challenged further.

Is there a role for mediation in rent review disputes? The speed, inexpensive and flexible approach which mediation brings to the problem may be usefully tried even in an area such as this. If the issue involves a straightforward question of valuing the market rent,

[4] *Finchbourne v. Rodrigues* [1976] 3 All E.R. 581, *Morgan v. Stainer* [1993] 2 E.G.L.R. 73.

[5] *Bandar Property Holdings v. Darwen* [1968] 2 All E.R. 305, *Havenridge v. Boston Dyers* [1994] 2 E.G.L.R. 73.

the parties are likely to be best advised by following the procedure in the lease for determination by a third party, particularly where he is to act as an expert and the process is uncomplicated. However, where there are wider issues affecting the landlord-tenant relationship, sending them for mediation as a "package" may well advance the interests of the parties more comprehensively.

Renewal of a business tenancy under the Landlord and Tenant Act 1954

9.2.11 The Landlord and Tenant Act 1954 (the 1954 Act) confers security of tenure on business tenants, subject to the landlord's ability to oppose the grant of a new lease on limited grounds. Such grounds most commonly include the tenant's failure to comply with repairing covenants,[6] the tenant's poor record in paying rent or complying with its other covenants under the lease,[7] the landlord's intention to demolish, reconstruct or carry out substantial works to the premises[8] and the landlord's intention to occupy the premises himself for business or residential use.[9]

In most cases the lease is renewed on terms settled by negotiation between the parties or their professional advisers. This may, and indeed should, involve an exchange between landlord and tenant of mutual, and sometimes contradictory, interests. A degree of flexibility and give and take is usually required to achieve a meeting of their minds on the terms of the renewed business tenancy. Mediation is very well-suited to bringing this to fruition. It is speedier, more informal and less expensive than the alternatives of court procedure or protracted correspondence between professional advisers.

Even where the renewal of the tenancy is opposed by the landlord, the picture may well be more complicated than at first appears. Where the ground of opposition is based on the tenant's past poor record of compliance with repairing obligations, an agreement on his part to carry out specified works, perhaps coupled with a deposit of a cash sum as security for the future, may meet the landlord's concerns. His interests may be better served by keeping the tenant he knows than starting again with an unknown quantity, particularly where the letting market is poor and the landlord is not confident about finding another suitable tenant. Where the landlord opposes on the ground of his intention to redevelop the premises or occupy them himself, the landlord's plans, or his ability to finance them, may be less certain than he cares to disclose. Equally the tenant may be chary of taking on the leasehold

[6] Landlord and Tenant Act 1954, s. 30(1)(a).
[7] *ibid.*, s. 30(1)(b).
[8] *ibid.*, s. 30(1)(f).
[9] *ibid.*, s. 30(1)(g).

obligation for too long in the future, particularly if business is bad or retirement has drawn closer. In these situations, which are commonly encountered in practice, the grant of a further tenancy for a limited period, and excluding it from the protection of the 1954 Act, may offer a far better solution to the parties. The court could not grant it without the agreement of the parties, but mediation could deliver that agreement.

Disputed rights under the lease

It is not uncommon that landlord and tenant fall into dispute over such matters as access to the premises, use of shared facilities in the common parts or other rights enjoyed under the terms of the lease. One party's unconsidered view of his own convenience, or ill-thought out flexing of negotiating power, may lie behind the dispute rather than questions of money. The introduction of a mediator in a calm informal setting is ideally suited to helping the parties to a better understanding of the other's position and to resolve their differences. Mediation is speedy and relatively inexpensive. By contrast, court proceedings involve costs and risks that may well be disproportionate to what is at stake. Worse still, the issue of proceedings may serve only to escalate the dispute and extend it out of tactical or retaliatory motives into other matters that were not contentious before. 9.2.12

Rights and obligations at the end of the tenancy

Leases of commercial property almost invariably provide that the tenant is to put the property into a specified state and condition at the end of the term. Disputes over the extent of the work required to comply with the covenant are frequent. Many a landlord's surveyor has been kept gainfully employed in producing lengthy terminal schedules of dilapidations. The tenant employs his own surveyor to respond in kind and the stage is set for a lengthy and doubtless expensive contest of wills. 9.2.13

The irony is that some of the expense at least may be quite unnecessary and even inappropriate. This is for the simple but far from well-appreciated reason that statute has capped the landlord's damages for breach of the tenant's covenant. The landlord cannot recover more than the amount (if any) by which the value of the reversion is diminished owing to the breach of covenant.[10] While the cost of putting the premises into the state of repair that they should have been left in by the tenant provides a *prima facie* indication of the extent of the damage to the landlord's reversion, this is by no means always the case. If, for example, the scarcity of property is such that there is an incoming tenant who for his own

10 Landlord and Tenant Act 1927, s. 18(1).

purposes intends to strip out the premises whatever their condition, paying the landlord the same sum by way of rent or premium as he would if the premises had been in full repair, there has been no diminution in the value of the landlord's reversion and the landlord has not suffered any damage.[11]

Another issue that can arise relates to fixtures. Where a tenant fixes goods to the property is he entitled, or bound, to remove them at the end of the term? The general rule is that the tenant is entitled (but is not bound) to remove his fixtures at the end of the term where this does not cause substantial damage to the property. Depending on the circumstances it may, or may not, suit the tenant's interests to remove them. Conversely, it may, or may not, lie in the landlord's interests to have them removed, irrespective of the legal position. To take as a simple example, if the property was a warehouse and the tenant has installed a goods lift that could not be removed without causing damage, the tenant would not be entitled to remove it, although he may have a use for it in another property. However, the landlord may have no wish to be left with the goods lift, and indeed may be intending to strip it out and throw it away. If suitable terms can be arrived at for the tenant to remove the lift and pay for making good, landlord and tenant have an identity of interest.

An early appreciation of factors such as these may save considerable time and money. At the end of the tenancy few landlords and tenants have any wish to prolong their relationship through lengthy correspondence and court proceedings. It would be to their mutual advantage to identify the issues *before* the lease comes to an end and attempt to accommodate their respective interests. This can be achieved through mediation without the parties incurring inordinate expense in drawing battle lines that may not become needed.

Landlord and tenant disputes generally

9.2.14 Behind these disputes is the reality that the landlord and tenant are tied by the lease into a relationship that may be long-term and that offers mutual benefits to each other. It is clearly in both their interests that the relationship is conducted constructively.

This is an area where the mediation process, which focuses on *interests* rather than *rights*, has a built-in advantage over litigation. The immediate subject matter of the landlord/tenant dispute often masks their medium to long-term plans which form the basis of the real issue between the parties. For example, the landlord may have plans for the redevelopment of the lease property that are not expected to ripen for several years, or for some indeterminate period that depends on the state of the market. Conversely, it may

[11] *Mather v. Barclays Bank* [1987] 2 E.G.L.R. 254.

be the tenant whose future plans dictate his desire to look for the means to end the lease commitment. Both could exist together—but neither is aware of it.

When the dispute eventually surfaces, mediation can achieve mutually beneficial results. The process should give the mediator an understanding of what each party is seeking to achieve. Having gained that understanding from the parties, separately and confidentially, the mediator is in a position to propose imaginative solutions. In the case postulated above, that might comprise an agreement by the parties to vary the lease by introducing a break clause that could be triggered at the option of either or both of them to take effect when it suits their respective plans.

THE ROLE OF COURTS AND TRIBUNALS 9.3

Commercial property disputes involve the jurisdiction of the courts rather than tribunals. The allocation of cases between the High Court and county court is dealt with by the Civil Procedure Rules. Their jurisdiction overlaps considerably. However:

(a) proceedings for a monetary claim may not be started in the High Court unless the value of the claim is more than £15,000;[12]

(b) possession claims must be started in the county court for the district where the property is situated,[13] subject to a right to start a claim in the High Court if there are "exceptional circumstances";[14]

(c) claims for a new tenancy under the Landlord and Tenant Act 1954 must normally be started in the county court for the district where the property is situated;[15]

[12] CPR 7PD para. 2.1.

[13] CPR 55.3(1)—a new provision dealing with possession proceedings that came into force on October 15, 2001.

[14] CPR PD55 para. 2.1, which lists the following as circumstances "which may, in an appropriate case, justify starting a claim in the High Court": (1) where there are complicated disputes of fact, (2) there are points of law of general importance, (3) the claim is against trespassers and there is a substantial risk of public disturbance or of serious harm to persons or property which properly require immediate determination. Para 1.4 adds that the value of the property and the amount of any financial claim may be relevant circumstances, but these factors alone will not normally justify starting the claim in the High Court.

[15] CPR 56—this is a new provision for specified landlord and tenant claims and miscellaneous provisions about land. It came into force on October 15, 2001. It provides that such claims can only be started in the High Court in exceptional circumstances. These are defined in the same terms as those in CPR 55 referred to in footnote 14, with the exception of (3).

(d) subject to any enactment, a claim should be started in the High Court if the claimant believes that the claim ought to be dealt with by a High Court judge by reason of its financial value, and/or the complexity of the facts, legal issues, remedies or procedures, and/or the importance of the outcome of the claim to the public in general.[16]

The parties can embark on mediation even before any proceedings are commenced. This may have the advantage of saving the considerable expense of fully preparing the claim to the extent needed for a contest in court. However, it may have the result that mediation fails if neither the mediator nor the parties have enough information to understand the extent of the respective claims or to assess their strengths or weaknesses. Provided there is sufficient information for this purpose, parties should not be discouraged to make an early attempt to mediate.

Mediation during the course of proceedings is provided for under the rules in a number of ways:

(a) The overriding objective of the CPR is that of enabling the court to deal with cases justly. This is defined as including saving expense, dealing with cases in ways which are proportionate to the amount of money involved, ensuring that the case is dealt with expeditiously and allotting to it an appropriate share of the court's resources.[17]

(b) The court *must* further the overriding objective by actively managing cases. Active case management includes "encouraging the parties to use an alternative dispute resolution procedure if the court considers that appropriate and facilitating the use of such procedure".[18]

(c) Alternative dispute resolution merits a definition in the Glossary to the CPR as "Collective description of methods of resolving disputes otherwise than through the normal trial process".[19]

(d) The court is given a firm steer to encourage and facilitate ADR by provisions built into the rules.[20] CPR 26.4 provides that a party may, when filing the allocation questionnaire, make a written request for the proceedings to be stayed while the parties try to settle the case by ADR or other means. This can be done by simply ticking the box con-

16 CPR PD7, para. 2.4.
17 CPR 1.1.
18 CPR 1.4.
19 CPR Section G.
20 See the illuminating discussion in CPR note 1.4.11.

tained in Part A of the allocation questionnaire (Form N150).

(e) The court may "of its own initiative" direct a stay of the proceedings for the purpose of the parties attempting settlement.[21]

(f) PD26 provides for the procedure to be followed when proceedings are stayed for the purposes of attempting settlement.

(g) Standard orders for case management directions in multi-track cases likewise make provision for a stay of the claim to a specified date "while the parties try to settle it by mediation or other means" (Form PF52).

(h) The Queen's Bench, Chancery and Commercial Court Guides each make specific reference to explain their positive approach towards ADR.[22]

(i) The Commercial Court Guide makes additional reference to the use of "early neutral evaluation" facilities available in that court.[23]

(j) Proceedings under appeal may also be stayed for mediation or other forms of ADR.[24] The Court of Appeal has an ADR Scheme under which the services of mediators are provided free of charge.[25]

If mediation or another form of ADR is attempted in the course of proceedings and succeeds in settling the issues, the settlement agreement can make provision for any order to be made by consent. In some cases an order of the court will be required[26]. In others, it may be sufficient simply to have the proceedings disposed of by consent on the terms stated as to costs or otherwise, such as by discontinuance under CPR 38.

THE ROLE OF ADR GENERALLY AND THE ADVANTAGES OF MEDIATION OVER OTHER FORMS OF ADR 9.4

In landlord and tenant disputes mediation and arbitration will be the principal methods of ADR. Arbitration is akin to litigation in that it is

21 CPR 26.4(2)(b).
22 See Queen's Bench Guide at para. 6.7, Chancery Guide at para. 17 and Commercial Court Guide at Section G.
23 See at Section G, para. G2.
24 CPR 52.10(1) provides that in relation to an appeal the appeal court has all the powers of the lower court.
25 See Court of Appeal Form 56A.
26 For example, an order excluding a lease from the protection of the Landlord and Tenant Act 1954 can only be made by the court.

essentially a formal and adversarial process (albeit at times less formal than proceedings in court). The preparation of a case for arbitration will require the same degree of detail and completeness as it would for the court. Thus arbitration is unlikely to produce any savings of cost as compared with litigation. The arbitrator is required to decide the issues put before him in making the award. As with litigation, the result of arbitration must always be that there is a winner and a loser on any given issue. Thus arbitration, like the courts, is concerned with the parties' *rights*.

By contrast, mediation is essentially informal and non-adversarial. It is much speedier and therefore cheaper than arbitration. It is more flexible as it focuses on parties' *interests* rather than their strict legal rights.

These advantages mean that in any contest between mediation and arbitration as the preferred method of ADR, mediation ought to win hands down!

Another approach is provided by *Early Neutral Evaluation* (ENE). Still in its infancy, ENE is a without prejudice, non-binding summary evaluation of a dispute or particular issues in it, undertaken by an independent person chosen by the parties. In the Commercial Court, provision is made for ENE by a Commercial Judge, if the parties are willing to agree.[27] The attractions of ENE are that it provides a speedy advisery opinion by an expert. This may be particularly helpful where the dispute, or a particular issue within it, raises a discrete point or points of law, and the parties are willing to be influenced by an early view given by an independent source whom they presumably consider to be reliable. However, where the dispute is more complicated, and particularly where there are issues of fact, ENE is unlikely to be productive in helping the parties to resolve their differences.

9.5 THE ROLE OF NEGOTIATIONS

Straightforward negotiations are a staple part of a good litigator's armoury. Many disputes are doubtless settled by deploying a flexible and imaginative approach at any stage. The difficulty lies in eliciting that approach without giving the appearance of being overly eager to settle.

ADR may be additional or alternative to negotiations. Where negotiations have failed, or neither party is willing to embark on them, it does not imply any weakness to suggest making an attempt to resolve the dispute by mediation. Most litigators are now reasonably familiar with the concept, even if they have not tried it

[27] See the Commercial Court Guide, para G2. If ENE is provided by a judge, that judge will take no further part in the case unless the parties otherwise agree.

in practice. The prospect of obtaining a sensible outcome for both sides without the costs and risks of litigation form a compelling incentive to make the attempt.

THE ROLE OF MEDIATION 9.6

Handling the client

Clients are generally receptive to the prospect of obtaining the gain of settlement without the pain of risk and cost. Where the case looks strong and the client is well able to afford to run it, mediation will be as unattractive to the legal adviser as it will to his client. Most cases are not that simple, and the benefits of mediation are more apparent. When the client has understood the process, and in particular that mediation is without prejudice, consensual and relatively inexpensive, consent to give it a try will usually be readily given. 9.6.1

Prior to issuing proceedings or after they are issued?

Proceedings define and crystallise the real issues and therefore concentrate the minds of the parties and their advisers on the essentials. They also place the dispute on the procedural path to trial, and under the Civil Procedure Rules the time lag between issue and trial has been substantially reduced. The process of negotiation undoubtedly improves against the background of procedural progress. The cost of beginning a claim and preparing a statement of case is relatively small. These factors militate towards issuing the claim before embarking on mediation. 9.6.2

If mediation is started before proceedings, there is a risk that the issues have not yet been fully defined. If the issues have not fully emerged it must follow that they cannot be settled. This raises the risk that mediation, even if successful, may fail to deal with the whole dispute. If, by contrast, the dispute has been defined by proceedings, a successful mediation is likely to include a term that all the issues in the respective claims and counterclaims (or even all issues now and in the future) have been settled, thereby preventing any party from raising them again in the future.

It is therefore preferable to initiate the claim and await service of the defence before embarking on mediation.

The approach to the other parties

An invitation to mediate is a neutral step that is designed to encourage all parties to adopt their own solution to their differences. It obviates the need to have recourse to the vagaries and expense of litigation. An approach that is formulated to emphasise these characteristics can therefore be made without implying any weakness or lack of confidence. 9.6.3

A good strategy for either claimant or defendant may therefore be to suggest that proceedings are issued (thereby underlining that your side has no fear of them), statements of case are exchanged, followed by a mediation.

The type of mediator

9.6.4 As with any other specialised area of law, it is advantageous, if not strictly necessary, for the mediator to be familiar with the legal background. An informed mediator is more likely to get straight to the heart of the issues. He will know the difficult questions to pose to the parties and how to concentrate their minds on the potential weaknesses of their case. These are vital in encouraging parties to move away from their entrenched positions.

In landlord and tenant disputes a barrister or solicitor with specialist knowledge and experience in this area is likely to be best qualified to act as mediator.

Who should attend the mediation

9.6.5 If the parties or any of them are individuals, and they are on speaking terms, it is recommended that they attend the mediation in person. Even if they are not speaking, they should attend, as it is not necessary for them to meet face to face. A mediation can be successfully conducted without the parties ever meeting, while the mediator shuttles between them until there is a meeting of minds, if not persons.

If the parties do not attend, their representatives should ensure that they have clear authority to enter into any settlement that results from the mediation, or perhaps any terms within stated parameters. If the representatives lack authority, there is a risk of the settlement unravelling if one or other of the parties refuses to ratify or implement its terms.

While any party who does not attend could be contactable by telephone in the course of the mediation, this is a poor substitute for being physically present to watch and hear the mediation process. At the very least the absence of a party is likely to lengthen the time it takes, with a consequent increase in costs.

What to give the mediator

9.6.6 In landlord and tenant disputes the mediator should be provided with (at least):

(a) the lease or tenancy agreement;

(b) any other relevant documents, such as deeds of variation, schedules of dilapidations, correspondence, etc.;

(c) the reports of experts;

(d) the statements of case in any proceedings.

Length of the mediation

One working day is usually enough! If the process becomes protracted much beyond that, it may be a sign that the parties are too far apart, or that they are tiring of the process. Obviously every case is different, and if there are numerous issues it may be necessary or desirable to hold the mediation over more than one day. If so, consecutive days are preferable, so that everyone involved (including the mediator) has the issues fresh in their mind without having to read back into the case. 9.6.7

The venue

There are no hard and fast rules in landlord and tenant disputes. In general, mediations are best held on neutral territory. However, if the premises that form the subject matter of the dispute have the necessary space and facilities, they may make a good venue, particularly if a site inspection would assist with an understanding of the case. 9.6.8

The settlement agreement

In a settlement of landlord and tenant disputes it may be necessary for the parties to enter into a deed or other document that varies the lease. If so, the terms of the variation should be annexed to the settlement agreement to obviate any doubts about the drafting later. 9.6.9

It may also be necessary for the parties to obtain an order of the court to give effect to the settlement, for example as to the terms of a new tenancy to be granted under the Landlord and Tenant Act 1954. If so, the agreement should commit the parties to indorse their consent to an order of the court in terms which should be annexed.

CHAPTER 10

PARTNERSHIP AND PROFESSIONAL PRACTICE DISPUTES

PETER GARRY

10.1 INTRODUCTION

The scope of businesses dealt with in this chapter

10.1.1 The classification "partnerships and professional practices" covers a multitude of business activities, across the various trading entity types.

Partnerships occur in almost every industry or profession, although partnership disputes over sums of a sufficient size to make involving lawyers or mediators worthwhile tend to arise for the most part in the professions (in the broadest sense), property, farming and the entertainment and leisure industries.

The essential elements which give rise to and fuel partnership disputes, and which are critical in seeking to resolve those disputes, also spill over into other forms of business entity used as the vehicle for professional activities, in particular limited companies, and latterly foreign (especially U.S.) limited liability partnerships with an established trading presence in this country.

Following the bringing into force on April 6, 2001 of the Limited Liability Partnerships Act 2000, we are more than likely going to see the establishment of a large number of U.K. limited liability partnerships ("LLPs"), either start-ups or (probably later) partnerships and other established professional practices which transfer their existing business into LLPs.

This new entity has, like all trading entities, a number of its own distinct features which may be breeding grounds for disputes and which will require special treatment from mediators and other dispute resolvers. It remains to be seen how many LLPs will be incorporated without an LLP agreement (the equivalent of a partnership deed or articles of association), thus relying on the very sparse, indeed deficient, default rules.

LLPs and their members are free to design their own bespoke governance structure, and as such we may see hybrid, and often homespun, entities, with little or no statutory or common law safety net. The perils will be aggravated by there being no requirement for an LLP agreement to be in writing, and further aggravated by the statutory recognition of implied terms in LLP agreements. These elements, supplemented by the incorporation of the companies unfair prejudice legislation into LLP law, are likely to lead to a decade or so of common law interpretations of the statutory code, unless of course the disputes which arise are resolved by alternative means before the judiciary is given the opportunity to rule on them. As with any situation where new law is being made, mediators may well be able to tap into the uncertainties so created in their efforts to achieve settlements.

The common thread

Despite the diversity of business activities and trading entities described above, there are nonetheless a number of common threads. What defines or distinguishes most if not all of the businesses to which this chapter relates is the importance of the skills, knowledge and reputation of the individuals who make up or run the entity, and the fact that the proprietors/shareholders are also the managers who carry out the day to day business of the entity. Another common factor is (usually) the close personal relationship and implicit trust between the proprietors, and between the proprietors and their clients or customers. There is also in professional businesses an overlay of regulation by and standards imposed by a professional body, the breach of which often constitutes grounds for expulsion of a proprietor from the business. **10.1.2**

A dispute within such entities cannot easily be side-lined or determined as it might be in a mega-corporation or medium-sized business, with the individuals concerned resigning or being dismissed and being escorted off the premises, whilst the faceless (but much trusted and respected) entity carries on with replacement managers or executives, with the perception of the outside world unaffected. Rather, in partnership and professional practice disputes the very constituent elements (the proprietor/managers) of the business entity themselves are in dispute with one another, destabilizing the business as a whole from within. In some cases, all of the proprietor/managers and in due course many of the staff fall under a malaise of uncertainty, jealousy and mistrust, turnover plummets, and the reputation and goodwill of the business are affected, particularly when disaffected or disheartened individuals start looking for alternative employment, or share their woes and opinions with colleagues and acquaintances both inside and outside the business.

Common contributing factors to such a malady are diminishing profits, top-heavy proprietor/management structure, the dominance of a group or an individual reluctant to share power and rewards, proprietors split down the middle by divergent interests, ambitions or agendas (often unspoken), or imbalance or perceived imbalance between individual contributions to the business, by way of turnover, reputation or management.

10.1.3 Rather than being neatly excised, such situations often fester and become exacerbated, which can result over a period of time in a series of expulsions, retirements (or worse—in the absence of a right to expel, refusals to retire), and in some cases dissolution or purported dissolution, or (in a corporation, and in due course in LLPs) an application for an order winding up the business or for one party or group to buy out the other (usually citing unfair prejudice in the form of exclusion from management, deadlock or other irreconcilable difficulty).

By the time a mediator is brought in, the business may have a serious financial problem, so that there may be uncertainty as to whether the business is viable, there may be uncertainty as to whether the practice has dissolved or will be wound up, and there may be any number of (often overlapping) groups of proprietors with competing (though not always declared) interests. Some proprietors or groups of proprietors may have made or be in the course of making arrangements to leave the business and take their clients or customers elsewhere.

Of course not all disputes in this category are so complex nor have such a cataclysmic background, but the same principles apply when seeking to resolve all such disputes, large or small.

10.2 TYPES OF DISPUTES

Partnership and professional practice disputes fall broadly into five categories. Many disputes fall into two or more of these categories.

Retirement

10.2.1 Very often there will be an agreement providing for retirement (voluntary or involuntary) in given circumstances, including reaching a defined retirement age and death. Normally such retirement will be on terms that the individual (or his estate) will take out of the partnership his fixed capital plus undrawn profits, or sell his shares to the other proprietors in accordance with a set formula. In partnerships, limited companies and LLPs there are no default provisions whatsoever as to what happens on retirement, so that in the absence of an agreement from the outset between the proprietors, when a proprietor leaves or dies the business may be wound up.

In cases where there is an agreement, disputes often arise as to the meaning of the agreement or how it is to be implemented. Most agreements require an account to be drawn up, normally on the same basis as the last account or accounts. Notwithstanding this, issues often arise as to how assets should be valued, and commonly continuing proprietors seek to introduce provisions into the account, for example in respect of over-rented leases, bad debts or ongoing claims against the business, thus purporting to reduce the profit for the outgoing proprietor's final year (and sometimes in the hope of reversing the provision in a later year to their but not the outgoing proprietor's benefit).

In the case of limited companies it is common to provide that the auditor will determine the value of the outgoing proprietor's interest, usually in the capacity of an expert, which as a matter of law makes the determination difficult to challenge. Nonetheless dissatisfied proprietors, outgoing or continuing, sometimes seek to undermine these decisions by pursuing litigation, if only to establish a negotiating position. Some corporate professional practices may adopt the partnership model as the basis for determining what sums a retiring proprietor can take out of the business.

As well as indemnifying the outgoing proprietor, continuing proprietors are often required to use reasonable or best endeavours to obtain the outgoing proprietor's release from direct obligations and covenants to bankers, landlords and other long-term creditors. Continuing proprietors are often reluctant to do this, particularly if a bank or landlord requires additional security as a pre-condition to releasing the outgoing proprietor. This very often happens in cases where the business is in financial difficulties. In such cases the outgoing proprietor may have a negative capital account; in other words he (and possibly the other proprietors) may have overdrawn against low profits, and indeed there might have been one or more loss-making years. The outgoing partner may be reluctant to repay his deficit until he has been released from direct liabilities to bank and landlord, contending that the continuing proprietors have not used sufficient endeavours and are thus in default of their obligations to the outgoing proprietor.

Expulsion

The expulsion (sometimes known as involuntary retirement) of one or more proprietors, often gives rise to a great deal of anger and resentment which fuel the ensuing dispute. 10.2.2

There is no automatic right of expulsion in any of the (U.K.) trading entities dealt with in this chapter, so purported expulsions in the absence of express provisions give rise to disputes as to whether the entity has been dissolved or should be wound up.

In cases of expulsion (pursuant to an express power) for cause, usually some form of undesirable conduct, there will be issues as to fact (did the expelled proprietor do what he is accused of doing?) and degree (was the conduct sufficiently "grave" or "persistent" or did it otherwise fall within the wording of the relevant agreement?).

Where there is a power for a majority to expel, without cause, one or more proprietors who are in the minority, issues arise (in a partnership) as to whether the power has been exercised in good faith and pursuant to the requirements of natural justice and/or the terms of the governing agreement, or (in a limited company, and no doubt in due course in respect of LLPs) whether the expelled shareholder/director or member had a legitimate expectation or the benefit of an implied (or indeed express) agreement to the effect that he would be entitled to continue to participate in the business.

Such considerations give rise to issues as to whether the partnership, shareholders' or, in LLPs, members' agreement has been repudiated or breached by those seeking to expel another, and consequently as to whether damages should be paid, a partnership dissolved, or a company or LLP wound up, and whether non-competition and other covenants can still be enforced.

In partnership expulsion cases there is often an issue as to whether the expelled partner in fact dissolved the firm before he was expelled, or as to whether the purported expulsion was inappropriate and thus itself repudiatory and leading to dissolution. This is particularly the case since a partner's entitlement in dissolution to a share of the assets of the firm is usually greater than it would be following expulsion.

Fraud, bad faith and misrepresentation

10.2.3 No consideration of expulsion is complete without special attention being given to fraud and bad faith (or breach of duty owed to a company or an LLP). It is also convenient to consider misrepresentation under this heading.

Against the background of the relationship of trust between proprietors of professional practices (although note that outside of express agreement the duties and relationships are subtly different in partnerships, companies and LLPs), and the absence in so many professional practices (particularly smaller ones, though larger businesses are not exempt) of adequate financial controls, fraud is easily perpetrated by proprietors who have lost the moral rectitude which their fellows take as read.

Common frauds include fiddling expenses (including surreptitiously passing off personal expenses as partnership expenses), receiving secret remuneration from clients or customers of the business (which would otherwise be billed through the business), receiving pay-offs from a client's opponent in return for unduly influencing the client, taking secret commissions from third parties in relation to a client's transactions, unauthorised drawing on client account (usually in the form of one large payment prior to fleeing abroad, but sometimes taking the form of long-term misappropriation of client monies which the client believes to be safely deposited at home or abroad for tax or investment reasons).

Examples of bad faith (or breach of duty to company or LLP) not always amounting to fraud as such include plotting with staff to decamp with clients to another firm, covering up negligent work rather than reporting it, and concealing minor misdemeanours. In some instances whereas the negligence or minor misdemeanors would not in themselves attract the sanction of expulsion, the concealment does.

Partnership agreements sometimes distinguish between fraud and bad faith, and there is often a fine line between fraud, bad faith, errors of judgement and non-culpable self-denial. Culpable conduct, when discovered or merely suspected, often leads to immediate expulsion, often before the full facts or extent are known, and issues then arise as to fact, construction, the bona fides of the accused and the accusers, and the quantum of damage, as well as accounting issues, since an expelled proprietor is nonetheless normally entitled to receive his capital and undrawn profit (subject to set-off for the loss caused by any default).

Conversely, sometimes there is a forfeiture clause (whereby in the **10.2.4** event of expulsion under certain heads of conduct the capital contribution and undrawn profit of the expelled proprietor become the property of the continuing proprietors), leading to even more bitter conflict.

In addition the professional reputation and ability of the accused to earn a living is often at stake, so the odds are even higher.

In the absence of an express power to expel, the immediate remedy for fraud is to dissolve the firm, appoint a receiver, and seek an account and damages. Issues then arise as to the entitlement (or lack of entitlement) of the accused and accusing partners respectively to continue to use and benefit from the assets and goodwill of the dissolved firm pending a resolution of the dispute and completion of the winding up.

Fraud, bad faith and misrepresentation sometimes also occur at the point of entry of an individual into a professional practice, and may be committed by the main body against the individual. Certain fundamental matters may (deliberately or otherwise) be misrepresented to or concealed from an incoming proprietor, such as the true value of certain assets, the true extent of certain liabilities (contingent or otherwise), the prospects for future fee levels, the intention of key proprietors to leave the business, and generally matters touching on the future prospects for the business.

In partnerships it is part of the duty of good faith to reveal such matters to an incoming partner. In corporations there may be written or oral representations which will often be translated into or supplemented by warranties.

Discovery of breach of the various duties of existing proprietors which may arise when a new proprietor joins a practice or business is often the catalyst for a proprietor exiting from a business and making a claim for damages, or is raised as a defence when an exiting proprietor is sued for breach of his own duties which he may, at least ostensibly, have committed (see in particular "Non-competition covenants, goodwill agreements, lock-ins and garden leave" below).

Dissolution and winding-up

10.2.5 Dissolution of a partnership can occur either pursuant to the partnership agreement, by way of dissolution by order of the court, or (more commonly) by operation of statute where the agreement makes no provision for retirement or continuance of the firm in the event of a partner leaving or dying, so that the partnership is a partnership at will terminable on notice given by one partner to the other(s).

The first issue in many dissolution disputes is whether the partnership has been dissolved at all. There may be issues as to what actually happened, whether the conduct complained of was repudiatory, whether the repudiation was accepted or alternatively the partnership agreement reaffirmed, whether there was an agreement providing for continuity of the firm in the event of retirement or expulsion and if so what its terms were, whether there was an agreement to retire, or whether a dissolution notice was given in good faith (since a dissolution notice given in bad faith may be ineffective).

Once dissolution has been established then there are often issues as to how the accounts ought to be drawn up, in particular whether adjustments ought to be made to reflect and/or compensate for conduct of a certain partner or partners.

There may also be issues as to conduct following the dissolution date, such as unauthorised appropriation of assets (particularly work in progress) or goodwill, failure to account properly or at all for post-cessation receipts, all manner of breaches of the continuing duty of good faith, and failure to contribute and/or to repay an overdrawn current/capital account.

Most of these areas of dispute in connection with partnerships translate over into corporate practices (or will translate over into LLPs). Thus one sees repudiatory breaches of shareholder agreements, applications to wind up companies under the "just and equitable" jurisdiction, and (post-liquidation order or resolution) misappropriation and misfeasance committed by current or former directors.

Non-competition covenants, goodwill agreements, lock-ins and garden leave

10.2.6 Partnerships and professional practices, being potentially such volatile entities, are often held together, particularly in difficult times, by disincentives to defection, for example common liabilities which fall to be paid by all proprietors, whether or not they remain in the practice, and whether or not the professional practice agreement is repudiated or the practice dissolves (for example, leases).

Other disincentives which are increasingly built into modern profession practice agreements are non-competition covenants and lock-ins.

It is a fact of life that professional practices (or indeed other businesses) will not normally recruit further proprietors (or sometimes indeed senior staff), unless they "bring something to the party" in the form of a following of clients, customers or contacts who will provide them and perhaps others in the business with work and thus enable them to generate turnover for the business which the business would not otherwise enjoy.

If proprietors (and others) can be prevented through non-competition clauses from taking clients with them when they leave a practice, then that may well have the effect of preventing or at least inhibiting them from leaving at all. Whilst often there will be a professional restriction prohibiting (and indeed a reluctance of the courts to effect) separation of a client from his professional adviser of choice, so that flaunting non-acting and non-solicitation covenants may bring short-term gains, the remedy of damages is always available to a professional practice when one of its proprietors leaves taking away clients in breach of covenant. The risk of being sued for damages is often a major consideration for departing proprietors.

There is also an increasing tendency to enter into agreements 10.2.7
whereby proprietors agree that in the event of their leaving they *may* take clients with them, but have to pay for the goodwill associated with those clients in accordance with a formula, for example 125 per cent of average billing to that client per annum over the previous two years.

Professional practices are also increasingly imposing lock-ins, so that proprietors cannot leave during a stated period, sometimes as much as five years, or only one or a limited number of proprietors can leave each year. Long notice periods are also common, six months terminating at a financial year end being more or less the norm in more regulated practices, and one year sometimes being asked for and agreed.

It is also common to require proprietors to take garden leave when they give notice, so that during the notice period they can be separated from their clients and contacts.

Not surprisingly, when proprietors make up their minds to leave a practice they try to find ways to escape from these restrictions, employing (consciously or sub-consciously) a variety of different strategies. These range from becoming an unpleasant person (in the hope of being asked to leave and being able to negotiate an exit on terms involving release of covenants) to finding or engineering grounds on which they can claim that the practice is dissolved or (if a corporation) should be wound up (or an order should be made requiring the other proprietors to purchase his shares), or that a partnership or shareholders' agreement has been repudiated, or was induced by misrepresentation and should be set aside, so releasing covenants and other obligations.

Issues also often arise as to whether the covenant is too wide and thus unreasonable and unenforceable (although covenants as between partners are more commonly enforced than covenants given by employees and salaried partners). Construction issues also arise, as well as issues of fact surrounding the alleged breach of the covenant, especially if it is a non-solicitation as opposed to a not to act for/do business with covenant.

10.3 THE ROLE OF THE COURT AND TRIBUNALS

Partnership disputes

10.3.1 The court derives its jurisdiction in partnership disputes not only through its general common law and equitable jurisdiction but also by virtue of specific jurisdiction under the Partnership Act 1890 (in particular to order dissolution in certain defined circumstances, including that it is "just and equitable" to do so).

The court also has power to appoint a receiver to get in and realise the assets of the partnership, or in some cases to carry on the business of the partnership (often to enable the goodwill of the practice to be preserved whilst issues are resolved which may enable one or more partners to succeed to the goodwill and carry on the practice in due course). Typically, receivers are appointed in cases of fraud or where partners cannot work together to manage the affairs of an otherwise viable practice, or to protect assets of a firm in dissolution. Injunctions are also commonly used to curb unlawful conduct.

Many partnership agreements include an arbitration clause.[1] Depending on the width of the arbitration clause, arbitrators usually have the same powers as the court, including the power to order dissolution and to take an account, but no power to appoint a receiver or grant interim injunctions, for which partners must go to the court. The court will also make orders in support of peremptory orders made by an arbitrator, although in many cases of non-

[1] Whilst some writers on ADR consider arbitration to be a form of ADR, in that it is an alternative to court-based litigation, in the partnership and professional practices sphere arbitration is as common, if not more common, a means of dispute resolution as litigation. This writer regards arbitration, at least in this context, as akin to litigation and thus not a form of ADR.

compliance by parties, arbitrators will use their powers to strike out or draw adverse conclusions.

An arbitration, rather than court proceedings, is usually regarded by the protagonists in a partnership dispute as desirable because of the extreme damage that can be caused to goodwill and professional reputation by a public airing of the issues, or indeed merely by publication of the fact that there is an internal dispute. However, not every partnership agreement contains an arbitration clause, and sometimes partners will use the threat of issue or continuance of court proceedings as a (cogent and often effective) threat to obtain what they want. It is not unknown for a party to deliver draft particulars of claim as a form of (lawful) blackmail. **10.3.2**

Arbitrations also have the advantage of enabling the parties to appoint their own choice of arbitrator (someone regarded by all parties as having the necessary expertise, experience and wisdom to reach the "right" result), although very often arbitration clauses provide, in default of agreement, for appointment of an arbitrator by the parties' professional or trade body or association, so that in those circumstances the outcome of the selection process can be impossible to predict.

The power of arbitrators to determine and tailor procedure as they see fit, and the ability of arbitrators to set a rapid timetable, are still attractive features of arbitration, though since the Woolf reforms were brought into effect in April 1999 judges have more of a "hands-on" role, and powers to match, and there is an emphasis on rapid resolution, including early identification of a "trial window", so that, whether before an arbitrator or a court, parties will fairly early on in proceedings know the likely date by which their dispute will be resolved. This is important both in terms of being able to make provision for the possible outcomes, and also in terms of knowing the timescale in which efforts to settle the dispute will have to be pursued.

Corporate/LLP practice disputes

Jurisdiction to order the winding up of the entity (limited company or LLP), is vested solely in the court. **10.3.3**

Foreign entities pose questions (beyond the ambit of this chapter) as to what, if any, jurisdiction the U.K. courts have in connection with their winding up.

Shareholder (or in the case of LLPs, member) disputes can be determined by arbitration if the parties have so agreed. It would appear that even questions arising from the particular jurisdiction afforded by sections 459–461 of the Companies Act 1985 (unfair prejudice) can be determined by an arbitrator, provided that the arbitration clause specifically grants this power or the parties otherwise so agree. Normally, however, there is no such clause or agreement, and this jurisdiction is exercised by the court.

10.4 The role of ADR generally and in particular the advantages of mediation over other forms of ADR

The advantages common to all forms of ADR, namely speed, lower cost, control of the outcome (no imposition of judgment), confidentiality, and party-selected facilitator, all have a great deal to commend themselves in the area of partnership disputes.

Example

10.4.1 To take a relatively simple example of a partnership dispute, a partner is expelled pursuant to an expulsion clause in the partnership agreement, and contends and claims as follows:

(a) The purported expulsion was based on trumped up grounds and was carried out in bad faith.

(b) Some of the expelling partners are guilty of much worse conduct than he has been accused of.

(c) By their conduct under the above items the expelling partners have committed a repudiatory breach of the partnership agreement (and he accepts the repudiation).

(d) He was induced into the partnership by misrepresentations as to the true value of assets on the balance sheet. The expelling partners will say in response that like many balance sheets the asset values given do not reflect the true value but are shown as part of an accounting convention, that in fact certain important figures were discussed with the expelled partner before he joined when he raised queries on them, and that even if that is found not to have occurred the valuations given did not induce him into the partnership, he would have joined even if the true values had been shown.

(e) By virtue of the above matters his non-competition covenants are thereby discharged (and he starts soliciting clients).

(f) The provision in the partnership agreement for accession of the expelling partners to the share of assets of the expelled partner does not take effect.

(g) He is entitled to a declaration that the firm has been dissolved or an order dissolving it on the just and equitable ground, for appointment of a receiver meanwhile, and for an account and payment of his share on dissolution to include a share in assets which ordinarily might not come into account on an expulsion (or indeed a retirement) such as off balance sheet work in progress and appreciation in the value of freehold properties.

(h) In addition he is entitled to damages based on his loss of income (despite efforts to mitigate) brought about by the demise of the firm, and loss of interest based on acceleration of tax payments (the catch-up charge).

The expelling partners now face the following dilemmas: **10.4.2**

(a) Their probity and honesty have been put into question, which is particularly difficult since there is no arbitration clause and the expelled partner threatens to issue court proceedings with a fully particularised claim form, a draft of which he delivers (some of the more embarrassing allegations are true, although not all of the expelling partners know this).

(b) The expelled partner threatens to tell the world that he is dissolving the firm.

(c) On hearing this, and/or on being solicited by the expelled partner, clients may stop instructing the firm, and contacts who refer work may stop doing so "until the problem blows over".

(d) Whilst the spectre of dissolution hangs over the firm it is going to be very difficult if not impossible to develop the firm through the recruitment of new partners (to whom a duty of full disclosure is owed), and yet candidates are already in the course of being recruited, and the expulsion of the expelled partner has left a gap in the firm's capability and expertise which urgently needs to be filled (to retain and attract clients and to avoid negligence).

(e) If a dissolution is ordered, the expelling partners will not necessarily have the option of acquiring the assets and goodwill of the firm—in many cases an open market sale will be ordered, and partners may end up bidding for their "own" firm. Whilst in many professional firms goodwill has no existence or value in isolation from the partners, equally in other firms goodwill might be valued as a multiple of profit or turnover. Partners trying to acquire goodwill in those circumstances will have to find additional funding/capital.

(f) The expelling partners cannot finalise accounts or distribute profits until the outcome of the dispute is known (in some firms the partners would stop drawing or draw less).

(g) Partner attention is distracted onto the dispute and away from fee-earning work and practice development. Morale is affected. Profits will almost certainly fall during the period of the dispute.

(h) The expense of litigation, even when shared amongst a number of partners, is considerable, and may never be recouped.

(i) The firm's bank may not be wholly supportive, particularly in the face of a dissolution claim, and in addition it may have lent money (particularly capital) to the expelled partner and it does not want to see him bankrupted.

10.4.3 The expelled partner has different dilemmas:

(a) He cannot get a job and, initially, has no income. When he attends interviews he is asked why he left, and has to admit that he is on the brink of commencing litigation or alternatively of being sued. Potential employers/partners are concerned about his solvency. So he sets up his own practice to cater for the clients/customers he has been able to solicit away, but no bank will lend him any money. He is a start-up over-shadowed by litigation—a very poor risk indeed.

(b) Even though he has been successful in soliciting clients/customers away from his former firm, if ultimately his non-competition covenant bites he will have to pay probably very substantial damages, so working hard now may bring no ultimate reward, in effect leaving him having incurred outgoings, but having his profit if not his entire turnover clawed back by his former firm.

(c) He is the one against the many. He is isolated and may have difficulty funding his side of the proceedings. Even if he is a solicitor he would need to work full-time on the case during certain busy periods, and he cannot afford the time. If he is not a solicitor his solicitor keeps calling for money on account, and may not be prepared to work without funding in advance. The expelled partner cannot hope to prevail as a litigant in person. He has no idea how to run a piece of litigation.

(d) If he loses he will be made bankrupt for certain (if he doesn't become insolvent first under the weight of the many financial pressures).

Both sides are advised to consider ADR. What are the advantages and disadvantages of the different types of ADR in these circumstances?

Early neutral evaluation ("ENE")

This can be a misnomer in that neutral evaluation can occur at any stage of a dispute, though clearly the earlier the better. **10.4.4**

A neutral expert who is known to and well-respected by both sides is instructed by both sides to study their submissions and the documents, and to produce a reasoned opinion (non-binding and without prejudice) as to the likely outcome if the matter were to come to be determined in court. The idea behind this method of dispute resolution is to enable both parties, but in particular the party whom the expert will predict to be the "losing" party, to face the reality of their situation so that having received the expert's opinion they then direct their energies and resources to settlement rather than continuing to contest the matter.

ENE does, however, have a number of drawbacks in relation to partnership disputes:

(a) Expert evaluators can comment on different outcomes in the event of (a limited number of) different findings of fact, but even in cases with restricted factual issues the value of an "if x then y" opinion may be limited in that it may not appear to be persuasive to one or both of the parties who might cling to the possibility of a finding of fact in their favour. An expert cannot properly make assessments of likely findings of fact without the benefit of hearing witnesses giving evidence.

(b) ENE *per se* does not therefore provide the best (or in some cases any) opportunity or forum for challenging the perceptions of parties as to the merits of their respective cases on issues of fact.

(c) As such the utility of ENE in partnership and professional practice disputes is limited. Disputes arising out of expulsion, or allegations of fraud, bad faith, or breach of covenant almost always involve numerous and complex issues of fact revolving around the day to day conduct, knowledge and intent of one or more parties, sometimes over a long period of time.

(d) Even accounting disputes, often thought of as the exclusive province of accountants, frequently involve underlying issues of fact such as what may or may not have been agreed, what is (under the terms of the partnership agreement) "just" (possibly influenced by conduct) or what accounting treatment reflects the custom or practice of the partnership (which can often be divined by accountants from the underlying historic books and records of the partnership) but sometimes requires clarification by way of supplemental factual evidence from the partners.[2]

(e) Of course some partnership accounting disputes have issues limited to the application of (often complex but nonetheless widely accepted) accounting conventions, not to mention simple audit and arithmetic, and as such can be wholly determined by expert accountants. Such disputes therefore lend themselves admirably to resolution through ENE.

(f) Equally, there is nothing to prevent parties putting out distinct issues to ENE, in the hope of adding to the weight of persuasion and pressure towards settlement if the expert finds for them. However, experience dictates that if parties are going to the trouble and expense of ADR they will want a "one stop shop" with the potential for resolving all issues, rather than dealing with the issues sequentially and/or in different forums. This is particularly the case in partnership disputes where commercial and emotional pressures so often dictate the preferred pace towards resolution.

10.4.5 In the above example of the expelled partner, most of the true issues are issues of fact which can only be resolved through witnesses being tested under cross-examination. The issue of balance sheet valuations could be put out to ENE, but that issue is going to be secondary until the issues as to what the partner was told about the balance sheet, and whether in any event he was induced into the partnership by the balance sheet have been determined, again through cross-examination.

If the evidence of conduct of partners and of representations made is comprehensively or at least substantially based on or supported by documentation (the authenticity of which is admitted) then there may be some value in ENE in a case such as this. However, experience suggests that it is rarely that simple, with parties putting forward contentions as to what happened or what was said at the time of or in between the coming into being of certain documents which (if found as facts) cast a different light on the interpretation of the documents or their relevance.

[2] For example, as to the type or quality of hotel accommodation or travel expenses normally reimbursed, or as to what has historically been considered by the partnership as a "reasonable" distance to travel to a morning meeting or go home at night after a late meeting rather than staying in an hotel, or whether spouses have historically been fed or accommodated at the expense the firm. These matters may sound relatively trivial but similar issues have in many cases given rise to lengthy and costly disputes, often with more than just the amount of the expenses themselves at stake, such as issues of bad faith or dishonesty (fiddling or overloading expenses) giving rise to expulsion.

Expert determination

An expert chosen by the parties or by a neutral appointing body, such as a professional organisation, considers the parties' written submissions (and/or other materials agreed to be provided) and then issues a determination which the parties have agreed in advance will be binding on them. The process by its nature is not without prejudice. 10.4.6

This method of dispute resolution is "alternative" in that it is an alternative to litigation or arbitration. However, purists might say that it is not ADR proper because (once the parties have agreed to be bound by expert determination) an outcome is imposed on the parties (as in litigation and arbitration) rather than the process leading to a consensual outcome.

Just as most partnership and professional practice disputes are not going to be suitable for resolution by ENE, for the reasons set out in the section on early neutral evaluation above, so an expert seeking to determine a dispute is going to face the same or similar problems, particularly where there are factual issues, or allegations of fraud or bad faith (knowledge or intention issues).

Again, certain accounting disputes and possibly other discrete issues may be suitable for expert determination within the partnership and professional practice dispute context.

Executive tribunal

One of the main advantages and purposes of an executive tribunal is to appraise senior executives and/or ultimate decision-makers of the reality of the circumstances giving rise to the dispute and what the true issues and merits are. 10.4.7

This is generally done in quasi-courtroom style, whereby the executives from each side comprise the tribunal (sometimes with a neutral facilitator or mediator as chairman). Presentations of case (often in the form of an opening address) are made by both sides' advocates (and may then be followed by each advocate giving a response to the other's address). Both executives thereby hear their case and the opponent's case put at its highest and also the best criticism which each side can level at their opponent's case.

In the context of partnership disputes, very often this is the first occasion on which a senior executive partner (for example a member of a management committee) fully understands all of the issues and the significance of the counter-accusations, without the "benefit" of précis and explanation from other partner(s) (who may be personally involved in the allegations and counter-allegations and may be protecting his/their own back) and/or legal representatives (instructed by the said personally-involved partner(s)). So very often a decision to expel or to consider expulsion is taken by a firm or management committee on the basis of a report by the partner most closely involved. The partner proposed to be expelled, in shock and reeling from the revelation of the accusations against him, does not put forward his best case, or in some cases has not yet had an opportunity to piece together what amounts to a conspiracy against him by others within the partnership. Not having acquitted himself well in his one opportunity to put his case, he is duly expelled. By the time of the executive tribunal however he is able, with the assistance of his advocate (or by himself if he cannot afford to pay a representative), to put forward a compelling case, or at least sufficient to make the senior executive partner pause for thought as to whether settlement may well be the best way forward.

A variation is for a presentation to be made by one side's advocate to the other side's executive(s), particularly where the case involves claim and defence but no counter-claim (although in partnership and professional practice disputes there is more often than not a counter-claim).

10.4.8 A further variation is to follow an executive presentation with a mediation, the mediator having been the third member of the executive panel to whom the presentation(s) is/are made.

A considerable advantage of this form of ADR, especially when compared to ENE, is that the parties set aside time to attend on the day, which gives rise to a much better focus on the issues than the arrival of an expert opinion in the post.

In partnership and professional practice disputes, typically it is one against the many so that on one side of the panel may be an individual partner (who for example might have been expelled) and on the other will be the representative of the continuing partners.

It is preferable that the executive appointed by the continuing partners is someone who has not been involved personally in the matters giving rise to any counter-allegations by the opposing partner or partners, or indeed in any matters in respect of which the facts are in issue, so as to give him or her the best opportunity of approaching the matter as objectively and unemotionally as possible, whilst at the same time being sufficiently senior and/or respected within his firm that his report and recommendation to his partners following the executive tribunal carries weight and is likely to be adopted (or indeed so that he has been vested with authority to settle on the day, clearly the preferred course to achieve speedy resolution). The tendency (and this applies to all forms of ADR in which personal attendance is required) is to send the managing and/or senior partner. In some cases they are the worst people to send if they have direct personal (and emotional) involvement in the matters in issue.

10.4.9 It is also important for the parties to be represented in equal numbers, otherwise the show of strength by, for example, the continuing firm may distract one or both parties from the actual issues, and may also inhibit or prevent one to one, face to face dialogue, which is so valuable in overcoming many of the barriers[3] preventing settlement.

Just like ENE, executive tribunals in themselves (without the optional mediation element) do not have a mechanism for examining and weighing up oral evidence (which is only really complete when challenged in the witness box).

Nonetheless, the executive tribunal is an opportunity for rehearsal, in a courtroom-like setting, of points worth making, including perhaps comment on the improbabilities of the other party's case on the facts (even though no factual issue can actually be determined), demonstration of a party's preparedness and command and knowledge of the perhaps intricate web of events, documentation and admitted or incontrovertible facts, and exposition of the conclusions which each party draws from them and believes a court or arbitrator is likely to draw from them.

Mediation

The essential elements of mediation are: 10.4.10

(a) facilitation;

(b) by a neutral third party (the mediator);

(c) of efforts to settle a dispute;

(d) on settlement terms which both parties are prepared (or become prepared during the process) to adopt;

(e) the process being non-binding and without prejudice.[4]

The mediation process blends a number of techniques and processes. Many of them are borrowed from other forms of ADR, and indeed from mainstream litigation, thus:

(a) In mediation, the parties (normally) meet on an appointed day or days, having set that time aside, and having prepared for the day both mentally and by way of preparing suitable bundles of documents and position statements (supplied to the mediator in advance). This is similar to litigation or arbitration, and also executive tribunals, in that the parties exclude all other matters from their thoughts in order to give

[3] Depersonalisation of (indeed demonisation of), and inability to empathise with, the opposing party(ies), lack of opportunity to apologise, inability to judge sincerity of apology, no opportunity to vent anger and frustration to permit of subsequent constructive debate.

[4] Unless and until a settlement agreement is signed at the end of the process.

their full attention to the business of the day, with a view to resolving their dispute once and for all.

(b) In mediation, the parties agree on a mutually trusted and respected person to determine their dispute or assist them to do so (as in early neutral evaluation, some arbitrations and most expert determinations).

(c) In mediation, the real issues quickly emerge into sharper focus, through the mediator gaining the trust of the parties and drawing out explanations for their contentions and conclusions. In litigation or arbitration this occurs at trial through probing by the advocates and by the trial judge or arbitrator.

(d) In mediation, ill-conceived "security blankets" are whisked away, through questioning by, and reasoned discussion with, the mediator. The parties find themselves facing up to the reality of their situation, with the alternatives of settling right away, or incurring more expense in order to fight on with the outcome remaining uncertain. In litigation so many settlements occur at the courtroom door, or after the first day of evidence, as one or both parties realise and accept that the settlement on offer may be better than the judgment which may be imposed.

(e) Like in some arbitrations (where the parties choose and appoint the arbitrator(s)), ENE and expert determination, in mediation, the mediator is selected and agreed by the parties. This is an indication from the outset that both parties have absolute trust in the mediator and vests him or her with authority based not on fear of compulsion (as with a judge or arbitrator) but on confidence that the person concerned has the best chance of resolving the dispute and a resolution that he or she should be given every assistance and opportunity to achieve that outcome.

10.4.11 To these borrowed elements are added unique elements not available or always fully available in other forms of dispute resolution:

(a) The mediator is non-judgmental. He does not suggest who he thinks is going to win, nor does he have power to impose a judgment or determination on the parties. It is in part because of this state of affairs that the mediator is able to gain the trust and confidence of the parties, and having done so they each (correctly) regard him as someone who genuinely wants to help them to resolve their dispute on a basis that they will both find acceptable. They accordingly, in absolute confidence (which the mediator respects absolutely), and by degrees, "bare their souls" to the mediator, which in so many cases leads the mediator to an insight as to the common ground which may resolve or help to resolve the dispute.

(b) The parties are given opportunities, either in private with the mediator, or (under the supervision of the mediator) face-to-face with the opponent, to vent their anger and frustration. This process so very often enables the parties to set aside emotional considerations and to focus on what is really important to them.

(c) Parties will often drop an issue or reduce or forgive a head of claim in exchange for a sincere apology, which the mediator can encourage in a suitable case (sometimes from both sides).

(d) Rather than the dawning of reality being an incidental by-product of the process,[5] the mediator carries out what is known as "reality-testing", testing the parties' respective contentions and assumptions, often with the benefit of material or points provided by the other party, honing that material as he journeys back and forth between the parties.

(e) The mediator is able to explore in detail with each of the parties what their best alternative to a negotiated settlement is and what it entails in terms of cost (financial and emotional), delay and risk (not only of losing but of a judgment or award in their favour resulting in the other party becoming insolvent).

(f) So very often there are ways in which the parties can assist each other or co-operate which can create value for one or both of them, as an alternative to or supplemental to the payment of money or whatever other remedy is sought. Mediators are able to explore such possibilities with the parties to enable them to reach beneficial agreements governing their future conduct which no judge or arbitrator would have jurisdiction to impose.

(g) With early neutral evaluation the expert has one opportunity to convince the parties as to the merits or otherwise of their respective claims. In court or during an arbitration the judge or arbitrator can ask a few pointed questions or indicate a tentative view, but opportunities are few and far between and a judicial indication is a blunt instrument compared with the

[5] As in litigation or arbitration in which regrettably on so many occasions reality does not dawn until just after the judge finishes delivering his judgment or the arbitrator's award is received in the post.

in-depth discussion a mediator can encourage and participate in. An executive tribunal offers an opportunity to discuss and negotiate afterwards but (unless supplemented with a mediation) does not lend itself to an ongoing analysis of the issues beyond that presented formally by the advocates. A mediation on the other hand is free-form. It develops and proceeds in response to the input and conduct of the parties. The mediator has numerous opportunities to narrow the issues, challenge assumptions and bring the parties closer to settlement.

A mediator therefore has more dispute resolution techniques and processes at his disposal, and more opportunities to apply them, than any other type of appointee in the dispute resolution field.

Furthermore, there are many special features of partnership and professional practice disputes which lend themselves to resolution by mediation:

Expense

10.4.12 Whilst exceptional profits in the professional arena are newsworthy, the average proprietor in a professional practice is comfortable but not exceptionally wealthy. A practice may be able to afford the cost of litigation or arbitration (although it will quickly impact on the "bottom line") but an individual very often will not, unless he is fortunate enough to have built up reserves (even then he may be reluctant to put them at risk). Partnership and professional practice litigation or arbitration, which fights all the way through to a final judgment, will often not leave much change from £50,000 plus VAT per party, and can in some cases cost many multiples of that figure, depending on the complexity of the issues and the quantity of documents which have to be considered (and in this sphere the issues can become complex and the documents numerous). Parties are exposed to the possibility of having to pay the other side's costs as well as their own if they lose altogether or lose particular issues. Even a summary costs order payable forthwith in respect of an interlocutory application can derail the finances of many a litigant. Individuals at odds with their former practice have to pay (and cannot recover) VAT on their legal advisers' bills and may not be able to offset their own litigation costs (nor the other side's if they are required to pay them) against their income for income tax purposes (whereas the continuing proprietors of the former practice usually can). Thus it is very important, particularly for an individual, to settle a partnership or professional practice dispute at an early stage. The cost of mediation is always going to be a fraction of the cost of litigation or arbitration.

Speed

10.4.13 As set out earlier in this chapter and in the example at paragraph 10.4.1 *et seq.*, a partnership and professional practice dispute is particularly damaging to the ongoing business because it is either going to be an internal dispute which causes the business to crumble from within, or one which in any event very often requires the ongoing development of the business to be put "on hold". For the individual, very often reputation and career development hang in the balance. Clients will not be receiving the best service whilst their advisers are distracted. Delay in resolving financial issues often puts parties, especially individuals, under extreme financial pressure. The sooner the dispute can be resolved the better. Despite continuing reforms, litigation and arbitration in partnership and professional practice disputes last anything from six months to two years or more. Mediation in partnership and professional practice disputes lasts from a (very long) day (normal) to a number of days (exceptional).

Complex factual issues

10.4.14 Litigation and arbitration are designed to achieve a just resolution of all issues, but regrettably often at very great expense. There is discussion earlier in this chapter of the difficulty posed by complex fact situations in other forms of ADR. Partnership and professional practice disputes are, as indicated above, often beset with numerous issues of fact. How does the mediator resolve these issues? Those familiar with mediation will know that he does not and does not need to. What he does do is present each party with the best points of their opponents based on the admitted facts, and the points which can be made as to credibility on facts which are in dispute. That can also be achieved in other forms of ADR. What distinguishes mediation is that the respective cutting edges of each side's points can be honed to a greater sharpness as the mediator goes back and forth between the parties, hearing their views on the points made by the other side, putting these points to the opponent in each case, and receiving a new point to take back. The mediator is not trying to win any arguments, or decide who has the best case. He is merely presenting each party with the reality of their situation. Ultimately it is each party sitting alone (or with a team of advisers), in between the many meetings with the mediator, who decides for himself how credible his case is or how likely it is to succeed, and makes his own choices on settlement accordingly.

Emotion

10.4.15 It is often said that partnerships are like marriages. Certainly the spurning of an individual by his partners often gives rise to emotions similar to those seen in divorce matters—anger, hatred, despair, feelings of rejection and a desire for revenge. These emotions will often cloud the judgment of an individual who may have been expelled or otherwise cold-shouldered by his partners. "I'll take them down with me", is a common articulation of these emotions.[6] In a mediation these emotions can be vented in an environment which is controlled in that it is expected that such venting will take place, and yet there is a mechanism, and more importantly a person, the mediator, available to umpire the confrontation, and to apply the energy released to constructive purposes. The realisation by continuing proprietors of the genuine depth and intensity of feelings of an ousted partner is a powerfully persuasive element when seeking concessions designed to mollify and to relieve possibly guilty consciences. The realisation by an individual that he has got his message across and that some restitution (if only a sincere apology) is being offered in respect of his emotional pain and suffering may give rise to concessions by the individual. Such concessions of course bring the parties closer to settlement.

Confidentiality

10.4.16 In circumstances in which there is no arbitration clause, and one party insists on proceeding in court, the professional embarrassment which can be caused can be considerable. Freelance journalists review the High Court cause book (a public document) on a daily basis and provide a claim form précis service to professional publications, which duly report fallings out, often with considerable relish and elaboration. It is not uncommon for clients of professional practices to read the publications concerned, which are often targeted not only at the professionals themselves but at their clients also. Very often individuals in the same profession make up an important component of a professional practice's client base. At trial the dirty laundry of incompetence, negligence, unfairness, duplicity and fraud is washed in public. Findings tend to be focussed upon acts of individuals (even if part of a collective design), as the judge reviews what occurred and who was instrumental in it. Reputations can be irreparably damaged, and even though a professional practice may win the battle and indeed the war, it may suffer unacceptable casualties. Furthermore, where adverse findings in a professional practice dispute are made public there is sometimes a regulatory follow-up by the professional body concerned, so that a bruising trial and judgment can be followed by professional sanctions. One might conclude that not taking time out for a day's mediation before all of this occurs is professional negligence (not to mention suicide) of the highest order.

[6] In the partnership and professional practices sphere this is sometimes a threat that the individual is in a position to put into effect.

THE ROLE OF STRAIGHTFORWARD NEGOTIATIONS 10.5

There is no doubt, as in all disputes, that negotiation has a role to play in efforts to settle all partnership and professional practice disputes. A partner or proprietor may well be prepared to walk away if the price is right. More complex settlements can of course also be negotiated. Negotiation should always be attempted before mediation, if only because it may narrow the issues and the gap between the parties that the mediator has to bridge.

In order to assess those situations in which negotiations may lead to settlement without the need for mediation, it is helpful to examine briefly why negotiations sometimes fail. The following shorthand list requires no further explanation:

> Focus on litigation rather than settlement; timetabling giving no opportunity to focus on settlement; failure to communicate (both between opposing parties, and between individuals within groups of proprietors or former proprietors on the same side); poor negotiation skills; lack of/different information; different interpretation of the same information; unrealistic expectations; over-optimism; positional bargaining; brinkmanship; "you go first"; principles; rights and wrongs; emotions; revenge; mistrust; fear of the unknown; fear of a superior's reaction; the burden of costs already incurred (own and other side's); problems unrelated to the issues in dispute.

By the time mediation is attempted, negotiation has very often hit one or more of these bottlenecks. Understanding and seeking to avoid or remove these bottlenecks will usually facilitate a negotiated settlement. If that does not work, by virtue of the factors discussed earlier in this chapter, mediation may well break the impasse.

PRACTICAL CONSIDERATIONS WHEN MEDIATING PARTNERSHIP AND PROFESSIONAL PRACTICE DISPUTES 10.6

Handling the client

In order for a mediation to occur it is of course necessary for the client or clients to be persuaded (or persuade themselves) that they want to seek a settlement and are willing to pay a mediator (and their legal adviser) for the opportunity to do so. Clients are unlikely to want to incur the cost and give up their own time before negotiations have taken place and have failed to achieve settlement. Happily, most professionals have heard of mediation and some have a good knowledge of the process and the merits, so advising them is made easier (although there is a danger of assuming knowledge which may even be claimed by the client but in fact does not exist or not in the depth assumed). With non-professional proprietors it is important to start from basic principles when appraising the client of the options. 10.6.1

A full exposition of the role of the adviser in a mediation is beyond the scope of this chapter. What can be said here is that it is important to remember that part of the role of the mediator will be to convey to each party in private meetings the nub of what the other party has to say on particular issues, in effect their "best points". It is a fact of life that sophisticated parties (which professional parties in this sphere tend to be) will endeavour to "play mind games" with each other by "winding up" (or put more respectfully, equipping) the mediator to persuade the opponent that in court the other party will prevail. It is important to explain the psychology of mediation to clients, so that they will understand that, in basic terms, as one of the techniques of mediation, the mediator's emphasis, when meeting with party A, will be on party B's best points and party A's worst points, and vice versa when meeting with party B.

Professional clients may want to speak for themselves. That is for several reasons desirable, in that they actively participate and thus perhaps focus more fully than if they take a "back seat", they offload their burden of anger and frustration (and any other emotions that have accumulated) and the mediator can get a better measure of them and what matters to them. On the other hand, professionals in an unfamiliar environment may demonstrate how too little knowledge can be a dangerous thing.

Non-professional clients should certainly do most of the talking in the first private meeting with the mediator, but thereafter may want the adviser to be the spokesman for the most part. It is nonetheless of vital importance to ensure that the client fully understands each point made by the mediator, and makes every decision himself. If he then wishes the adviser to communicate that decision or other matters then no harm is done.

Prior to issuing proceedings

10.6.2 As with litigation in other fields, prior to the issue of proceedings the issues are usually not as well-defined as they will later become. It is important to make a list of the other side's actual or anticipated best points and what your client has to say about each one. Also make a list of your client's best points, what the other side is likely to say in response to them, and what the reply to that response will be. It is important to have the issues and the answers to the other side's points well-rehearsed, so that the mediator can be sent back to the other side each time with a better answer than might have been expected. In the heat of the moment or as tiredness overtakes the participants it is all too easy to forget points that ought to be made, unless there is some form of checklist.

After issuing proceedings

10.6.3 The points at paragraph 10.6.2. apply, with the added complication that statements of case designed to define the issues may give rise to as many questions as they answer. Ideally, serve a request for further information and refuse to mediate until the answers have been provided. If that cannot be achieved at least have a list of questions to pose to the mediator for him to pose to the other side.

The court will normally be prepared to make an order staying the proceedings, usually for a month, for the purposes of mediation. Arbitrators also have this power.

Making contact with the other parties—the approach

To avoid appearing to be "weak", the points usually made when seeking to negotiate can be made when seeking to agree mediation, namely that whilst the client has confidence in his case he recognises that it will be a lengthy and expensive process and it appears to be in the best interests of both parties to seek a resolution through mediation rather than before the court or an arbitrator. **10.6.4**

The approach can either be made direct or through a mediation organisation, most of which will agree to approach the other side and at the same time recommend a shortlist of suitable mediators. Some parties will respond more readily to a mediation organisation, and mediators recommended by such an organisation are more likely to be regarded by the approached party as neutral.[7] Having said that, there is nothing to prevent a party from asking a mediation organisation to recommend a particular mediator from its pre-existing panel, who may be known to that party (or perhaps both parties) as a reliable and able mediator, and whose neutrality cannot be put in doubt by either party.

The type of mediator

Whereas it is often said that a mediator need not be an expert in the field in which he is mediating, in professional practices disputes it is often thought of as advantageous if a mediator is, or (following retirement) has been, a member of the profession concerned. The particular ethos of and rules governing a profession will be ingrained into such a mediator. A mediation offers the opportunity not only to hand-select such a person to facilitate settlement, but also for that person to explore with the parties at length the particular issues, incentives and threats which professional status gives rise to in the context of the dispute. **10.6.5**

Where accounting or taxation issues are likely to arise it is also helpful if the mediator has experience of dealing with such matters either in his personal or in an advisery capacity.

7 Experience suggests that often any mediator proposed by one party direct (not through a mediation organisation) will be rejected almost as a matter of course by the other party, or at the very least enquiries will be raised as to any earlier association (including other mediations) which the proposing party or his solicitors may have had with that mediator.

A mediator who has been involved in running his own business may bring fresh insights to resolving disputes in this area.

The mediation agreement

10.6.6 In the case of a partnership, the likelihood is that at least one of the signatories will be signing on behalf of himself and others in the firm, so consideration should be given as to who are the contracting parties, given that:

(a) a firm has no legal capacity in its own right (so the agreement should not be signed "for and on behalf of XYZ & Co" but rather, for example, "on behalf of himself and B, C and D, as partners in the firm of XYZ & Co");

(b) any salaried partners should be expressly excluded from any collective description (for example, "all of the equity partners of XYZ & Co");

(c) often one party will still be a partner of the firm which he is in dispute with, or there will be a dispute as to whether or not one party is or is not a continuing partner in the firm (so use wording such as, "for and on behalf of the equity partners of XYZ & Co excluding [(should he still be a partner)] E").

In the case of a limited company or LLP dispute, remember that the dispute is (normally) between shareholders and/or directors, and consider whether or not the corporate entity needs to be (perhaps separately) represented in the mediation (and thus included as a party to the agreement).

Who should attend the mediation?

10.6.7 Any parties who have a common interest (such as continuing partners) can be represented by one person provided that he has the requisite authority. It is as well for such a person to have his authority documented,[8] but this would not normally be provided to the other party or to the mediator.[9]

As indicated earlier in this chapter, in respect of continuing partners/proprietors, it is not always advisable for the persons most directly involved in the matters in issue to attend the mediation, particularly if there is a counter-claim containing conduct issues relating to such persons. The ideal representative of a group of partners or proprietors is a senior (not necessarily *the* senior) partner/proprietor who has not been personally, or at least not directly, involved

[8] For his own protection and the avoidance of future disputes within the firm, particularly where there is a limitation placed on that authority.

[9] Both of whom can in most cases rely on ostensible or statutory authority.

in the matters in issue. Such a person will tend to be more objective, and will carry less emotional "baggage" than someone who has been involved in the detail of the matter, and may have had accusations of misconduct levelled against him.

That is not to say that the personally involved partner should not attend at all. Indeed it may be desirable that he does, for a number of reasons:

(a) he has a grasp of the detail of the matter;

(b) if he is in the right then the opponent may be less likely to reinforce assertions made against that partner, particularly in joint meetings;

(c) if he has not told his partners the full story then when damning new evidence is produced by the other side for effect at the mediation he will be there to explain himself and the true position to the representative partner;

(d) he is available to make or receive (or both) a personal apology, if agreed.

What papers should be passed to the mediator prior to the mediation?

It is normal practice in a mediation to provide the mediator in advance with core documents that will help to give him an overview of the matters in issue. 10.6.8

In partnership and professional practice disputes, the following documents are more or less obligatory:

(a) partnership agreement, articles of association/shareholders' agreement or LLP agreement;

(b) last agreed accounts and any draft and/or management accounts since then;

(c) minutes of relevant internal meetings;

(d) documentation dealing with or effecting (purported or actual) retirement, expulsion and/or dissolution;

(e) if proceedings of any sort are extant, statements of case, replies to requests for further information (or the requests if not yet responded to), and any witness statements;

(f) copies of correspondence or other documents setting out the parties' respective positions (both open and without prejudice).

Length of the mediation

A (very long) day is adequate for most partnership and professional practice disputes. 10.6.9

The venue

10.6.10 Neutral territory is preferable, subject to considerations of cost. Professionals and other sophisticated businessmen, especially when accompanied by advisers, are well used to meeting the opposition on the opposition's home ground, so this may not be too much of a problem if there is no alternative. Having said that, if there is no strictly neutral territory which can be used it is preferable by far to hold the mediation at the premises of one of the parties' advisers, rather than at the premises of one of the parties. Arrangements should in such circumstances be made to isolate the mediating parties and the mediator from everyone else in the building. If that can be done the location soon ceases to have any significance, and should not normally interfere with the mediation process.

The cost of the mediation

10.6.11 Cost varies enormously depending on who the mediator is, whether he is provided through a mediation organisation, what part of the country the dispute is in, and what amount is in issue between the parties.

Given that disputes in this area are commercial in nature, charges are based on a commercial scale.

Often a fixed fee will be quoted to encompass administration (including approaching the other side and setting up the mediation), reading-in by the mediator before the day of the mediation (up to a given number of hours), and a day's mediation (any number of hours until the parties settle or decide they must break for sleep). For time spent beyond these limits there is usually an hourly charge.

Overall, mediation charges in this kind of dispute (whether fixed fee or hourly or a mixture of both) tend to reflect standard hourly rates which would be charged by a partner in a mid-sized professional firm in the geographical region in question, plus say four or five hours if a mediation organisation is involved in providing the mediator and setting up the mediation.

The settlement agreement

10.6.12 Taking a simple case where money is the only or main ingredient in a settlement, there are essentially two forms of settlement. Either the parties can agree that one of them pays an agreed sum to the other, or they can resolve the issues as to how an account should be taken[10] and then carry out the accounting themselves (with the

[10] For example, whether provision for certain future liabilities should be made in the account for a partner's final year, what provision should be made for bad debts, how profit should be divided (if not in fixed shares), whose assets are whose in a merged and now de-merging practice, and how work-in-progress should be accounted for.

assistance of their accountants) on the basis that all that remains to be done is the arithmetic.

In the agreed sum type of settlement, care must be taken to state in the settlement agreement how the sum paid is to be treated for accounting and therefore tax purposes. Is the sum to be accounted for as a capital repayment (no tax payable by the recipient), as payment of undrawn profit from previous years on which tax has already been paid (no tax payable by the recipient) or as undrawn profit for a more recent (typically the final) year (tax not yet paid so tax payable by the recipient)? If a capital sum is to be paid to a partner in excess of the capital contributed, then effectively the difference comes out of the net of tax income of the paying partners.[11]

If the agreement is to include new covenants in restraint of trade, care must be taken to ensure that they are drafted in such a way that they are enforceable.[12]

It is wise to provide expressly which parts of the partnership (or shareholders' or members') agreement survive the settlement, and which do not and are effectively replaced or simply abandoned. This applies particularly to provisions designed to survive the end of a proprietor's participation in the business, such as non-competition covenants, indemnities, annuities and accounting and repayment provisions.[13]

Provision should also be made as to how any current arbitration or court proceedings will be finalised, and what is agreed in relation to each party's costs of the proceedings.

The agreement should be easy to enforce. Clearly-stated obligations, without use of the "R-word",[14] are important, as are rigid timetables for compliance, and easy conversion of entitlements into debts which can be enforced by statutory demand.

11 Because capital is a tax-paid fund and the capital accounts of the paying partners will have to be adjusted downwards. Monies to build them up again, if required, have to come from taxed income, or from borrowings that have to be repaid out of taxed income. Or if not built up again, on subsequent dissolution or retirement the remaining partners will receive a smaller tax-paid capital sum.

12 Although as a general rule covenants given by equity partners are more likely to be enforced than the equivalent covenant by a salaried partner or other employee. Increasingly partnership agreements and settlement agreements impose no bar on competition but have agreed methods of calculating the purchase price to be paid by the outgoing partner for the goodwill in respect of any client which transfers its business to him. Because there is no breach of contract in taking the client, the payment cannot be characterised as damages and therefore even quite punitive formulae cannot give rise to the debate as to whether that part of the agreement is a liquidated damages clause or unenforceable as a penalty.

13 The latter providing in particular when payment of sums due to the outgoing partner will be made.

14 A large proportion of post-settlement disputes arise out of differences in interpretation of the words "reasonable" and "reasonably".

Post-settlement issues

10.6.13 As with settlements in all practice areas, disputes can arise post-settlement, either in relation to interpretation of the agreement, or because of non-compliance.

It is common following settlement of partnership and professional practice disputes for outgoing proprietors to breach non-competition provisions, and in consequence for agreed instalment payments not to be made by the ongoing proprietors.

Agreements to use best or reasonable endeavours to secure the release of an outgoing proprietor from personal liability to banks, landlords and other long-term creditors sometimes are not honoured or, more commonly, the endeavours are half-hearted. Drafting may have created a duty to attempt release once only, or a duty to continue indefinitely trying to secure release. A frequently-raised issue in this context is: does "best" endeavours mean "all possible" endeavours? If necessary to secure release of an outgoing proprietor from say a long-term loan from a bank, do ongoing proprietors have to realise the equity in their homes, or give them up as security, or raise monies in other ways, in order to discharge the liability if the bank will not otherwise release the outgoing proprietor?

10.7 Ten key points to remember

(1) With proprietors being pitched one against another, the survival of the business itself is at risk.

(2) Whilst the dispute continues, the ongoing development of the business is hampered, if not altogether prevented, and the business may go into decline, all of which is an incentive to settle early and move on to more profitable associations.

(3) In professional practices the preservation of reputation and client goodwill is of paramount importance.

(4) For that reason professional practices are particularly sensitive to their internal disputes becoming public knowledge, and the threat or perceived threat of this happening often precipitates a compromise.

(5) The strength of individual proprietors' respective negotiating positions may depend in part upon actual or perceived differences in their skills, reputation, or ability to attract and retain clients or customers.

(6) In partnerships and professional practices, hidden agendas, shifting allegiances, personal enmity and skeletons in cupboards are all commonplace, and can be impediments to settlement unless detected and explored.

(7) Unusually in the sphere of commercial disputes, partnership and professional practice disputes are frequently driven as much by pride and (often very strong) emotion as by pure logical analysis, and the importance of releasing this emotional tension cannot be over-emphasised.

(8) Shared (personal) liabilities such as outstanding loans, long (and sometimes over-rented) leases and obligations to employees often bring parties to partnership disputes to settlement, since it is a sobering prospect that the business might fall apart leaving those liabilities with the partners.

(9) In drafting settlement agreements it is critically important to consider not only taxation issues but also the interplay between the settlement agreement and the partnership (or shareholders' or members') agreement (which usually continues to govern at least some rights and duties).

(10) Given the often complex nature of this type of dispute and the uncertain ability or willingness of the parties to implement some elements of the settlement agreements which arise from them, it is wise to consider putting a mediation clause into the settlement agreement.

CHAPTER 11

SHIPPING DISPUTES

JONATHAN LUX, WILLIAM MARSH AND CATHERINE BLOOMFIELD

11.1 TYPES OF DISPUTES

It is conventional to categorise shipping matters as either "wet" or "dry". Roughly speaking "dry shipping" is all about the commercial use of ships and "wet shipping" is all about marine casualties. It follows that dry shipping disputes are almost invariably disputes relating to contracts. Contractual issues, however, are often only peripheral to wet shipping disputes which are more likely to have as their basis tort rather than contract—as, for example, in the case of a collision between vessels. That said, however, a marine casualty will usually lead to contracts of one sort or another being made, for example, with salvors engaged to provide salvage services in connection with the casualty; bonds and other securities given in the immediate aftermath of the casualty and contracts between the parties involved in the maritime adventure which is the subject of the casualty—these will include the shipowner, the charterer(s), the owners of any cargo carried on the ship and the insurers of the respective interests.

Traditionally, those involved in the shipping industry have tended to "do their own thing" when disputes have arisen, with the result that a number of specialised, industry-specific dispute resolution vehicles have evolved. Against this background the traditional dichotomy between wet and dry shipping has led to further diversification of the infrastructure for dispute resolution. The way, for example, that collision and salvage matters are dealt with bears very little resemblance to the way charterparty matters are dealt with. Limitation actions are entirely *sui generis* (see below). For these reasons an overview of the use of mediation and other ADR techniques in relation to shipping disputes can only be obtained against an overview of how those disputes have traditionally been resolved.

Whilst it is convenient in this chapter to deal with some aspects of wet and dry shipping separately, it is germane at the outset just to outline the sort of things which can arise under each of the two heads.

Wet shipping has four main arms—collision, salvage, arrest and limitation. The terms collision and salvage are self-explanatory. Limitation in the shipping context is *not* limitation of time. Rather it is limitation of liability: by international convention a shipowner is entitled to limit his liability for loss or damage for which he would otherwise be responsible to a sum calculated by reference to the tonnage of his vessel.[1, 2] The right to limit may be invoked by the shipowner commencing a limitation action in the Admiralty Court or by way of defence to a claim brought against him whether in court or other dispute resolution forum. The former may be classified as a pure "wet shipping" matter and is dealt with at paragraph 11.2.7 below. The latter, however, is really a dry shipping matter in that if the right to limit is pleaded as a defence, then it is just the same as any other defence. As to arrest, strictly speaking this is simply the means by which the jurisdiction of the Admiralty Court is invoked in relation to claims against the ship which is arrested. The arrest of a sister ship has the same effect. Service of the claim form on a ship whilst in the jurisdiction will commence *in rem* proceedings in just the same way as service of the claim form on a person within the jurisdiction will commence *in personam* proceedings. The advantage of an arrest is that it produces security for the claim, since the vessel will only be released against the provision of acceptable security. Otherwise the vessel is at risk of being sold by court auction in satisfaction of the claim. International Conventions[3] and the applicable statutory rules[4] and rules of court[5] detail the claims in relation to which arrest is permissible. Once a vessel is arrested (or released against the provision of security) the proceedings will continue in precisely the same way as *in personam* proceedings in any other court. The shipowner or, in practice, his P&I Club on his behalf, will take over the defence of the claim and the handling of the litigation. Accordingly, although arrest is traditionally regarded as a wet shipping matter the disputes which led to the vessel being arrested in the first place are just disputes and are in principle as

[1] The U.K. is a party to the 1976 Convention on Limitation of Liability for Maritime Claims. This supplements the 1957 International Convention Relating to the Limitation of the Liability of Owners of Seagoing Ships to which many countries are still parties. See s. 17, Sched. 4 of the Merchant Shipping Act 1979 and now s. 185, Sched. 7 of the Merchant Shipping Act 1995.

[2] Tonnage limitation should be distinguished from package limitation. Under the Hague and Hague Visby rules (*infra*) the carrier may limit his liability for cargo claims to a sum calculated by reference to the number and size of the packages carried.

[3] The International Convention for the Unification of Certain Rules Relating to the Arrest of Sea-going Ships 1952 (the Arrest Convention); The International Convention on Certain Rules Concerning Civil Jurisdiction in Matters of Collision, 1952 (the Collision Convention).

[4] Supreme Court Act 1981, ss. 20 and 21.

[5] Section 2A CPR (Special Proceedings under Part 49).

amenable to resolution by mediation or any other ADR process as any other shipping dispute. The only real specialist matters relating to arrest are things such as the order of priorities[6] for claims on the fund established if, having been arrested, the ship is subsequently sold, the proceeds paid into court and the total claims on the fund exceed the amount of the fund. By and large these matters are subject to set procedures and well established rules which, given the potential number of parties involved, do not easily lend themselves to compromise.

As to dry shipping there are numerous different types of ship—ranging from passenger ferries, to dry bulk and liquid bulk carriers, through livestock carriers and reefers to RoRos and ULCCs—and numerous different commercial uses to which they can be put. It follows that there is no end to the permutations of the factual bases upon which disputes might arise. In practice, however, most dry shipping disputes are contract disputes and the most common contracts relating to a ship are charterparties (under which all or part of the ship is hired either for a particular time or a particular voyage), bills of lading (under which cargo is carried by the ship) and ship sale and purchase, repair and newbuilding contracts. It is likely that a time charter, a voyage charter and a bill of lading contract will exist at the same time for the same ship on the same voyage. The same set of facts may give rise to different disputes between different parties involved in the adventure, often with the outcome of one dispute determining the outcome of another and with indemnities passing up and down the contract chain.

11.1.1 The sorts of disputes which typically arise in relation to the various contracts include the following:

(a) *Time charterparties*—[7] disputes very often centre around who, as between the owner and charterer, is responsible for a particular loss; the liability of the charterer for damage to the ship caused by defective bunkers he has supplied to it;[8] whether the shipowner, acting through the Master, is or was obliged to follow particular orders given by the charterers[9] and whether or not the charterers' obligation to pay hire for the vessel is suspended at any particular time.[10] Disputes

[6] See generally N. Meeson, *Admiralty Jurisdiction and Practice* (2nd ed. LLP, 2000), Chap. 6.

[7] The most common form of time charterparty for dry cargo vessels is on the standard New York Produce Exchange Form (NYPE). The latest version is the 1993 version—references to NYPE 1993 are references to this. It is now very common for vessels to be chartered on the NYPE form for single voyages only—these are known as time charter trips.

[8] *E.g.* cl. 9(b) NYPE 1993.

[9] *E.g.* cl. 8 NYPE 1993.

[10] *E.g.* cl. 17 NYPE 1993.

often arise as to the condition of the vessel on delivery under the charter or on redelivery after it.[11]

(b) *Voyage charterparties*—again disputes very often centre around who, as between the owner and the charterer is responsible for a particular loss: whether to the vessel—as in an unsafe port claim, or to the cargo for which the ship-owner may be liable to the cargo owner under the bill of lading; as with time charters there may be disputes as to the condition of the vessel on delivery[12] under the charter or, on redelivery after it. There may be disputes as to the length of time taken to complete a particular voyage(s).[13] Disputes relating to demurrage (liquidated damages payable by the voyage charterer for failure to load or discharge the cargo within a pre-agreed time[14]) are common.

(c) *Contracts of affreightment*—under a contract of affreightment the carrier undertakes to perform a number of cargo liftings on the same or different vessels within a given period of time. There are, essentially, a series of individual voyage charterparties and in addition to disputes relating to the overall agreement the whole range of voyage charter disputes can arise.

(d) *Bills of lading*—amongst other things a bill of lading evidences the contract of carriage between the carrier (the shipowner or charterer) and the cargo owner. The most common disputes under bills of lading relate to loss of or damage to the cargo during the voyage, delayed or non-arrival of the cargo and misdelivery of the cargo.[15]

(e) *Second-hand ship sales*—these are usually completed on the basis of a standard form contract such as the Norwegian Saleform. The most common disputes relate to the condition of the vessel on delivery to the buyer.

[11] *E.g.* cl. 2 (Delivery) and cl. 35 (Redelivery) NYPE 1993.

[12] There is a strict common law duty that the vessel should be in a condition at the start of the voyage such that she can perform the contract voyage in safety.

[13] It is an implied term in all charterparties that the owner proceeds with reasonable dispatch on the contract voyage and on the approach voyage.

[14] Laytime—this may be calculated by reference to a fixed number of days (either calendar or conventional) or by reference to a daily rate of loading/discharge—*e.g.* 500 tonnes per day.

[15] Bills of lading may be subject to the Hague Rules (the Brussels Convention 1924), the Hague Visby Rules (the Hague Rules as amended by the Brussels Protocol (1968)) or the Hamburg Rules (the UN Convention on the Carriage of Goods by Sea 1978). The Hague Visby Rules are enacted into English law by the Carriage of Goods by Sea Act (COGSA) 1971. The Hague, Hague Visby and Hamburg Rules impose duties on the carrier as regards care of the cargo under the contract. As well as to bill of lading contracts any of the rules may apply to charterparties (time or voyage) if they are expressly incorporated by means of a clause paramount.

(f) *Shipbuilding contracts*—disputes commonly relate to the condition of the "finished product" and whether it meets the contract specifications.

(g) *Overlap with wet shipping*—as mentioned at the very beginning of this chapter marine casualties usually give rise to some sort of contract dispute. To take just a few examples: where limitation is pleaded as a Defence, where a casualty gives rise to unsafe port issues and in relation to general average ("GA")[16]—the Master might declare GA following the casualty, GA bonds and guarantees might be posted on behalf of the different interests involved in the adventure *(e.g.* the cargo owners), the claims adjusted and then disputes arise as to the meaning and application of the York Antwerp Rules[17] which the parties have agreed in their contracts are to govern the adjustment of general average.[18]

(h) *Associated marine matters*—there are numerous other matters associated with shipping which can give rise to disputes—for example, claims by and against the suppliers of bunkers and necessaries and claims by and against port and harbour authorities.

(i) *Insurance*—it is important to bear in mind that many maritime disputes have insurance aspects and in reality a dispute is very often simply between subrogated insurers.

The general consensus is that if a dispute can be settled then it can be mediated—even one involving allegations of fraud—and that the only cases where mediation might not be appropriate are cases where a precedent is required or publicity is wanted. However, even as regards these two points there may well be a role for mediation. For example, as to precedent, mediation might still be useful to secure agreement on all points save for the one issue which might then be taken to the court on a construction summons; and as to publicity, it might be a term of the mediation settlement that something, *e.g.* an apology, is to be published. The precise role of mediation in relation to shipping disputes is addressed in more detail at paragraphs 11.4–11.6.

Since the vast majority of maritime disputes are in fact settled before a final hearing, it might be thought that mediation is, at

[16] General average is a form of mutual insurance designed to cover extraordinary sacrifices/expenses incurred by one of the interests in the voyage (ship, cargo or freight) for the benefit of all—*e.g.* where cargo is thrown overboard to save the ship and enable it to complete the voyage with the remaining cargo.

[17] The York Antwerp Rules govern how general average will be applied in a given situation.

[18] *E.g.* cl. 25 NYPE 1993.

worst, simply a means to expedite that outcome. However, as indicated above, the infrastructure for dispute resolution in the shipping world is already quite sophisticated and it is necessary first to consider how it all fits together.

RESOLVING SHIPPING DISPUTES IN COURTS AND TRIBUNALS 11.2

By the end of the nineteenth century the great majority of ships trading in the world were built in the U.K. and owned or operated by British owners. Consequently most shipping contracts were governed by English law. At the end of the nineteenth century the "Commercial List" was established to deal with mercantile disputes, including shipping disputes.

The commercial scenery has, of course, long since changed. British interests in shipping are the exception rather than the rule and shipping is now a truly international industry. The legal scenery, however, has not changed: it is still the norm for shipping contracts to be governed by English law—albeit most of them by virtue of an express choice of law clause rather than any factual connection of the vessel, its cargo or the parties involved in the adventure with England or the U.K. Similarly, most differences between "shipping people" continue to be resolved by utilising the dispute resolution machinery established in England under English law.

The Commercial Court in London and the Business List of the Central London County Court are the courts for resolving shipping disputes. However, for very many years the method of dispute resolution preferred by those involved in the industry has been arbitration. In the early years arbitrators were typically drawn on an ad hoc basis from the ranks of members of the Baltic Exchange. The London Maritime Arbitrators Association (the LMAA) was established in 1960. Detailed written terms to be applied to maritime arbitration under the aegis of the LMAA were introduced in the early 1980s. Those terms were substantially revised and enlarged in 1984, 1987, 1991, 1993 and most recently in 1997 following the entry into force of the Arbitration Act 1996.

In many other areas of commerce arbitration is considered to be another form of ADR. For a very long time, however, arbitration of shipping disputes has in fact been the norm. It has now developed a degree of complexity and formality such that a shipping arbitration (at least one on the full LMAA terms) is very little different—certainly in terms of time and expense—than a Commercial Court action. At least in the shipping context it is not really apt to include arbitration in the category of ADR techniques.

Most shipping contracts contain an express arbitration clause— 11.2.1
this is the norm for example in charterparties, shipbuilding and ship sale contracts. Bills of lading, however—even those issued pursu-

ant to a charterparty—rarely have such clauses (although they may be expressed to incorporate the terms of a charterparty, that will not be sufficient to include a charterparty arbitration clause unless that clause is specifically and individually incorporated[19]). Most "dry shipping" arbitrations are conducted pursuant to such an express clause and most are conducted on the LMAA terms. Often the clauses do not specify that the arbitration is to be conducted on those terms. A very common form is for the clause to specify simply that the arbitrator(s) be "commercial men". However, the established maritime arbitrators are all members of the LMAA and none will accept appointment other than on the LMAA terms. There are a number of categories of LMAA arbitrations: those on the full LMAA terms, those on the LMAA small claims terms, those on the LMAA FALCA (Fast And Low-Cost Arbitration) terms and those on documents alone.

Although in practice much rarer, other forms of arbitration are also possible for the resolution of shipping disputes—for example, the London Court of International Arbitration (LCIA) or the International Chamber of Commerce (ICC). It is also possible to have private ad-hoc arbitrations. Some contracts—especially large scale shipbuilding contracts—have a clause requiring technical disputes arising in the course of performance of the contract to be referred to the arbitration of the vessel's Classification society. The vast majority of shipping arbitrations, however, are on the LMAA terms.

Whatever the specific terms, all arbitrations governed by English law are subject to the provisions of the Arbitration Act 1996 and the supervisory jurisdiction of the Commercial Court.

The procedural steps for an LMAA arbitration

11.2.2 The procedural steps for an LMAA arbitration are governed by the applicable part of the LMAA terms. The documents alone, the small claims and the FALCA procedures are all variants of the same sort of thing—there is no hearing and everything is done on paper.

The LMAA small claims procedure was introduced in 1989 as a quick and cheap way to resolve smaller claims. It was specifically introduced for use where neither the claim nor any counter-claim exceeds U.S.$50,000 (originally U.S.$25,000)—although the parties are free to modify those limits. There is a sole arbitrator whose award is based on a simple sequential exchange of Letters of Claim, Defence and Reply together with relevant documents. The arbitrator's fees are limited to £1,000 plus VAT. He is also limited in the level of costs he can award to either party. The whole thing is supposed to be over within a month of final written submissions.

The LMAA commentary says of this procedure specifically:

[19] *Thomas v. Portsea SS Co.* (1912) A.C.1. *Cf. The Merak* (1965) P.Q.Q. 3.

> "It is not suitable for use where there are complex issues or where there is likely to be examination of witnesses. On the other hand the procedure may be suitable for handling larger claims where there is a single issue at stake."

If the small claims procedure is used, the right to appeal to the court is excluded.

The LMAA FALCA rules were introduced in July 1996, the intention being to provide an arbitration procedure one up from the small claims procedure but still cheaper, quicker and less cumbersome than the full LMAA procedure. The rules are specifically aimed at claims between U.S.$50,000 and U.S.$250,000—the LMAA commentary to the rules refers to the "middle range of maritime disputes", although as with the small claims procedure the parties are free to modify the upper and lower limits. The FALCA rules also provide for a sole arbitrator, no oral hearing (save in exceptional circumstances) and that by agreeing to the rules the parties are deemed to waive any right of appeal to the courts. Strict time limits are set down so that the time between the appointment of the arbitrator and publication of his award is no longer than eight months. Unlike the small claims procedure, however, there is no fixed fee and the arbitrator may charge and assess costs on the basis of normal costs principles. Nevertheless there is a limit of £7,500 on the amount which can be claimed and ordered by way of security for costs—although that limit can be relaxed where the arbitrator orders that, due to the particular circumstances of the case, it should not proceed on documents alone and there should be an oral hearing.

Whether because of the financial and costs limits or the exclusion of rights of appeal, arbitrations on the LMAA small claims and FALCA terms have not proved hugely popular in practice. Where, however, the factual evidence is clear on the papers and there is no real need for witnesses to give evidence in person, often the preferred choice is to agree to proceed on documents alone. Such an agreement can be made even after a full LMAA arbitration has been commenced and in such a case there will be no hearing and the need for factual and expert witnesses may be dispensed with altogether. There is simply an exchange of written submissions (usually sequential with the claimant having the last word as is the norm in all LMAA arbitrations—which in fact reflects the court practice), the tribunal then considers the papers and submissions and publishes its award. There are, however, no time limits by when the arbitrators should do this.

Prior to the introduction of the LMAA Guidelines on Procedure arbitrations on the full LMAA terms were procedurally very similar to Commercial Court actions. In outline the steps in both were as follows: 11.2.3

(a) commencement (service of claim form/arbitration notice);
(b) service of pleadings/submissions;
(c) disclosure of relevant documents;
(d) exchange of factual witness statements;
(e) exchange of experts' reports;
(f) trial/hearing.

Now, however, the LMAA Guidelines stipulate the following simplified procedure after commencement of the arbitration, which procedure it is stated, should be followed in all but exceptional cases. This reflects the general duties of the tribunal as set out in section 33(1) of the Arbitration Act 1996 and cl. 12(a) of the LMAA Rules 1997 which provides that "It shall be for the tribunal to decide all procedural and evidential matters, subject to the right of the parties to agree any matter":

(a) Sequential service of submissions of Claim, Defence and Counter-claim and Reply with in each case supporting documentation attached.
(b) Both parties ask each other for any documentation which they consider to be relevant but which has not already been disclosed. This two-stage procedure marks a significant departure from the previous rules and the Guidelines specifically state that formal pleadings with later disclosure of documents will be the exception rather than the rule and that the arbitrators have no obligation to adopt any of the rules of civil procedure that apply in courts of law unless they or the parties have decided or agreed that they should.
(c) Hearing (fixed after agreement between the parties as to the necessary procedural and evidential steps leading up to it or, absent agreement, by the tribunal following the submission of detailed questionnaires.)

A significant difference between the procedure in the Commercial Court and in full LMAA arbitration is the Case Management Conference (CMC). However, the arbitrators in LMAA arbitrations will routinely issue directions as to the conduct of the arbitration, and in so doing they must have in mind the general principles set out in section 1 of the Arbitration Act 1996. These re-confirm that the object of arbitration is to obtain the fair resolution of disputes without unnecessary delay or expense and that the parties are at all times free to agree how their disputes are resolved, subject only to such safeguards as are necessary in the public interest. The

Arbitration Practice Direction which regulates the court's supervisory role is founded on these general principles which it describes as "the overriding objective"—thus bringing the terminology into line with that in the CPR.

Wet shipping matters

With regard to, specifically, collision, salvage and limitation—because of the limited and very specific nature of the points which are in issue there are very specialised dispute resolution mechanisms which are in place. **11.2.4**

Collision

Obviously because of the nature of a collision there will not be a pre-existing contract between the parties which provides for arbitration and so everything must be resolved in court. There are two basic issues which arise in relation to any collision—liability and damages. Which of the two colliding ships is liable for the collision and to what extent is decided on the available evidence by the Admiralty Judge assisted as necessary by the Elder Brethren.[20] Then, liability having been decided, the damages flowing from the collision (*e.g.* the cost of repairs and loss of use claims) are assessed by the Admiralty Registrar (not the Admiralty Judge). In the past the Admiralty Registrar was assisted by merchants but nowadays he conducts the assessment alone on the basis of the evidence submitted by the parties. **11.2.5**

The sequence of events/procedure in a collision case is as follows:

(a) Collision.

(b) Proceedings are commenced by the service within the jurisdiction of an "*in rem* Claim Form" on the colliding vessel or a sister vessel. Technically the parties to the proceedings are the two vessels.

(c) The parties file with the court their "preliminary acts". These set out the parties' case as to what happened and why they believe the other vessel is at fault.

(d) The parties then exchange these preliminary acts.

(e) There is a Case Management Conference at which the court gives directions leading up to the trial on liability.

(f) Damages are assessed by the Admiralty Registrar.

[20] The Elder Brethren are Master mariners and members of Trinity House who are appointed to sit with the Admiralty Judge to advise him on matters of ship navigation and handling.

There are normally a number of different parties involved in a collision case – including the H&M underwriters who might have paid out in respect of collision damage and collision liability; the vessels' P&I Clubs which might have paid, for example, pollution damage claims arising out of the collision and claims in respect of cargo lost or damaged in the collision and, of course, the shipowners themselves (each for their uninsured losses—*e.g.* hull deductible, cargo liability deductible, loss of profits).

Salvage

11.2.6 The vast majority of salvage services are performed under Lloyd's Standard Form of Salvage Agreement (LOF) which is a standard printed contract, the signature of which by the Master is an admission of the shipowner's liability to pay salvage. It is not, however, an admission as to the amount due. That is assessed by an arbitration conducted in accordance with the rules annexed to LOF.

The sequence of events/procedure in a salvage case is as follows:

(a) LOF signed.

(b) Salvor performs the salvage services.

(c) The salvor demands security.

(d) That security is provided to Lloyd's which then appoints an arbitrator—who will usually be a Queen's Counsel practising at the Admiralty Bar. The parties to the arbitration are the salvor and the salved property (the ship, cargo, bunkers, freight and stores). The arbitration follows the procedural rules annexed to LOF.

Limitation

11.2.7 If a shipowner wishes to limit his liability arising out of a casualty, the procedure is simply to issue a limitation Claim Form and then serve it on one potential claimant. The Claim Form must be supported by an affidavit stating, *inter alia*, how the claim in respect of which limitation is sought arose, the amount of the claim, the amount of the limitation fund and an explanation as to why the party seeking to limit is entitled to limit.[21] A limitation decree is an "all or nothing" type remedy (if, indeed, it can accurately be described as a remedy) and is an issue which arises at the very front end of a dispute. Further, given that under the 1976 Limitation Convention limits are virtually unbreakable and there is a more or less automatic right to a limitation decree, limitation simpliciter is not something in relation to which disputes often arise.

[21] The procedure in a limitation action is set out in s. 2A CPR (Specialist Proceedings under Part 49).

THE ROLE OF COURTS AND TRIBUNALS 11.3

Against the background of how it all works it can be seen that the role of courts and tribunals is in fact wider than simply providing a means of dispute resolution in their own right. They also serve a useful role both as a backdrop to the various ADR techniques, all of which are, in principle, available to the parties at any stage after a dispute has arisen, and as a vehicle whereby those techniques—specifically mediation—might be introduced.

Courts and tribunals as a vehicle for ADR/mediation

Where the dispute is the subject of court proceedings, the court 11.3.1
may order a one month stay in the proceedings for the parties to consider mediation. The court may make this order of its own volition or at the request of one of the parties. If a party does not co-operate there might be serious costs penalties against that party if the matter proceeds to a full hearing, even if that party is successful. When the dispute is the subject of arbitration, however, the situation is less clear. Although modern shipping arbitrations cannot really be regarded as a variant of ADR and arbitration clauses are often simply standard form clauses in standard form contracts which the parties have had little or no opportunity to negotiate, the fact remains that technically the parties are arbitrating only because that is the way they have chosen to resolve their dispute. All English law arbitrations are subject to the Arbitration Act 1996, s. 1 of which provides:

> "1. **General Principles**
> The provisions of this Part are founded on the following principles and shall be construed accordingly
>
> (a) the object of arbitration is to obtain the fair resolution of disputes by an impartial Tribunal without unnecessary delay or expense;
> (b) the parties should be free to agree how their disputes are resolved, subject only to such safeguards as are necessary in the public interest;
> (c) in matters governed by this Part the court should not intervene except as provided by this Part."

Whilst an arbitral tribunal might consider that mediation would be the fairest, quickest and cheapest way of resolving the dispute, it is bound to give effect to the parties' agreement. On a general level also, one feature of the post-Woolf era is that the court system is regarded as a public resource which, like any other public resource, might be the subject of rationing: access to the courts and judges might be restricted to ensure that no one case is allowed "disproportionate" use of that resource. Mediation therefore has a role in siphoning out cases which would otherwise use valuable court time. An arbitration, on the other hand, is a private commercial matter and unless the parties have agreed to it in advance it is not open to the arbitrators to ration the service which they are being paid to provide. There would also in any event be something of a commercial conflict of interest insofar as professional arbitrators are concerned. It is doubtless for this reason that although the LMAA does have a set of "Conciliation Terms" which provide expressly that conciliation includes mediation and any other form of dispute resolution other than litigation or arbitration, those terms only apply when the parties are seeking an amicable settlement of their dispute and have agreed that the terms apply. Otherwise the LMAA terms do not refer expressly to ADR or mediation and the LMAA panel of mediators (which for the most part comprises the LMAA Arbitrators) has rarely been used. The mediation clause in the procedural rules attached to the LOF 2000 put the point in no stronger terms than this:

> "The Arbitrator shall ensure that in all cases the representative parties are informed of the benefit which might be derived from the use of mediation."

11.3.2 There would therefore be grounds to object to an arbitration tribunal of its own motion ordering a stay of the arbitration for the parties to consider mediation. However, if in the course of the arbitration both parties agree to try to resolve their dispute by mediation, then arguably it would be the tribunal's duty under the 1996 Act to order such a stay. An interesting question would arise if just one party were to apply to the tribunal for a stay pending mediation but the other objected. At first blush it would seem that since arbitration is in theory a consensual means of dispute resolution the tribunal would be bound not to grant the application. A similar situation arises where, once an arbitration has been commenced on the full LMAA terms, one party wishes it to proceed on documents alone but the other wants a full oral hearing. In the past LMAA Arbitrators were extremely reluctant in these circumstances to agree to allow the short cut—giving deference instead to the other party's right to have everything "proceed by the book". In this way it was possible to use as a litigation tactic the threat of the delay and additional expense associated with an oral hearing. More recently however—especially since the introduction of the LMAA Guidelines[22]—LMAA Arbitrators have been more willing to entertain contested applications to convert the arbitration to "documents alone" if on an objective basis the dispute is apt for decision without a hearing. Section 33 of the 1996 Act sets out the general duties of an arbitration tribunal. They include in section 33(1)(b) a

[22] Above.

duty to adopt procedures suitable to the circumstances of the particular case, avoiding unnecessary delay or expense. Section 33(2) provides that this is an overriding duty with which the tribunal should comply in conducting all aspects of the arbitral proceedings. Accordingly, whilst it remains to be seen what view will be taken of a contested mediation application in an arbitration on the LMAA terms one argument might be as follows:

(a) by agreeing to English law arbitration the parties have agreed to resolve their disputes by an arbitration governed by the Arbitration Act 1996,

(b) the arbitrators in all such arbitrations are bound to resolve the dispute in such a way as avoids unnecessary delay and expense,

(c) mediation is intended to avoid unnecessary delay and expense,

(d) the arbitrators are therefore bound to consider the use of mediation and because of this,

(e) they must have an implied power to order mediation; accordingly,

(f) by agreeing English law arbitration therefore the parties have agreed that their disputes might ultimately be resolved by mediation.

Courts and tribunals as a backdrop to ADR/mediation and the role of straightforward negotiations

Until the development of ADR in its modern sophisticated form there were really only two ways of resolving shipping disputes once they had arisen: by simple negotiation or by formal legal proceedings in the appropriate forum—whether that was court or arbitration. Obviously it is always preferable if the parties (direct or via their lawyers) can negotiate a satisfactory agreement. Even in one-off cases when broader commercial considerations do not apply the delay and expense of the alternative to negotiation can be prohibitive. It is only if settlement through direct negotiation proves impossible that the other layers (mediation/arbitration/court) enter into the frame. From one point of view the single most important role of courts and tribunals is a negative one: to provide a spectre of potentially open-ended costs and delay. This at any rate is true for many dry shipping disputes where the sums involved and the complexity of the issues and dispute resolution procedures have grown with the complexity of the ships themselves. This "backdrop" role, however, is much less pronounced in collision and salvage cases which, unlike pure contract-based cases, are invariably fact based and so often do need to go through some formal investigative process before they can be 11.3.3

resolved. For example, in collision cases without prejudice negotiations will commence almost immediately the collision has occurred and whilst for the purposes of those negotiations liability and damages will be dealt with together rather than separately as in the formal court and Registry proceedings, it is still very often necessary to go through at least the preliminary stages of the formal liability assessment. This is because it is only in this way that it is possible to ascertain what the other side's case is (as set out in the Preliminary Act), whether the papers support that case and hence what the judge's likely finding will be on the apportionment of liability for the collision. This will, of course, be directly germane to the amount of damages which might be recoverable. Collisions are, by their nature, unexpected events and are not preceded by anything in writing from which the precise issues and arguments might be identified.

However, things do tend to be much speedier so far as wet shipping disputes are concerned. Because of the lesser bulk of work, references to the Admiralty Judge and the Registrar can be brought on comparatively quickly and in salvage arbitrations the time scales are fixed such that they are normally over within six to nine months of the LOF being signed in the first place.

11.4 THE ROLE OF ADR GENERALLY AND IN PARTICULAR THE ADVANTAGES OF MEDIATION OVER OTHER FORMS OF ADR

ADR has been developed to do precisely that which its name suggests—*viz.* to provide a means of alternative dispute resolution. In the context of a shipping dispute this means an alternative to resolution either in the Commercial Court or in arbitration. It is not really alternative to resolution by straightforward negotiation since that has always been and will certainly remain the preferred method of dispute resolution. As will be seen, however, mediation, which is the most common form of ADR, is usually used as an adjunct to negotiation—to kick start it/put it back on course if it has broken down. The rest of this chapter is concerned with how mediation might be utilised to resolve shipping disputes and is intended to provide a practical guide to the initial decision/order to try mediation, the lead up to and procedure at the mediation and then what might happen after the mediation. Initially however, brief mention should be made of the other forms of ADR which may be appropriate to resolve a shipping dispute. These cover the whole spectrum from structured negotiation techniques (of which mediation is one), through case appraisals to binding third party intervention.

Structured negotiation

11.4.1 The *mini-trial (Executive Tribunal)* involves a tribunal consisting of senior executives from the disputing parties and an independent chair. The executives have no previous involvement in the dispute, they will often be advised by experts on technical or legal issues and, after a procedure which resembles an abbreviated trial—with legal representatives making submissions on behalf of the parties —a decision is made. However, that decision will not be binding unless the parties agree beforehand that it should be. This form of ADR may be suitable where a more formalised presentation of the evidence/arguments is required and where it is anticipated that the involvement of objective senior executives may enable a commercial deal to be concluded.

Case appraisal

Early Neutral Evaluation (ENE) involves a "judge" (or other mutually agreed neutral person) reviewing the evidence submitted by each party and then providing a preliminary view on the merits. For this reason the "judge" will usually have a legal background and might be, for example, a retired judge, senior Counsel or solicitor. The judge's view is non-binding and is designed to give the parties an indication of how the court or arbitration tribunal may regard the merits of their case should the matter proceed to a full hearing. The idea is that the neutral evaluation will facilitate direct negotiations between the parties. **11.4.2**

Third party intervention

Expert determination/adjudication—here the parties appoint a neutral expert or adjudicator who reads or hears the submissions of the parties and then delivers a legally binding decision. Expert determination/adjudication is sometimes used in disputes which are technical in nature. An adjudicator may also be used to give non-binding decisions on disputes during the currency of a contract (*e.g.* a long-term time charterparty or a contract of affreightment). The parties may reject the decision and proceed to arbitration if they wish. **11.4.3**

Hybrid methods

Customised ADR—in certain cases a hybrid process may be devised combining, for example, mediation with expert determination or ENE; Med-Arb (mediation-arbitration) is a process whereby the parties agree that if the mediation does not result in a settlement, then the mediator converts to an arbitrator and makes a binding award. This procedure, however, although quite open to the parties to agree, is subject to the obvious question-mark about the appropriateness of a "neutral" who may have acquired confidential information as a mediator switching roles to that of arbitrator. **11.4.4**

The principal difference between these other ADR methods and mediation is that they all tend to produce a "win/lose" result in very much the same way as court or arbitral proceedings do. However, the aim of mediation—which is effectively just assisted negotiation—is to produce a "win/win" result—*i.e.* a deal: an *agreed* not an imposed resolution of the dispute.

11.5 THE ROLE OF MEDIATION

Mediation is a useful means of breaking a deadlock in negotiations between lawyers and/or their clients. It is an effective way of bringing forward the resolution of a dispute.

There are times when considerable costs and effort are expended in negotiations which appear to be making little, if any, progress. There may be many reasons why negotiations are not working. It may be, for example, that the lawyers are too afraid to be seen to be making the first concession in case they appear weak and the other side takes encouragement. Sometimes the problem is that one of the lawyers does not fully understand his client's case and has therefore not evaluated its merits sufficiently accurately. The lawyer may not be advising his client properly and may even have ulterior motives for keeping the case going. On other occasions it will be the clients that are the stumbling block. The dispute may have become personal with one party obstinately refusing to give way. The client may be subject to internal pressures. One party may simply wish to delay the inevitable for as long as it possibly can. For whatever reason, negotiations may be slow and costly.

The role of the mediator is to find a way of overcoming the obstacles to settlement whatever they may be. This is what the mediator has been trained to do.

What actually happens during a mediation?

11.5.1 There are no hard and fast rules about mediation. One of its great strengths is its flexibility. The more experienced practitioners become, the greater use they are able to make of this flexibility. In brief, though, the process is usually as follows: the parties each prepare a brief statement of case which is sent to the mediator and to the other parties. This will set out each party's position. It should be brief, clear, concise and reasonable. These statements are not formal documents and the parties are not bound by them. They are, as is everything to do with the mediation, entirely without prejudice. Their function is to enable the mediator to understand the case, where each party is coming from and what factors are important to each party. The mediator is also provided with some of the documents in the case. This is dealt with in paragraph 11.5.11 below.

At the beginning of the day all the parties meet together with the mediator. Each party then makes a short presentation of its case. This may be made by the lawyer or the client. Who does it will depend on the type of case. Generally speaking, presentations are more effective if made by the client. If the case turns on legal points, however, or is particularly complicated, they may be better done by lawyers.

The mediator may then give the parties an opportunity to respond to what they have heard and may encourage parties to vent their feelings. If there are any emotional overtones in the case, it is usually a good idea to encourage them to be articulated as this will usually facilitate settlement later in the day.

When the mediator feels that the group session is no longer serving any useful function, he will send the parties back to their own rooms and will arrange for a series of meetings to take place in "caucus". The mediator will visit each party in their own room to explore their case with them. This part of the process is called "reality testing". The mediator will probe and challenge each party, testing how realistic its position is and trying to uncover what it is that each party really wants and what obstacles each party is putting up to hinder settlement.

Views differ as to how much the parties should tell the mediator. 11.5.2
Mediators would obviously like to know everything so that they can find a path between the true positions of the parties. Lawyers will try and play the mediator and concede as little as possible. Take this too far and the mediation will last much longer than necessary and may fail altogether, which is not likely to be in the best interests of the clients. A point always to bear in mind is that the clients will witness how their lawyers deal with the mediator. If the client wants to settle and his lawyer is being too difficult, he will not be impressed. Another point to bear in mind is that if the mediator perceives that a lawyer is hindering settlement for his client, he may ask to meet the client without his lawyer. Such a request should not be refused. It is the clients' day and they may settle on whatever terms they wish, irrespective of their lawyers' views. Stories abound of clients who have only disclosed some critical fact to their lawyer after the mediation has taken place. It is not only lawyers who adopt tactics!

As the day progresses, the mediator may meet with different groups. He may, for example, meet with just the parties' lawyers, just experts or simply with one or all clients. As a settlement approaches, it becomes more likely that the mediator will meet just with clients.

Hopefully a settlement is eventually achieved. The lawyers will then draft the settlement agreement. The case is concluded and everyone can go home or out to celebrate, as the case may be.

Mediations are often intense experiences, especially as the day progresses. A momentum is built up which encourages clients to focus on the consequences if they do not settle. When it becomes clear that a settlement may be possible, clients rarely want to walk away. Mediations can therefore often achieve in one day what might take many weeks or months to achieve by conventional negotiation.

Sometimes mediations fail. The mediator will then usually call the parties back in a room together and try and finish on as positive a note as possible. Sometimes the parties may agree to reconvene the mediation at a later date.

Handling the client

11.5.3 Mediation is now part of the dispute resolution landscape. Too much scepticism will not benefit your client and may well backfire if your client subsequently comes to appreciate the benefits of the process. The first point, therefore, is to be positive. There are few down-sides to giving mediation a go.

Solicitors have a professional obligation to advise clients on mediation and this should be done as early in the case as possible, especially in court cases where there may be financial penalties against a party who refuses to mediate. Clients need to be aware that the court may order that the parties attempt to resolve the dispute by mediation and that if it fails, the parties will be required to report back to the court (although not usually in any detail). There are points to be won and points to be lost by the parties depending on how they deal with mediation. A party who is quick off the blocks in proposing mediation may obtain a tactical benefit.

It is advisable to explain as much about the mediation process as possible to the client. In particular, they will need to be quite clear that a mediator does not impose a solution on the parties. Any settlement lies in the hands of the clients themselves.

Lawyers would do well to remember that they will be spending several hours with their clients during the mediation day. There are often long periods of sitting around with nothing very much to do whilst the mediator meets with the other side. This time is an opportunity to strengthen relationships with the client.

11.5.4 It is obvious that on the mediation day itself lawyers will be performing in front of their clients (not to mention the other side's clients). If you are not well prepared and do not know your case well, you can expect to be exposed. If you lose your cool under pressure at a mediation, you will lose respect. You will be on display the whole time and can expect your client to compare you with the other party's lawyers.

The mediation is really the client's day. It is therefore essential to ensure that they are properly briefed and that they have realistic expectations as to the merits of their case. If they have been misled in some way, this will be exposed during the course of the mediation.

The mediator will encourage the parties to vent their feelings, even though these may be strong or misguided. It is advisable to prepare your client for this. Encourage him to vent his feelings, but equally importantly, encourage him to listen properly when the other side express theirs. It costs nothing to acknowledge an opponent's feelings but can result in a significant costs saving if this allows the parties to move on to the substantive issues. By the same token, if there is some matter to apologise for, encourage your client to apologise. Acknowledgement of feelings and apologies do not equate to admissions of liability. They may, however, unblock the path to settlement.

Never push your client too hard into agreeing a settlement he does not want or you may well be blamed later. Even when the pressure is on to settle, the lawyer should remain objective and give objective advice.

Prior to issuing proceedings

Generally speaking, the earlier the mediation takes place, the greater the costs saving. There will often be a concern, however, that some information may come to light later in the case that fundamentally affects the merits of the parties' positions and that settlement would then be achieved on better terms. It is always difficult to advise properly if there are large gaps in the evidence. However, these factors must be weighed against the potential costs savings and savings in management time if a case settles early. **11.5.5**

Given the pre-action protocols (which apply in substance to actions in the Commercial Court and which the LMAA has indicated should be followed insofar as relevant in arbitration subject to the LMAA terms as well) and the front end loading under CPR, there is no obstacle to parties proposing mediation at an early stage. Indeed, there may be tactical advantages to proposing mediation early in a dispute. Not only does the party making the proposal seize the initiative, but in the case of court proceedings, it may well win some favour with the court.

The days when proposing mediation was considered a sign of weakness are now gone. Whether a party considers itself in a position of strength or is concerned at potential weaknesses in its case, the earlier it mediates, the greater the benefits.

Be sure when proposing mediation not to miss limitation periods for commencing proceedings—these are often very tight in shipping cases.

After issuing proceedings

Mediation can be proposed by any party at any stage. In High Court proceedings the parties are asked whether they would like a stay in order to mediate when they complete their allocation questionnaires. In the Commercial Court, the issue will usually be raised at the Case Management Conference. Quite how the courts deal with **11.5.6** mediation varies from judge to judge. Some have a better understanding and are more proactive than others. ADR is still a relatively recent innovation in English court proceedings and there is therefore not yet much case law. This is likely to change with time. In the meantime, it is best not to be seen to be reluctant to mediate a case.

In some cases the parties do not properly focus on settlement until close to trial. Suddenly the risks are more apparent and the consequences of losing more concerning. Costs start to mount and the realities of the situation strike home both with lawyers and their clients. In such cases, mediations may not take place until quite close to trial. There are still significant costs savings to be had and the elimination of risk becomes a more influential factor.

Making contact with the other parties—the approach

11.5.7 The suggestion is usually made by one party's lawyers but may also be made by clients or by one of the various available ADR and mediator service providers at the request of the client or his lawyer. Suggesting mediation may be a sign of strength as much as a sign of weakness. It may reflect a more commercially-minded party. In today's world making the approach is rarely a problem.

Where all lawyers involved in a case are experienced in mediation, agreeing to mediate and setting up the mediation is usually very straightforward. Problems may arise, however, where one lawyer has no experience and is concerned that he will be taken advantage of in some way. In such circumstances many of the mediation service providers (those bodies who supply mediators) will happily speak to the resisting lawyer on a confidential basis. As a neutral organisation, they are better able to deal with the concerns and fears of an anxious lawyer.

Occasionally a mediation proposal may be rejected on the grounds that it will only waste costs. If that is the obstacle put forward it is easily refuted by agreeing to pay the costs of the mediation. These will usually be insignificant in the context of the dispute and will no doubt be taken into account by the paying party when he calculates his costs for the purpose of the settlement negotiations.

A more common obstacle put forward is that a party does not have all the information it requires. This is best dealt with by enquiring what further information the party would like and then providing it.

If a party refuses to mediate in the context of court proceedings, his attention should be drawn to the Overriding Objective in CPR and the costs provision in CPR Pt 44. This correspondence (which should obviously not be without prejudice) can then be produced to the court at a later stage on the issue of costs.

It is advisable to be as reasonable and helpful as possible when setting up the mediation. In reality there are no points to be scored here. Tactically speaking, it is the more laid back and reasonable party that will have the edge.

The type of mediator

The most important consideration is to appoint a mediator who is skilled at mediation. Check that the proposed mediator has been trained and accredited as a mediator and that he has sufficient experience. Being a retired judge, silk or solicitor does not make someone a good mediator. **11.5.8**

Many appointments are made on the strength of recommendations from colleagues. Alternatively, mediators may be obtained through mediation service providers. There are now numerous such bodies which hold lists of trained mediators. The usual practice is for CVs of three mediators to be provided by the mediation service provider for consideration by the party which requested them. If you wish to reject one or more of the proposed mediators, further CVs will be sent until you have three possibilities with which you are happy. These CVs can then be sent to the other side for them to consider.

Mediators are impartial. There is, therefore, no point in rejecting good mediators proposed by the other side simply because they have proposed them.

One of the areas of debate in mediation is whether or not the mediator should have subject-matter knowledge. In some disputes it is obviously not essential. However, in specialist areas such as shipping it may be an advantage (or may not be if you are on weak ground). If a matter is complex it may be worth trying to find a mediator who understands the industry and the language. It will avoid time having to be spent explaining it to someone with no knowledge or experience and may avoid confusion. It may also increase the client's confidence if the mediator speaks his "language". As already mentioned, some of the LMAA Arbitrators are now trained as mediators. Also, the Admiralty Solicitors Group has a mediation sub-group and a pool of trained and accredited mediators with expertise in shipping-related matters.

Mediators' styles vary between facilitative and evaluative. The facilitative mediators tend to ask more questions with the aim of drawing out the parties' concerns and the underlying issues. Evaluative mediators are more inclined to form a view as to the merits of a case and to challenge the parties to have more realistic expectations. Barristers and judges are often unable to avoid being evaluative, which may or may not be helpful. Parties may experience evaluative mediators as more robust and as having a tendency to "bang heads together". Facilitative mediators have a more gentle approach.

The parties will need to have confidence in the mediator. He will therefore need to be patient, have good listening skills, be diplomatic, considerate and persuasive.

The mediation agreement

11.5.9 When parties agree to mediate, a mediation agreement is usually entered into. This avoids confusion as to how the mediation will proceed.

If the mediator is coming via a service provider or if he is someone who mediates regularly, he will usually provide a draft mediation agreement. These are usually short and uncontroversial. As well as identifying the parties, mediator, venue, date and time, some provision is usually made for exchange of documents and the written statements of case. There should be a confidentiality clause and the mediator may insist on a provision that he will not be called by any party as a witness in any proceedings relating to the case.

Most agreements currently provide that the mediator will not be liable if he is negligent. This is a rather dubious clause. Mediators should carry their own insurance and should be liable for their actions in the same way as are other professionals. You may or may not be able to persuade the mediator to remove this clause.

Who should attend the mediation?

11.5.10 This is a question which should be carefully considered and will depend on the case and personalities involved. The starting point is that someone with authority should attend from each party. Serious problems may arise if one party attends without full authority to settle. Prudent lawyers will always check not only that their own clients have authority to settle, but also that every other party will also be represented by someone with that authority. If there is any change to the identities of those attending, all parties should be informed immediately.

Most mediations are attended by lawyers as well as clients. Occasionally it is helpful for Counsel or experts to attend. This will depend on the nature of the dispute and on what may be required to bring about a settlement.

It is not uncommon for senior representatives of the parties to be encouraged to attend. If the case has been handled by someone who is perceived as a potential obstacle to settlement, the mediation may provide an opportunity to bring in someone more senior within the organisation to listen to the debate with the hope of bringing a more objective and commercial approach to bear. Senior executives are less likely to be concerned with the detail and are more likely to focus on achieving a cost-effective resolution to the matter.

If the dispute is a multi-party dispute and one party refuses to participate in the mediation, this will usually undermine the process and make settlement impossible to achieve. It is now possible in Commercial Court proceedings to obtain orders to mediate which contain a condition precedent that a third party, not yet joined to the court proceedings, participates in the mediation.

What papers should be passed to the mediator prior to the mediation?

The short answer to this is as few as possible. What the mediator will be interested in is what is most important to each party. Minor details and side debates will become irrelevant. The mediator will not have the time or the inclination to wade through files of documents. He is not Counsel. He needs to understand what the case is about, what matters are in dispute and why and what the underlying issues are for the parties. If the parties will require him to carry out extensive additional reading, they will have to pay for it. It will probably also mean that the party who makes that demand does not have sufficient understanding of its case to prepare a concise statement of case. **11.5.11**

The statement of case is usually best done when drafted with numbered paragraphs and headings and is presented in double spacing. It is usual to give the mediator a copy of any pleadings. Witness statements and experts' reports may be provided if necessary. Key documents may also be submitted. Usually the parties try to agree what will be given to the mediator and this is certainly not an issue to fall out over. No party can stop another party from showing the mediator any document they wish. If a document is not sent across in advance, it can always be produced at the mediation (most parties usually bring their files with them to a mediation in case something emerges unexpectedly).

Documents may also be passed to the mediator on a confidential basis. An example might be a draft expert's report or a document not yet disclosed.

It is unwise at the mediation to try and ambush opponents with new documents. At the very least, it will do nothing to create a climate for settlement. It will waste time and there will be a real prospect that the mediation will be adjourned or even abandoned. If the mediation is court ordered, such conduct may be reported back to the judge.

Length of the mediation

Most mediations last a day, usually starting at 9.30 a.m. or 10 a.m. and often not finishing until late at night (it is sensible to warn clients of this). Large multi-party mediations may take several days; small cases may be time-limited to half a day. **11.5.12**

Sometimes mediations are adjourned to enable the parties to

deal with matters arising in the mediation. Adjournments may last weeks or even months.

The venue

11.5.13 The venue is actually quite important as the parties may expect to spend several hours, if not days, in their respective rooms.

One room big enough to sit everyone attending will be required. Each party will also need its own room. Windowless, poky rooms are not a good idea as parties become irritable and impatient which may prejudice the process. Refreshments (including lunch) will need to be available.

Law firms are often able to provide rooms, often at no cost to the parties. Inexperienced practitioners may feel uncomfortable at mediating on the other side's territory. In reality, however, it makes no difference.

Other sources of venues are the mediation service providers and the various organisations which provide venues for arbitrations.

The cost of the mediation

11.5.14 The cost of the mediation is usually divided between the parties. There is, of course, nothing to stop a party being paid its costs of the mediation as part of the settlement agreement.

The most commonly promoted benefit of mediation is its cost-effectiveness. Direct costs are usually limited to the mediator's fees, room hire and refreshments. The other most significant cost is that of lawyers' fees preparing for and attending the mediation. In reality, the time is usually usefully spent even if the case does not settle at the mediation. Other costs may include experts' fees and travel expenses if clients are overseas.

Costs will usually be insignificant compared to the cost of continuing with litigation, especially if the matter proceeds to trial.

The settlement agreement

11.5.15 If the mediation results in a settlement, best practice is to draft and sign the settlement agreement before concluding the mediation. Many mediation agreements contain a provision that there is no binding settlement until the terms of a settlement have been reduced to writing.

The inexperienced practitioner would be well advised to give some thought to the terms of any settlement agreement in advance of the mediation, although the mediator will probably assist in drafting any agreement if necessary. Heads of agreement are less satisfactory than an agreement setting out full terms as there is always a real risk of further disagreement arising, possibly even resulting in the collapse of the settlement.

It is best to keep the settlement agreement as simple as possible.

In addition to the terms of the settlement, details of the parties, etc., there are a few other clauses to bear in mind in shipping disputes which, by their nature, are often international. For example, the agreement will presumably be subject to English law but should any proceedings be commenced in the High Court or by arbitration? This may well depend on considerations relating to enforcement. It is often sensible to have a service of suit clause in case any proceedings arise out of the agreement, especially when dealing with companies based in "state of convenience" countries. An irrevocable agreement that the parties' London solicitors' address be the address for service of any process relating to disputes arising under the settlement agreement would suffice.

If the settlement is in the context of court proceedings, consider whether a Tomlin Order is required. Alternatively, if the backdrop is arbitration, consider whether to draw up the settlement agreement as a Consent Award.

Post settlement issues

If the mediation results in a settlement there will be a few house- **11.5.16**
keeping matters to deal with. The formalities of discontinuing any court or arbitration proceedings will need to be attended to on whatever terms have been agreed. Witnesses, experts, Counsel, etc., will all need to be notified and the terms of the settlement agreement will obviously have to be performed.

If the mediation does not result in a settlement, parties to court proceedings will certainly wish to give consideration as to whether a Pt 36 offer should be made. The parties will also have to report back to the court on the mediation (this is usually a brief letter, but may be the opportunity for complaint if one party has not mediated in good faith).

TEN KEY POINTS TO REMEMBER **11.6**

(1) Know your case thoroughly—both law and facts.

(2) Calculate your client's costs to date (not forgetting to include unbilled costs and the costs of the mediation and the costs of any arbitration).

(3) Calculate your clients' future costs should the case proceed to arbitration or a court hearing. Calculate all costs on a fairly generous basis to allow room for error—clients may well remember the estimates given and these may come back to haunt you.

(4) Calculate the value of the claim/counter-claim. Do not forget to include interest (compounded quarterly if this is what you would hope to recover in any arbitration).

(5) Make a note of all previous offers made and received. The mediator will almost certainly ask for this information and it may help to narrow the parameters of the settlement discussions.

(6) Brief your clients thoroughly on the procedure, how to handle their opponents and on the strengths and weaknesses of their case.

(7) Make sure your clients and all other parties have full authority to settle.

(8) Evaluate any offers made during the mediation objectively. Do not be sucked into pressing for a settlement which your clients may later regret. The idea is not to settle at any price.

(9) Always mediate in good faith.

(10) Always be seen to be reasonable (even if you are not) and never lose your cool.

CHAPTER 12

PROBATE AND TRUST DISPUTES

GEOFFREY GREENHOUSE

WHY MEDIATE? 12.1

The benefits of using mediation to settle disputes with or without other alternative dispute resolution methods are clearly apparent in probate and trust cases.

The parties will probably have had a long ongoing relationship. Perhaps they are members of the same family with deep rooted mutual enmity and hostility going back over many years, not necessarily connected to this particular dispute. The testator or settlor might well have known of these antagonisms and have written the Will or Trust hoping to avoid his beneficiaries becoming embroiled in costly litigation. Indeed, in probate cases, it is not unusual for the deceased knowing there would be a dispute in the family to have refused to make a Will believing that the matter would best be sorted out by the family having their entitlement in accordance with the law of intestacy hoping the law would provide a benchmark as to what was fair and correct.

But as every lawyer knows there are substantial costs both financial and emotionally in having to ask the courts to resolve a dispute and the law is often less clear cut and even more subjective than most people recognise. Judges base their decisions on their interpretation of the law and lawyers can never be sure what a judge will do in a particular situation. Not only are there the uncertainties and the costs but the very real likelihood that neither party will be the winner or have the decision which is to their satisfaction.

Let me take an actual case to illustrate the difference in approach and result between litigation on the one hand and mediation on the other. In so doing I will spend some time considering the litigation process as it shows how starkly it contrasts with dispute resolution using mediation. I have of course changed the names and certain facts so as to protect the parties' anonymity.

A DEATH IN THE FAMILY 12.2

In a suburb of London lived a mother and father with their two little girls. They were a very happy family but suddenly the mother died leaving the father with his two daughters then aged six and eight. The father re-married and the years went by. The daughters grew up and moved out of the house and had families of their own. Twenty-five years after having re-married the father died. He had made a Will giving his second wife the right to live in the house and the benefit of his pension. There had been no children of the second marriage and he left his residuary estate to his daughters.

The second wife (whom I shall call the step-mother), having been informed of the terms of the Will, complained that there was no way she could make ends meet living on her husband's company pension and she considered the terms of the Will unfair.

12.3 ENTER THE LAWYERS

The step-mother went to see a solicitor. He thought the Will was unclear as to whether she had a life interest in the house or merely the right of occupation. The Will did not make sufficient provision to reflect her 25 years of marriage and dependence upon her late husband and she certainly had a very good case. She would probably receive a life interest in the property together with a life interest in part or all of the residuary estate and perhaps even a lump sum. This would depend partly on how much savings she had of her own. He recommended obtaining an opinion from Counsel.

The opinion which was many pages long commenced with an analysis as to whether or not the Will created a life interest of the house and advised that there probably was but that it was somewhat restricted. Counsel then went on to consider the rights of the step-mother. Following up on a further detailed analysis he came to the conclusion that she would be entitled to an unrestricted life interest in the property together with a capital payment at this stage and a life interest in the whole of the residue. This was, however, subject to a number of factors such as her outgoings and income and capital. It might be that either or both of the step-daughters could show that they have special requirements which might give them an immediate entitlement. The solicitor was advised to obtain a professional valuation of the property. In the meantime the solicitor should take steps to ensure the assets were frozen pending the outcome of the case.

The daughters had by now received a letter from the family solicitor who was administering the estate. He told them that their step-mother had taken independent legal advice that this had resulted in the estate being frozen and advised them to obtain independent legal advice. They told their solicitor that they had never got on with their step-mother and they did not think their father had either. The father and step-mother had lived in separate rooms and she had remained in the house only as a matter of convenience. They had never liked their step-mother and if their father had been a stronger person he would have thrown her out and in any case she had worked full-time until retirement and they believed she had substantial savings. It was for these reasons their father had made these provisions in his Will. Their solicitor advised that their step-mother was probably entitled to a life interest in the house and although her behaviour or the state of the marriage might be a fact to take into account there would have to be substantial evidence. It was also important to find out how much she had in savings and whatever other income she might have. With the agreement of the daughters the solicitor obtained Counsel's advice which like his colleague's, contained a detailed analysis of the law and stated that the step-mother would obtain a life interest in the house and depending upon her personal circumstances a capital sum and a life interest in most if not all the residuary estate.

LITIGATION COMMENCES 12.4

For the next year the solicitors battled it out in correspondence. Notwithstanding that Counsel's opinions were similar, the parties were now further apart than ever. They were also angry and frustrated. The allegation that there had been no real marriage and that the step-mother had substantial funds was met with the response of incredulity and that "no progress could be made if this was the attitude of the daughters". The step-mother refused to disclose her savings on the basis that with this level of hostility it was obvious that the step-daughters would not be interested in reaching a settlement and the matter would proceed to court. Probate was obtained and an application on behalf of the step-mother was filed in the High Court under the Inheritance (Provisions for Family and Dependants) Act 1975. An application was also made for an interim payment and this was met with an application for an order that she disclose details of her assets. The hearing date was fixed for some three months later but a week before the date the step-mother gave what were believed to be full details of her assets. Counsel on both sides advised that this would not make a substantial difference to the eventual court hearing but they were uncertain as to what exactly the judge would decide. The application for an interim payment was withdrawn by consent without any order as to costs.

By now, almost two years had passed and the case had not yet been fixed for a final hearing let alone a hearing date fixed. Both parties had paid out thousands of pounds to their lawyers and neither side had seen any results. There was a complete stalemate. The correspondence between solicitors slowed down and comprised of without prejudice letters and repeated threats of requesting indemnity costs unless the matter was settled on the terms demanded by the parties' respective solicitors. Each party, unbeknown to the other, was expressing serious concern to their solicitors as to the thousands of pounds which had already been spent and that they did not have further money and certainly could not afford the cost of a trial. The executors and their solicitors were also becoming increasingly anxious as they had not been able to complete the administration of the estate and pay the bills. It was in these circumstances that one of the solicitors thought about mediation. The other, in desperation, agreed in the hope that there might be a slim chance of an agreement being reached.

12.5 THE MEDIATION PROCESS

It is usual for parties wishing to mediate a dispute to approach a "mediation provider", being an independent organisation or perhaps a firm of solicitors who provide the names of a number of mediators and their CV. This enables the parties (usually through their solicitors) to choose someone in whom they feel they can have confidence. This is the first step for the parties in taking back responsibility in finding a solution for their problem. The mediation provider then discusses with them the fees and for those new to mediation explains the process and its benefits.

Having been asked to act as mediator I spoke by telephone with each of the solicitors. I explained that I was not a judge or arbitrator, that I was to remain impartial and to help facilitate the parties coming to their own settlement. The process was without prejudice and confidential and prior to mediation both parties would sign an agreement confirming first, that they wished to mediate and secondly, that any agreement would only be binding if a settlement was reached in writing and signed by the parties or their solicitors. Furthermore, they had to agree that I could not be called into court to give evidence so that everything said and done at the mediation remained without prejudice and confidential unless agreed otherwise (in writing) by the parties. Each party had to pay one half of the mediation fees as this showed the commitment to the mediation process. The first stage was for the parties' solicitors to prepare a summary of their case (which is without prejudice) and agree the documents to be given to the mediator prior to the mediation. The documents usually comprise the statement of case and other essential documents, the parties being encouraged to keep it to a minimum.

Mediation commences with the parties and their advisers meeting together with an introduction by the mediator to explain the purpose of mediation and how it works. Each party (or his advisers) is given the opportunity of stating his case and asking the other side points that might be relevant. The discussions will continue until the mediator decides the stage has been reached to meet each of the parties "in caucus", that is, separately with their own advisers. The idea is that by meeting the parties separately and being able to hold information confidentially with the assurance that it will not be passed to the other side, the mediator can explore each side's interests and needs and move away from purely positional bargaining. The benefit is that without the presence of the other side a party is likely to be more open disclosing information they might otherwise hide. Having confidence in the mediator allows for a fuller and freer exploration of options and meeting separately gives the mediator a chance to better understand each parties' point of view. During the mediation the mediator will shuttle between the parties perhaps bringing them together for joint meetings and sometimes asking the lawyers and experts from each side to meet with the other.

In probate and trust disputes it is, however, frequently the case there is such antagonism between the parties that they refuse to sit together in the same room. There is little purpose in forcing them to meet if they do not wish to do so. The mediator is not a psychotherapist or analyst. I do not consider it as part of my remit to repair the relationship between the parties. I am there to help them reach a settlement which focuses upon their interest and needs and to enable them to go beyond legal right based arguments and the sedimented and entrenched feelings which perhaps prevent them and their legal advisers from moving forward. If this is done without the parties meeting then notwithstanding the departure from the usual mediation style and provided it is the parties who come to the agreement, it can be said that the mediation has been successful.

MEDIATION COMMENCES 12.6

In this case the daughters refused to meet their step-mother. I asked them to tell me why. They said how resentful they were of their step-mother. They considered her an opportunist who had taken over when their mother had died. She had never treated them properly and they did not think their father got on with her either. I then asked them what it was they really needed. They said they had their own families and they both desperately needed money now. The lawyers were, however, talking about a life interest and they did not wish to wait for about 20 years before they got anything. The house should be sold and they thought it would be fair if each of them received one-third of the estate.

I then met with the step-mother and her solicitor. She told me she was bitter that after all the years of looking after the two daughters they refused to meet with her. She had given up the best years of her life and made a welcoming home for them yet they refused to have anything to do with her. I then asked her what she really needed. Surprisingly, she told me that she did not wish to stay in the house as it was too large and expensive to maintain and she certainly did not want the daughters constantly enquiring as to her health and whether she was still alive. She wanted to own her own home in her own name and this could be a one bedroom flat near her sister who lived in North England. She was prepared for the estate to be settled one-third each so long as there were sufficient funds for her to buy her own property. I then had a joint session with the solicitors. They needed to go away and do some research. How much would a property cost, what was the current value of the family home (a professional valuation having been undertaken two years earlier) and what would be the value of the net estate after taking into account the costs involved?

The mediation was adjourned for one month and when we resumed it appeared the one-third share would not be sufficient to purchase a property and for the step-mother to have sufficient funds in the bank for her to feel financially secure. The daughters' solicitor (we had resumed the joint session with the solicitors) then came up with a novel suggestion. The daughters could lend to the step-mother part of their one-third share and this could then be secured by way of a mortgage. This got around having a life interest and enabled the step-mother to own a property outright and meant that the daughters received most but not all of their share. The mortgage would be repayable when the step-mother died and it would be administered by the solicitors so that the daughters would not be involved in granting permission if, for example, the mother wished to move. The daughters were more than pleased to come to this arrangement. Their main interest was in receiving part of the estate at this stage and this had been satisfied. They were surprisingly co-operative in agreeing the loan. A settlement in the form of a Tomlin Order was agreed between the parties.

12.7 Why a Settlement was Reached

The importance of the above case study is that it shows first, that a settlement can be reached which satisfies the interest of both parties but which is totally different to any order which would have been made had it been left to the courts. Secondly, that the agreed settlement did not result in either party giving up their legal rights or coming away worse off than had they gone to court.

Mediation gives an opportunity for the parties to look at their interests. It enables them to look beyond their personal emotions and inter personal frictions with the resultant posturing by their legal advisers. Where negotiations are structured around a series of offers and counter offers there is little or no opportunity to find out what the other side really needs or to explore options together. Had this case not gone to mediation it would probably have been settled at the trial door but the settlement would have been imposed upon the parties without their having any real input or their being satisfied as to the outcome. The step-mother would have been stuck in the house for the rest of her life and the daughters would have had to wait perhaps 20 years to receive anything.

USING MEDIATION AND OTHER ADR PROCESSES **12.8**

Why then should the parties and their legal advisers involved in a trust or probate dispute consider using mediation with or without other ADR processes?

(a) It enables the parties to find a solution to the problem which is workable and acceptable to them rather than having a settlement imposed upon them.

(b) It can help build bridges or stop the breakdown of ongoing relationships such as that which might exist between family members or trustees and beneficiaries.

(c) Parties can at the same time decide other issues so as to create a continuing ongoing relationship and prevent further disputes.

(d) It results in substantial savings on the cost of litigation.

(e) It reduces the stress and aggravation suffered by the parties in litigious situations.

Most important of all, however, is that the parties' involvement, together with their legal advisers, in determining the outcome of their dispute increases the likelihood of settlement. This is because parties are more likely to accept support and work towards a solution that they thought of themselves rather than that imposed upon them by the courts.

INDEX